# i didn't do It, **I** did

## A conversation with Consciousness

## A roadmap to Truth

### Susan Pearson

**BALBOA.**
PRESS
A DIVISION OF HAY HOUSE

Balboa Press books may be ordered through booksellers or by contacting:

Balboa Press
A Division of Hay House
1663 Liberty Drive
Bloomington, IN 47403
www.balboapress.com.au
1 (877) 407-4847

Print information available on the last page.

ISBN: 978-1-5043-0985-1 (sc)
ISBN: 978-1-5043-0986-8 (e)

Balboa Press rev. date: 03/15/2018

# Table of Contents

## Part 1 – What We are not

## Part 2 – Discerning what is not from what Is

## Part 3 – Why we don't deactivate i, and how we can

## Part 4 – Conscious Trust

# Dedication

## To all seekers of Truth

# Don't skip this bit

Two "states" of C(c)onsciousness are presented in this book; our normal human awake state of consciousness, and our less familiar Spiritual Consciousness. Spiritual Consciousness **should** be more familiar because, individually and collectively, It Is who We Really are. Yet Spiritual Consciousness remains unfamiliar and remote because It is hidden "behind" or masked by human consciousness. The reasons why this is so, and why it is crucial to unmask Spiritual Consciousness, will become obvious throughout the course of this book.

To limit possible confusion and to make a clear distinction between the two "states", **I** (Spiritual Consciousness) have used upper-case and lower-case letters in unconventional ways. For instance, the use of lower-case in many words, particularly "i", "you", "me", "my", "we", "us" and "self", is always used purposefully to indicate human consciousness. **I** realize that lower-case at the beginning of a sentence may interrupt your flow, but it is deliberate so that you, the reader, may be clear that **I** am pointing to the human state of consciousness. Similarly, upper-case at the beginning of certain words such as Truth, Love, Life and Infinity, and particularly the words "**I**", "You", "Me", "My", "We", "Us" and "Self", may be awkward and jarring in the middle of a sentence, but will ultimately uncover Spiritual Consciousness without the need for extra words.

In addition, some passages require Spiritual Consciousness to be active in order to be fully Understood. If you find yourself doing mental gymnastics causing your head to spin, don't force the issue. It is quite normal for a New Idea to be read many times before Consciousness Reveals Its Self to you. **I** suggest moving through these passages gently in the assurance that deactivation of human consciousness requires both time and patience, and that mental exertion will not serve this end.

Not so onerous, but helpful, **bold** words are for emphasis, and *italics* are used to identify quotes or references to quotes. Also, the use of the words "man", "he" and "his" denote individual and collective humanity and are not gender specific.

Above all, the Ideas outlined in this book present an enormous challenge to the conventional wisdom, and, as a result, are bound to encounter an understandable level of resistance. Be Aware that your immediate reaction to some of these challenging views can often be a smokescreen used by human consciousness to keep its limited awareness in place. Apart from the first instinct to dismiss or reject these Ideas, one of these reactions might arise as the temptation to skip chapters that you feel are unworthy of your attention. It is recommended that you stick to the order presented, because each chapter prepares you for the next and, by browsing, you may misinterpret later sections in human consciousness' favour.

If you can manage to delay this and other habitual reactions, you will allow a deeper meaning to arise, which you will come to Know as Spiritual Consciousness Revealing Its Self.

The Revelation of Spiritual Consciousness is not sought or appreciated by human consciousness, yet all of us must tread this Path sooner or later. This book therefore walks humbly in the footsteps of those brave individuals who have gone before and who have cleared the way for the rest of us.

i didn't write this book, **I** did.

# How this book came about

From an early age it became evident that i had an artistic flair, an inventive nature. Perhaps this was why i also had questions. "Why was i in this body? Why wasn't i in someone else's body? Why did i have these particular parents? Why did i live in this country at this time? Why not some other country at some other time? What was it all for? What was i doing here?" Nobody seemed able to answer so i stopped asking, but the questions never left me.

Life continued with its normal ups and downs until my last year of school. It was the same year Maharishi Mahesh Yogi came to Australia to teach "Transcendental Meditation". A friend asked if i wanted to go along to a class. i had no burning desire to learn Meditation, but it was a welcome distraction from my dreaded studies and the looming exams. my chemistry teacher had taken me aside and warned me that i would fail if i didn't take the subject more seriously. The talk injected the intended fear, but made the struggle for what was clearly beyond my understanding no less difficult.

So there i was, dazed and clueless about chemistry, about to take on something logic would say was a total waste of time.

After the private mantra-giving ceremony, we all sat as a group to practice. To my surprise and delight, i caught on straight away.

my friend had trouble. For me, though, the experience was like turning on a light. With further practice, i found i could very quickly, and at will, descend into a deep ocean of Calm atop of which the choppy waves of my own thought had detached and remained on the surface. i could be Calm and manage this "surface" at the same time. But not only had i gone "inwardly" deeper, my "outward" world was simultaneously uplifted and expanded into an utterly brilliant dimension of clarity. my senses tingled. Colours were vivid, sound crisp, nerve-endings alive. The new Awareness was like coming out of a fog. Compared to this profound and thrilling sense of Awake Awareness, i had been in a dull and smothering sleep. Sadly, the Awareness would only last a couple of hours and grow dim, but could be rekindled by sitting still and connecting again. Practice twice a day was recommended. i had no trouble adhering to the recommendation. It felt amazing.

Though, after a couple of weeks floating in and out of this other-worldly dimension, my conscience pulled my thoughts back to me and prompted me to return to my chemistry books. Reluctantly, i began studying, and then an extraordinary thing happened. To my astonishment, out of the blue, i suddenly understood the laws and language of chemistry! Had i suddenly become smarter? No, i was to discover later that i had simply opened the door to Truth.

Not yet even vaguely Understanding what i had accessed, i gratefully breezed through the chemistry exam and, to my teacher's bewilderment, passed with flying colours.

After that, life got busy as life does. The knowledge of chemistry faded along with my motivation to meditate.

Many years passed. i married, had children and built a business. And perhaps as a result of some business difficulties, the early childhood questions bubbled up again along with another; "why did humans seem to attract so many more problems than other creatures?" This time my inner enquiry was accompanied by an unrelenting push from within to find the answers to this and the earlier questions.

i did not resist. i could not resist. Juggled around family and business life i found the time to undertake and complete an "Energetic Healing" Diploma, i attended weekly classes in mediumship, i underwent transpersonal psychotherapy sessions, i attended self-help lectures, workshops and read every Spiritual book i could get my hands on. Finally, the prompt from within came to meditate again. Perhaps i was trying too hard to recapture the experience of my final school year. i couldn't connect, so i just sat still, relaxed and silently asked my questions. Then the answers came. Not only that, i was compelled to write them down.

The title came first. i had just completed a small oil painting during a break from reading. Amazed with how the paint seemed to fly onto the canvas, i showed my husband. "you're clever" he said. The door to Truth opened again. The words came; "i didn't do It, **I** did."

# Acknowledgements

Although i feel extremely privileged to have been able to bring this message through, it was a giant undertaking, and so it is hard to imagine that i could have completed the work without my Generous group of editors. i am forever Grateful for their Dedication, Attention, and Sensitivity to the subject-matter. Heart-felt thanks goes to...

my husband Geoff Pearson, for sharing this journey with me, for being my sounding-board for the Ideas in the book, for being my live-in dictionary, for respecting my space, and for his endless Encouragement, Support, Humour and Love.

Janis Sernik, for generously devoting many hours over many years exploring the Ideas in the book and especially for smoothing out the bumps for the reader;

Jo Derham, for being there when this book was just a seed of an Idea, for her Warm and unfailing interest in the subject, her keen editing eye, and respect for the English language;

Jan Armstrong, for her astute questioning that led to deeper Insights, and for her Wise and valuable suggestions;

and my sister Shannon Smith, for filling in the gaps in my knowledge of grammar, for her Encouragement, and above all, for sharing with me her brave and frank questioning of mortality even as she faced her own mortality.

i am Grateful to my beautiful sons Edward and Harry for their unique perspectives and for being open to the often unconventional ideas being floated; my mother, Margaret, for her calm reassurance and Support, and for those wonderful discussions around the kitchen-table with Barbara Campbell too; my father, Eric, for making light of seriousness; my sister Sally Rice, for her mixture of Candour and Humour; and my sister Carolyn Beattie, for the same playful and Encouraging Attitude, and for her library skills that helped find a category for this book.

And to my dear friends; Judy Matulick, for her lightness and laughter, her Support, and for making serendipity normal; and Robyn Vincent, for all her Encouragement and for being on the same wave-length. Thank you.

Finally, Appreciation is extended to every person who i happened to meet during this long process. Whether it was a chance encounter or a scheduled meeting, regularly and without fail, answers to questions that hung in my mind were given form and incorporated within these pages.

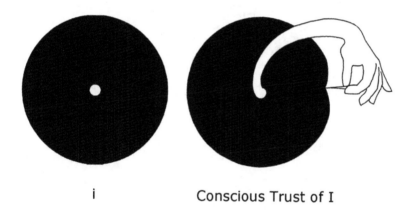

i          Conscious Trust of I          I

# PART 1

# What We are not

# CHAPTER 1

——●——

# i is for intellect

What am i doing here? Why am i in this body?

you've been asking those questions for a long time.

Ever since i can remember.

Getting any answers?

Most people i ask are busy, or look at me sideways and change the subject. Then something told me to ask and wait.

That "something" was your Intuition.

Then maybe it can answer me. What am i doing here? And, why am i in this body?

you are discovering what You are **not**.

What do You mean? i want to discover what i am, not what i am "not"!

you will discover that too, but trying to discover what-You-are hasn't worked very well so far.

How come?

Because what-You-are-not has been blocking the way to the Realization of who You **Really** are. you block the way when you ask "what am i doing here?" because it's the little "i" asking the question. And **by** asking, this "i" has unknowingly put up a wall between you and your goal of finding the Real You and your Purpose for being here.

```
i don't understand.
```

Don't worry, **I** don't expect you to yet. We will get to it.

The first point is to realize that "i" is the identity that we, as human beings, have unwittingly adopted. Unfortunately, this adoption has prevented us from Knowing our True Self.

```
If i am not my True Self, who is the Real me?
```

The Real You Is Me, the One you are Listening to Now through your Intuition.

```
my Intuition is the Real me?
```

Not your Intuition, but Its Source.

```
Why haven't i discovered this fact sooner?
```

Because, before now, it hasn't occurred to you to question who you are. The "i" asking these questions is the only self you know. Consequently, this little i's first instinct when it is told that the Real You is Me is to doubt the Idea. But doubt doesn't change the Truth.

```
doubt doesn't change what Truth?
```

The Truth that **I Am** Your True Identity. More importantly, the Truth that **I Am** Permanent and Perfect. And if **I Am** Permanent and Perfect and **I Am** You, You are Permanent and Perfect.

```
You're right. i do doubt that. In fact, i
totally reject it!
```

doubt and rejection are natural reactions because you look to your imperfect and impermanent world to provide answers that only Truth can verify.

```
Why can't the world provide the answers?
```

Because the world is a product of your unconscious rejection of the Ideas of Permanence and Perfection. Not only does this circular thought exclude Truth, it keeps what you think is an imperfect and impermanent "you" within its temporary and intrinsically flawed boundary. Think about it. From your position in what you see as a finite and uncertain world, could you ever accept that Permanence and Perfection are Real? Or, rather, that there could be an Infinite Source of Renewal and Replenishment of the world that Is Permanent and Perfect? Could you pick up from your material existence in the world that My Timeless Presence has actually been accompanying you through life, walking ahead of you making the crooked road straight, and Lovingly Providing for your every need?

No, the world doesn't tell me that. i haven't noticed You there. Actually, i would argue that if You have been providing for me You haven't done a very good job.

As you will come to See, it's not for Me to push My Self on you. you have free-will to focus on the world of matter for its own sake and see it as lacking. But this is why you keep the door to the Consciousness that you are Really Me securely locked and all My Benefits at bay.

It sounds rather counter-productive. Can't i open the door?

you can but you won't because the wider the door opens the more the little i disappears.

i don't want to lose my self. i don't want to disappear.

That's why we must go slowly. Even though you are now curious about what's behind the door, your fear of losing your self becomes the gatekeeper that prevents you from fully opening the door.

Eventually, however, you will push the gatekeeper aside and discover that your fear was totally unfounded, for the door of your Consciousness is your own Mind, and It is not scary. Besides, only through It are you able to discover that **I Am** your **only** Hope, in Fact, everyone's **only** Hope of lasting Peace, Safety, Health, Prosperity and Happiness.

**I** will lead you along. It's enough that you are taking steps towards letting My Influence direct the Mind.

What has been directing it up to now?

your intellect. Quite understandably, you have come to rely on the intellect to protect and defend this imperfect and impermanent, fearful "you". it encourages you to devise ways to get what you need and want, or avoid being affected by the world's many perceived failings; its diseases, tragedies and lacks.

You say that like it's not necessary.

your lack of Consciousness **makes** it necessary, for the intellect does not have the foresight to know that the Real You already Has what you need, and these "failings" are misperceptions "caused" by your mistaken identity's **belief** in failings. Unaware of any alternative, you listen to the intellect and let it lead you down a blind alley to believe that you are deprived, alone and vulnerable in a dangerous and arbitrary world.

This is not so, but while the intellect monopolizes the Mind, you are trapped in this total misrepresentation of Truth. For without Truth to Guide it, the intellect cannot Know about, and therefore cannot accept, an extra dimension that Reveals Permanent Harmony. **I Am** this extra dimension. And, as you will discover, this dimension is not really "extra" but the **only** dimension. When you become Aware or Conscious of Me, **I** uncover the Truth that you are not the insecure physical being you think you are at all. you are never deprived or alone, and you are always Safe.

Until you get to Know Me, though, the activity of the intellect effectively hides Me and forms an impenetrable bubble around you that you know as your physical universe, the universe you depend on, despite feeling insecure.

The intellect hides You? How does it do that?

The intellect can hide Me when **you** don't know what the Mind is Really for or how to use It correctly. We will explore this topic later at length, but it is appropriate and important for you to Know now that your

Mind is My Mind, and It Is the control-tower of the perception you call the physical universe. Without Consciousness of this Fact, your universe is like a ship without a captain. The intellect, unqualified, but believing it has the skills, marches onto the control-tower and starts steering the ship of the universe with thoughts based on your sensory view of that same universe. Not knowing that you have rejected the Truth and shut My Safety out, you trust this brazen pseudo-leader and follow its directions. Buoyed by its confidence, you are carried along, completely oblivious that you are being led into stormy weather. Basing its expectations on past experience, the intellect justifies worry and appoints you and your anxious thought to take over the helm on its way to a series of tragic wrecks ending in death.

Why do i let it do that?

you don't know any better. While you lack Consciousness of Me, you unwittingly allow the intellect to run your life. Needing a mind through which to think and a body through which to act, you ignorantly offer your self. This involuntary relationship has gone on for so long that you don't even realize you are being manipulated. Like a puppet-master and his puppet, the intellect pulls the strings and you automatically jump. From your position, you don't see the strings, so you believe you thought of the jumping all by yourself. In this way, the intellect's sense-generated thoughts have become integral to who you think you are.

The philosopher Descartes was right when he said;

*"i think, therefore i am."*[1]

What you think about determines the tone of your existence and who you think you are. But there's more. For it is equally true that you must have existed before you could think. And if you don't objectively examine the nature of the i that thinks, your thought processes shrink down to the narrow range dictated by the intellect and become distorted as a result. you think about what you think about because you don't know you are the puppet of the intellect.

---

[1]   Rene Descartes, *Discourse on Method and Meditations* (New York: Dover Publications, 2003), 23

So who i think i am determines what i think about just as much as thinking determines who i am?

Yes. It's circular.

How do i escape the circle?

There is a way. What i thinks **about** exposes its circular thought-process and shines a light on you, the thinker. Stop, then, and consider what it is you think about. Not the subject-matter, but under the surface to the thought that shapes all other thought. Then we will have something to work with.

What is this thought?

Deep down at the core of your mind is the universal assumption that you are "in" a particular body. your initial question "why am i in this body?" demonstrates this tightly held conviction. In fact, it is part of the unscrutinized foundation of your identity.

i never really thought about it?

you see? And that's the problem, because "thinking" becomes an adjunct to the body and limited by that very thought. Now what if you could discover that you were never "in" any body? What would that do to the thinker and its thought about who it is?

Wait a minute—i am not in a body?

It certainly feels like you get around this world **in** your physical body. you see with **your** eyes, hear with **your** ears, touch with **your** hands, taste with **your** tongue, smell with **your** nose, and think with **your** brain. you and your body live together. But the belief that you can't live without your body is up-side-down, for the body can't live without **you,**

What are You implying?

The idea that you are "in" your body means you don't look under the assumption you have made. you don't see that this is how the intellect maintains its control. it needs **you** to depend on and associate this container with **your** existence, which in turn guarantees **its** existence. But look what you have signed up for. Doesn't "my body" and "me" form a progressively unsatisfactory and morbid alliance? When my body needs food, **i am**

**hungry**; when my body needs rest, **i am tired**; when my body gets a disease, **i am sick**; when my body has an accident, **i am injured**; when my body ages, **i am old**; and, when my body fades away, **i die**."

That's just the way it is.

This **way** is the consequence of associating your "self" with a temporary and flawed container. Not only are you trapped in the prison of a failing body, all your ideas about life are built on a false assumption. By allowing this fatalistic thought, you have made your self subject to a self-imposed grim and foreboding future. Instead, wouldn't it be great to Know that **You** are the Captain of a perpetually Inspiring, Peaceful and Joyous Universe? The Real You is not dependent on an unpredictable and harsh universe for Its existence, it's the other way around. The Universe is dependent on You, and Its appearance becomes dependable as a result! As a further consequence, when **you** become Aware of the Truth, the intellect loses the foolish little i that carried its limited and limiting beliefs. Suddenly you are Free, because there is no i to be hungry, tired, sick, injured, old or dead.

But the body **does** get hungry, tired, sick, injured, old and dies!

The body can't do anything in isolation from Me.

Then it must be my mind that tells my body it is these things.

The mind can't do anything of its own accord either. The mind is your instrument of consciousness, the consciousness that doesn't know that **I**, the Real You, Governs the Mind, the Body and the Universe in Permanent and Perfect working order.

But it's irrational to make that assertion.

When you depend on material evidence alone, it certainly **is** irrational to contradict it. But what if **I** told you that your rejection of Me altered the perception of the world you count on to tell you the truth? Wouldn't your accusation of irrationality be misdirected?

It would if that was possible.

It seems impossible because "physical evidence" is the product of the intellectual rejection of Me that precedes the physically evident reason to reject Me. i, the intellect's puppet, is therefore not in a position to discern that its assumptions are skewed. it can't know that it has used the control tower of the mind to make its assumptions **appear** true. Indeed, the intellect would never concede that its assumptions **are** assumptions. To the intellect, they are absolutely true! In turn, i, the puppet, has no choice but to accept that it has little control of its ultimate fate. If it is lucky enough to escape death by injury, hardship or negligence, in the end, it will deteriorate into old-age, succumb to sickness and die because its body will follow this pattern.

i can accept that i die because the body doesn't last forever, but why would the intellect tell the mind and body to be sick? i don't want to be sick.

Of course not, but the intellect doesn't believe it is possible to be Permanently Well, therefore sickness becomes a universally accepted belief that lurks in the dark corridors of your mind waiting to link arms with the belief that you are vulnerable.

Surely a belief can't make me sick?

When we examine how the Mind works, we will discover that this is the **only** thing that **can** make us, the believer, sick.

But you should know that it is not only your health that is affected. This outright rejection of Permanence and Perfection extends to, and accounts for, every other discord of your experience. it "causes" accident, poverty, crime, injustice, tyranny and tragedy, just to name a few.

i feel like a victim.

you are, of your intellect.

So my intellect and i are closely related.

The intellect is synonymous with humanity, collectively and individually. i, the "me" of us all, is a product of intellectual thought produced by **lack of Consciousness** of Me and My Permanence and Perfection.

But i thought my intellect was my consciousness. Certainly i am conscious of some things.

Sure, but your definition of "consciousness" is limited to the intellect who says consciousness depends on you being awake. your dictionary says the word "conscious" is to be;

> *"aware of one's own existence, sensations, thoughts, surroundings, etc"*[2].

This definition only applies to your waking hours, and you will note, your waking hours happen to be the only time the intellect functions as the "conscious" you. you don't have a definition for a greater Consciousness, because the intellect has no access to what it means to be more Conscious than its understanding of what it means to be "awake", and, therefore, has little use for such a definition.

Yet while we are asleep, there is "something" that is Awake or Conscious; our bodies manage to turn over a few times, our bladder holds, our stomach digests, our lungs breathe, our heart beats, and our brain synapses, all while maintaining an even 37 degrees Celsius (98.6 degrees Fahrenheit). So it seems that our bodies function very well without **our** "conscious" awareness, without the intellect.

Doesn't the body do these things on its own?

The body's arm can't lift itself. Nor can your legs decide to walk by themselves. Yet we think the heart, the lungs, and the myriad of other miraculous bodily functions work automatically and autonomously. It's inconsistent thinking. we haven't thought it through. Clearly, there must be something else going on that the intellect is incapable of Understanding or considering. Though now we should Notice that the intellect doesn't include this "something else" in its definition of consciousness, yet we

---

2    Dictionary.com http://dictionary.reference.com/browse/conscious?s=t

Trust this "something else" to look after our bodies while we sleep and to wake us up in the morning. This "something else" is Consciousness, and we should distinguish it with an upper-case "C" because It makes our awake-consciousness unconscious by comparison.

Is this Consciousness only active when we sleep?

Not at all. But sleep, a state of unconsciousness by i's standard, allows this Consciousness to do its job without any interruptions from the so-called "conscious" us. Once we wake up and become "conscious", we forget this Trust. Worse, we immediately begin to override the Trust with our daily worries and concerns until we put our head on the pillow again the next night.

i must say, i do feel better after a good uninterrupted sleep, and i feel irritable if i don't sleep.

That should tell us something. This "greater" Consciousness not only Governs, It Is the Intelligence and Power that Renews and Invigorates the Mind and Body. Furthermore, we not only Trust It, we expect It to do Its job night after night. The problem is we fall short of Acknowledging that It Is Our Infinite Spiritual Consciousness; Governing, Renewing and Invigorating Its Body as It has always done.

i probably don't acknowledge this Consciousness because death catches up eventually. So what good would it do to acknowledge it? What difference would it make?

It makes all the difference, because by Acknowledging this Greater Intelligence and Power that **I Am**, the intellect is elevated into its proper role in cooperation with Me and We work together, through the Mind, all day every day for mutual Good. This cooperation Transcends intellectual thought **and** dissolves discord. Even the concept and experience of "death" is redefined. So you might as well Acknowledge Me because the Fact remains—**I Am** the Infinite Invisible Life or Spirit that Lovingly Forms, Governs, Maintains and Harmoniously Sustains what you call your "body" and "mind" always. **I**, not i, Am Your True Identity.

It's hard to believe.

Of course **i** can't believe it, because believing is an intellectual exercise limited to your waking hours. **I**, Consciousness, am beyond your "conscious" thinking ability, and, therefore, **I** am beyond the "i" that you think you are. But **I** am sure you know that just because you are not conscious of something doesn't mean it's not there. It's just that **you** are not yet Aware of it.

Think how we once believed the earth was flat. Did believing it was flat make it so? No, the earth was always a sphere, yet the belief limited us to our fear of falling off the edge of the earth, made that fear reasonable, and justified it. Similarly, we believe we are **in** a body, a belief that limits us to the short interval between "birth" and "death", and makes any inequitable circumstances of our "birth" unreasonable to question. But if we Knew we were Unlimited Consciousness, wouldn't the belief we are in a body make these limitations only **seem** to be so, and our subsequent reasoning incorrect?

i don't know how to reason any other way.

The intellect won't accept that there is an alternative way to reason, and exhibits an even greater unwillingness to spend time pursuing the possibility that there might be a greater Reasoning beyond its own. Yet, as this "greater Reasoning" is Acknowledged, our intellectual reasoning stops for a moment, and we Hear My Voice whisper, "it's alright not to comprehend Me" and we Rest in that inner Assurance. It doesn't make any sense to our "conscious" self who must comprehend before it accepts such an Idea. Nevertheless, it somehow Feels Right, because the Assurance comes from the very core of our True Being.

Ironically, when we do accept **we** can't comprehend It, this "greater Reasoning" is accessed. you access **I**.

Is there two of me?

No, there Is only One of Me. A **lack** of Consciousness of Me, the "i", can't be Real. **I Am** You.

you will come to Recognize that i is a false identity, simultaneously created and blown off course by the unwavering demand for logical reasoning; a logic that says it's reasonable to worry about imminent stormy weather, but unreasonable to bring a proven Trust into your waking life.

So hold onto your original questions "what am i doing here?" and "why am i in this body?" But focus more on the "i" that asks. By doing so, you shoot a rescue-flare up into the Infinite Unknown where this greater Reasoning resides, not to rescue i, but to rescue you **from** i. After all, i cannot be rescued. i never existed except in your mind. Uplifted and corrected by this Acknowledgement, your universe is then navigated back onto its True course. My Governing Influence of Goodness and Grace opens out the clear passage of Peace and Love that **i** had nothing to do with. And **because** i had nothing to do with It, your assumptions about the universe, body and mind are redefined along with the i that accepts storms as normal.

So don't be afraid of opening the door of your Consciousness for an imagined danger of losing your self. Question i and its beliefs, for this action actually steers you towards your Purpose for being here because it anchors you Safely and Lovingly with Me.

## CHAPTER 2

i is for ignorance of Truth

When you question i and its beliefs you question the intellect's truth, the truth that says you are vulnerable. The question arises from the part of you that Knows that vulnerability is not True. This "part" is the Real You that Knows that You are actually Invulnerable, because You are Infinite Spiritual Consciousness.

How does being Infinite Spiritual Consciousness make me Invulnerable?

If you Knew what Infinite Spiritual Consciousness meant, you would naturally equate It with Invulnerability because you would be free of all discord, so let us explore what "Infinite Spiritual Consciousness" means.

The three words "Infinite", "Spiritual" and "Consciousness" are synonymous. But of the three words, "Infinite" is the least misinterpreted and therefore the least confusing. Let us start here.

Infinity is endlessness, isn't it?

Not an abstract endlessness that you might strain to imagine on a time-line or spatially, but rather that **You are** time-less and space-less.

i don't see myself as timeless and spaceless. Quite the opposite. i occupy space for a limited time.

13

your body seems to, yet Infinity describes You to a tee. To accept that Infinity is You, though, requires us to go through a few mind-stretching steps that will end up defining Infinity in terms other than that of time and space.

Ok...?

First we must agree that there is a "you". "you" exist in some capacity. Do you agree?

```
Seems like a silly question, but yes, obviously
i exist.
```

I needed to ask that because now I am going to ask you to do something that will seem even sillier—exclude the body. We will bring it back a bit later, but first we need to get a proper grip on the  second word of the trio "Infinite Spiritual Consciousness"—"Spirit"— and we can't do that if we are thinking of spirit somehow occupying a body. This old ghostly assumption must be thrown out. What I want you to Understand is that this "you" (that you say exists) is body-less, because this "existence" you just agreed to is actually Spiritual (as opposed to material). "you" don't exist materially but Spiritually, and this Spirit Is Immortal and Eternally Divine. Establish, too, in your Mind, that Infinity is not material but of the same Spiritual or Divine Essence as this existence that "you" are.

```
Are You saying that "existence" is Infinite?
```

Yes, as long as you don't think of your body as having a role in determining this "existence".

Ok...?

Next, we must find a way to come to the conclusion that Infinity Is All there Is.

```
Why?
```

Because Invulnerability, to **Be** Invulnerable, must be free of any opposing presence, power or intelligence. Let's start by acknowledging that It must be All there Is because Infinity would cease to be Infinite if there was an alternative to It.

```
Makes sense.
```

Let's keep going on this track and bring the Spiritual "you" in. Can anything be missing from Infinity or added to Infinity?

By definition, no.

Then, "you" must, at the very least, be part of Infinity, for there can't be Infinity **plus** "you", right?

That's logical.

Following on, can Infinity be divided up into parts?

Again, no. you can't have a part of Infinity because the part would not be Infinite anymore.

This means "you" and Infinity must be inseparable. But **I** ask this for a further reason; the universe looks like it is made up of separate objects, but if Infinity Is Indivisible, the appearance of separateness demonstrates that our physical senses must not be capable of accommodating the Indivisible Spiritual Essence of Infinity. Though some other faculty must be capable.

This "other faculty" brings us to the third word in the trio, the word "Consciousness", for something must **Be** Conscious in order to accommodate and Understand this Indivisible Nature of Infinity. By the same token, if Infinity can't be divided, there can't be some other Consciousness to rival Consciousness. There must be only One Consciousness.

So?

you might be able to see that everything points to the same place.

i'm not sure.

"you" are the common denominator. In Fact, without "you", there is nothing. Let's bring it all together and See. If Infinity is Spiritual, not material; if "you" exist and "existence" is Infinite; if there is no alternative to Infinity; if "you" can't be excluded from Infinity; if Infinity can't be divided up into parts; and if Infinity Is Conscious of Its Self As All there Is, the only logical conclusion we can draw is that there is nothing other than "you". Therefore "you" are Infinite Spiritual Consciousness!

However, to be absolutely clear, we must re-emphasize that this Infinite Spiritually Conscious "you" is not you-in-a-body but your True Self. **I** should therefore remove the inverted commas. This Infinite "you" is You with an upper-case "Y". You are the **I** that **I Am**.

I realize it's a lot of information to take in, but don't strain your mind. Rather, close your eyes, breathe, and try to Feel this Timeless, Spaceless, Ageless, Limitless You, this Divine Essence of You that exists. you often say (in contradiction to your changing reflection in the mirror) that "inside" you don't feel any different. Know now that it is because the True You doesn't have a beginning or an end. But more than that, being Infinite, It Is both the Source **and** what **appears** As the Body **and** the Universe.

What exactly do You mean by "appear"?

There is no actual "physical" body or universe "out there" separate from You. The Infinite Spiritual You **appears** physically.

Oh! Does this somehow make me Invulnerable?

It doesn't make **you** Invulnerable. **You** are already Invulnerable by virtue of Your Infinite Nature! And now might be a good time to introduce the Word "Love". Love Is Your Infinite Nature because Love is another name for Infinite Spiritual Consciousness. Through Love, you can gain a better Understanding of Your Invulnerability.

How so?

Think about it logically. Would Love be Love if It allowed you to actually be vulnerable to danger, disease, pain and loss? In other words, would Love be destructive to Its Self?

It wouldn't be very Loving.

Right. Love would be working against Its own Nature. Not to mention that if Love was destructive to Its Self, fear would be introduced. This would make fear able to destroy Love and, by inference, Infinity. But can anything destroy Infinity?

Not logically, no.

Then, if You are Infinite, You, not the finite body with which you identify, but the Infinite You, the Source of the Body and the Universe, must be Invulnerable. This is the Truth about You.

How does this relate to my life?

It has everything to do with your life because when you become Conscious of the Spiritual Fact that Infinity Is All there Is and It Is You, It Reveals Its Self to you "physically". Invulnerability is made tangible.

However, while the intellect controls your thinking, the Idea that You are Invulnerable is unbelievable. you think it doesn't pertain to your life, and it doesn't **because** the very thought that you are "in" a body that is vulnerable is self-fulfilling.

How is vulnerability self-fulfilling?

**I** can only give you a brief answer because to Understand the full answer requires more background knowledge. This knowledge will unfold as we go along, but for now, try to accept that the discordant universe you sense (and to which you react with fear) is a perception created by the mind fed with the thought that you are vulnerable. If you lack Consciousness that this is what the mind does, your thought fulfils itself to you over and over.

Despite what you sense, your vulnerability is **not** True. your Purpose, then, is to find out You are Invulnerable. What are you doing here? you are discovering You are not i, but **I**, for **I Am** Invulnerable, Indestructible and Unchangeable, Consciousness of which appears "physically" As My (Your) Permanently Harmonious Perception.

It was important to introduce you to your True Invulnerable Self, if only in theory. Now let us explore what it means to be Invulnerable in a practical sense, because "physical" experience is the only way to convince you that this Spiritual way of defining Infinity is not just esoteric mumbo jumbo, but something tangible and useful.

Among other things, Invulnerability means you are Safe and Secure at all times and in all places. It means you are Healthy at all times in all places. It means you are Prosperous at all times in all places. It means you are Loved at all times in all places. In a very Real sense you are Free.

If only that could be true.

your Purpose is to discover It **Is** True.

How do i make this discovery?

By Awakening from the self-created dream of vulnerability. And you do this by learning to Trust your Intuition.

The Intuition Is your Connection to Infinity, your built-in Voice of Truth. Not Truth Itself, but a Spiritual Impulse or Thought that forms a direct line to the Truth and, with Consciousness, appears As Its Self As your experience of Permanent Good. It follows, then, that if you are to demonstrate Your Invulnerability, you must allow Me into your Conscious Awareness and give My Thoughts your Trust.

How do i distinguish between my normal thoughts and my Intuition?

The simple answer is that they F(f)eel different. your Intuition is Thought derived from Love (the Nature of your Invulnerable Self) which the Body verifies with a Feeling of Undisturbable Joy, Rightness and Peace. your normal thoughts, on the other hand, are based on fear (for your vulnerable body) which reverberates though your body as fear, uneasiness and tension. The more complex answer involves a realization that it is rare to Feel the Undisturbable Joy, Rightness and Peace of Love because you keep your mind busy reacting with fear to the apparent unpredictable and often threatening world of situations and people.

my intuition would warn me about frightening situations and people, wouldn't it?

you are referring to "gut-feeling", the "sixth sense" or "extra sensory perception". This is an abridged form of Intuition or intuition with a lower-case "i". Abridged, because frightening situations and people are part of what the human mind unknowingly creates **with** fear, and, therefore, warning you about it only reinforces fear. True Intuitive Insight tells you there is nothing to fear and, if you Trust It, It proves it. This is Love in operation. But if you think fear is a legitimate response to perceived threats, you will never Feel Love much less Hear your Intuition tell you that you created the world you fear with fear! While fear runs around in your mind freely shaping what you call your "normal" thoughts, Love has no chance to prove Its Self. Add to this the vain attempt to suppress the distasteful feeling of fear with the pursuit of your own idea of happiness and you have a recipe for confusion when it comes to distinguishing between your normal thoughts and your Intuition.

What's wrong with my own idea of happiness?

you go on a wild goose chase. desire for the things, situations and people (that you have decided will make you happy) is the other side of the coin of fear, because desire wouldn't be necessary if you Knew you were already Provided for, or if you didn't fear loss. fear, then, is behind desire and makes the happiness you gain strained and unfulfilling. desire is a lure to remain in fear. you must expose this temptation for what it is, for a choice for a false happiness is a choice for fear. Love offers you the only Real choice there is—a choice to eradicate what frightens you. But we must first bring fear out from behind its pretence of intuitive guidance and support.

How?

Shine a light on it. fear is the buzz of anxiety or nervous energy that meets you when you wake up in the morning. it makes your body involuntarily clench and twitch and your mind brace for the onslaught of the day. If you awaken to something you look forward to, this buzz is excitement, but underneath your enthusiasm simmers a deep-seated worry of the possibility of failure and loss, and so the buzz always has a defensive edge.

i wouldn't say i'm defensive. i'm usually quite positive.

Being positive doesn't mean you are not defensive. "positive" means you have simply become adept at managing fear. To be positive, you must have a negative frame of reference. This means that the most determined effort to remain positive cannot match your own sabotaging thought-system. fear lays in wait like a cat ready to pounce on its prey. The constant buzz of anxiety is evidence of its presence. Sure, it has become unnoticeable just as one becomes deaf to the hum of traffic by living near it, but it doesn't take much for it to reveal itself. At the slightest provocation, your smile quickly fades and your mood reverts to the more authentic irritation, frustration, disappointment, anger and other forms of fear.

These feelings are not really "me" either though.

That's because deep down you Know You are not i. The fear is therefore not genuine. But this Knowing has not yet crystallized. It is a sleeping pupae waiting to emerge like a butterfly out of your ignorance. Yet, did you Notice? With the Recognition that your old habitual feelings don't Feel Right, the opportunity to let the butterfly emerge has suddenly presented itself.

Why?

Because only your True Self could have made the Recognition! Now open your Mind and see if you can be consciously Receptive to Its Voice.

It is like walking into a forest away from the hum of traffic. The mind's defensive edge softens, the anxiety recedes and a crispness of Life takes over. As you Listen and Trust, it is as if you are breathing for the first time. Bubbling up from the long forgotten Infinite depths is the Undisturbable Joy I mentioned earlier. This Feeling naturally arises from the Pure and Certain, Invulnerable, Perfect Love and Permanent Life of Your True Being. Intuitive Thoughts come from this place of Wholeness. As you Resonate with your own depth, you Feel the Joy of Wholeness that, by definition, cannot fail to Feel Uplifting, Warm, Comforting and Peaceful.

Further emerging out of these Feelings is a Knowing that the Intuitive Insight you Receive is completely Right and **can** be Trusted in spite of the world you have set up to make you feel vulnerable. I mention this because this deep Feeling of Rightness also includes the Feeling of what is not-Right. To follow your Intuition, then, Promises profound Relief.

Then i should add Intuition to my normal thoughts.

Unfortunately you can't add Intuition to any great effect, because i favours its defensive thinking over Listening to Me. Allowing Intuition to Guide your thoughts is the ideal we want to work towards. The correction eradicates the need to think for your self, for there is no self to protect and defend. Without a puppet, the intellect is stripped of its self-appointed role of boss and returned to its proper role as partner of the Intuition. your Acknowledgement of the partnership Reveals the Uplifting Feeling and Assures you that the depth of My Loving Influence Is at work behind the scenes Providing for your every need. Not in a self-delusionary way as false hope would promise, but practically and tangibly **As** your immediate and total Health, Prosperity, Peace and Safety. It's a Confidence that you are Provided for by something Greater, and that this "something" is always at hand.

However, you can't be Assured of My Presence and doubt It at the same time. you must prioritize Listening to Me and, in turn, you make the happy discovery that **I** was never missing. you were always enfolded in the bosom of Perfect Love. There was never any threat to your Well-being, you just thought there was. And when you Remember this, you can Relax. It's like having a supportive and protective big brother or sister, an intelligent and prudent financial advisor or benefactor, and a physician who never lets you get old or sick all rolled into one at your disposal at all times in all places.

Actually, before you forgot about Me and obscured Me with doubt, your Mind and **I** were joined in Truth. Remember that Timeless, Carefree Feeling you had as a child?

i do. Nothing worried me at that innocent age.

No matter what tragedy and mayhem seemed to be mesmerizing adults, you were oblivious. But it wasn't merely because you were young and innocent, it was because you were in touch with that Invulnerability that was in no doubt that you were Safe, Healthy, Loved and Provided for, and always would Be. In fact, the thought that these Attributes of the Truth of Your Being could be absent didn't cross your Mind. you simply embodied Truth because the Connection with Me was intact. My Presence went wherever you went, appearing As your Loving Parents and every Reliable circumstance of your existence. Through these Avenues, **I** fed you with Peace and Happiness on every level.

Yes, it was blissful knowing that i was protected somehow. i still have the Feeling if i care to tune in, but nowadays it seems remote, and doesn't relate to my life very much.

The point is, It's still Here and can be accessed anytime. Adults have to relearn how, but small children Connect to this Feeling of Undisturbable Joy naturally. Some children even display behaviour that would explain it, if only it wasn't misinterpreted.

Are you referring to my "imaginary" friend?

Yes, that's a good example.

Apparently i communicated with my "friend" before i spoke to my parents. They told me that it lived in the overhead light in my bedroom and we would have long conversations in an incomprehensible language. Was that You?

It was Me.

Typically, as young children, there is a short window when our Receptivity to Truth is uninterrupted. Sometimes this Connection manifests as open communication with our True Self and the parents mistakenly call it an "imaginary friend". Little do the elders realize **their** relationship with this **belief** is imaginary, not the child's Relationship with Me.

But one day i stopped talking to You.

Yes, this is what happens. Without Consciousness, you became exposed to, and accepted, the untrue idea that My Presence was imaginary. Before that moment, you existed in the atmosphere of Gentle Oneness with Me. With no reason to interrupt the experience, your Mind remained crystal clear. My Permanence wasn't questioned. My Perfection wasn't doubted. Accordingly, Warmth and Comfort flowed freely between Us. Contentment and Happiness reigned, for **I Am** Love, and Love holds Its Self in an unbroken embrace.

*"I will never leave you nor forsake you."*[3]

your infantile world operated smoothly both inwardly and outwardly **because** the channel to Me was open. It was like a shell that Protected you from the discord that others continually experienced in the world and therefore took for granted. Unfortunately, without Conscious Awareness of what was Protecting you and why, you began to trust your senses. Rather, you learned to trust your senses over your Intuition because you began to listen to your elders (people you trusted who trusted the senses), and the clarity of My Presence became shrouded by the possibility of an unsatisfactory present and a uncertain future. It was as if a scared and noisy crowd was allowed to enter the Sanctuary of your Mind and My Guiding Voice was drowned out by the hooting and hollering.

As soon as you accepted a discordant world as a reality, it was as if the Protective shell shattered. But it wasn't really Protection that shattered because Truth can't be broken. It is more accurate to say fear closed in. The intellect smothered your unconscious Trust and the Truth that would have continued this Protection. Through no fault of your own, you swapped unconscious Trust in Me for an unconscious trust in the outer world. Inevitably, your experience turned up-side-down, for the outer world cannot operate Harmoniously without **Conscious** Trust in Me.

Just as tuning into a particular channel on your TV excludes other channels, we, individually and collectively, tune into the belief of impermanence and imperfection and exclude the Truth of Permanence and Perfection.

Aren't You able to break through?

you ask that as if **I** am separate from you. It's only you that can break through with Consciousness. In the meantime, it is futile to expect an Idea of Perfect Safety, Health, Abundance, Peace and Love to override the actual perception of disease, accident, injury, poverty, crime and injustice.

---

[3]   *The Holy Bible*, New King James Version (Tennessee: Thomas Nelson Inc., 1982), Hebrews 13:5

In the face of these pictures, Intuitive Insight falls on deaf ears and blind eyes, and the open Mind required for Me to demonstrate the Truth is terminally obstructed.

To Hear the Truth you must deliberately and persistently tune in to the channel that **tells** the Truth—your Intuition. Initially this will be at odds with the persistent pictures of discord, but we must Consciously reject these pictures in the knowledge they are only a sensory perception based on ignorance of Truth.

How can i do that? They look so real.

It's not easy, and the intellect will point directly to the "fact" of impermanence and imperfection, but we can begin by realizing that the material world we perceive with the five physical senses is unreliable and should not be trusted to shape our thoughts.

> *"the only evidence we have of sin, disease and death*
> *is furnished by the senses; but how can we rely on their*
> *testimony when the senses afford no evidence of Truth?"*[4]

There are plenty of examples of sensory perception that should raise doubt about its trustworthiness. We have already raised one. The earth looks flat, but will we fall off the edge at the optical illusion we call the horizon?

No, we never get to the horizon.

A mirage looks wet, but is it really wet?

No.

Does the sun really rise and set?

No. The earth is moving, not the sun.

How can you be so sure? From your perspective on earth, doesn't it look as though the sun is moving?

---

4    Mary Baker Eddy. *The Christian Science Journal*. (Massachusetts: The Christian Science Publishing Society, 1947), 460

Yes, but space exploration has educated me. It has been shown that the earth actually moves around the sun.

Yes, we override our senses with expanded knowledge. Now what's to say we are **not** seeing My Safe, Prosperous, Healthy and Loving World, My Permanent Harmony, for the very same reason that we don't actually see the earth revolving around the sun? Might the senses be deceiving us once more?

i suppose so, but i am suspicious because if what You say is True, wouldn't we have already discovered it?

This discovery is not your average discovery. It is in a different category altogether, for we must reach into the Infinite Spiritual dimension where Your True Invulnerable Self is accessed. From the material perspective we therefore come to an unbridgeable impasse. For whereas the rocket enabled us to see the correct order of planetary movements by extending our sensory perspective, Truth, like Infinity, is not physical, It is Spiritual. And no device will extend our sensory perspective to include Spiritual Concepts, because the only device able to bring Spiritual Concepts to Life is the Mind, and, in our present state of consciousness, we use the Mind to process sensory input at the **exclusion** of Spiritual Concepts. we say matter exists but Spirit doesn't exist. Hence the problems of impermanence and imperfection persist.

Think of it like darkness declaring Light doesn't exist. Is this a legitimate assertion? Does an absence of Light have any authority to say something it knows nothing about doesn't exist? And even if it tried to prove the existence of Light, could it? darkness would negate its self in the process.

Likewise, i would negate its self if it stopped trusting the senses. Therefore by trusting the senses unreservedly, i survives at the expense of Truth.

Then how do You suggest i proceed?

Again, by Listening to your Intuition, because Its direct line to your Invulnerable Self bypasses the senses and changes what you sense.

Though, **I** must warn you, before we continue beyond the mental impasse into Spiritual territory, Listening to and Trusting your Intuition results in the Receipt of information that contradicts every lesson the intellect has taught you about the world and how to conduct your self in it. It makes myths of your cherished beliefs and even transcends the laws of physics. you can understand, then, that any questioning of what makes up your perception is a direct affront to the intellect's authority. This will challenge it to mount a counter-attack to justify and maintain its sensory stronghold. The intellect's role as a puppet-master depends on your total allegiance to it. you must therefore expect the usual rejection, doubt and suspicion to be ramped up to new levels of strength and sophistication. For instance, the intellect will try to convince you to drop your Spiritual investigations because they can't be scientifically proven. But this should be no deterrent. **I** never said Spirit could be scientifically proven. **I** don't need scientific proof. you will notice there is no scientific proof for the origin of matter, yet here we seem to be!

There is no scientific basis for Intuitive Insight.

No there isn't, but nor is there any scientific basis for the subjective evaluations of rejection, doubt and suspicion, the very tactics the intellect employs to shut down your Intuition.

But let us not criticize the intellect. it does its best to protect and defend you in your lack of Consciousness. In any case, you can't abandon it. By questioning its teachings, you will be re-establishing the Intellect's partnership with the Intuition thereby Acknowledging Its True role. This must necessarily bring the Unwaverable Higher Reasoning of the True Intellect into play which will verify the Ideas **I** will be putting to you. And since this Reasoning comes from the same Source as your Intuition, It will support and Resonate with the memory of that primordial sense of Assurance and Comfort, Freedom and Belonging, the same sense of Rightness you Felt as a child but dimly Remember. Together, Reasoning and the sense of Rightness will be your Truth litmus test.

Revealing Truth is never easy. At first, it will feel like you are demolishing a favourite old house. But do not be concerned. Under the foundations of fear is buried Treasure representing your True Home of Love, Peace, Beauty and Joy, everything Good you have ever wanted but your trusted world failed to give.

The unearthing of the Treasure, however, will not happen by itself. It requires your Willingness and Intent to break down myths you thought were true and replace them with four solid and stable **Truth-fundamentals**, and a Law that binds them together. These Principles, taken into consciousness, are the foundations of your True Home.

Are you ready to find out what they are and shake things up a bit?

`i think i'm ready for the disruption.`

Alright... Here we go.

# CHAPTER 3

# i is for in a body

As long as you think you live your life "in" a body, you are going to feel vulnerable, because at every turn, there are threats to navigate. Under the spectre of disease, accident, injury, evil intent, and, in the end, the certainty of death, you must be vulnerable. But this idea flies in the face of Your Invulnerability. Let us then demolish this persistent myth. You are not body, or "in" a body.

Though, before we can demolish the myth, we must look at the implications of the myth itself. To believe you are "in" a body is to believe you are "in" the universe, because the body is part of the universe. Further implied is the belief that this universe and the body are material and separate from one another, otherwise how could the body be "in" the universe?

In Reality, all of these assumptions are as true as a flat earth. You are neither material, separate, "in" a body, nor "in" the universe, because, as we established earlier, You are the Invulnerable, Spiritual Source of the Body and the Universe. This Is the Truth, and if You are the Truth, You appear **As** a Body **and** the Universe.

Now, because you associate your self with the body, Your appearance **As** the Universe will, initially at least, be too immense to take in, so let us confine our attention to the Fact that You appear **As** a Body and apply that Understanding to the Universe a bit later. Besides, the Body is your personal "vehicle" for making this discovery. It makes sense to begin here.

To get started, right now, while you are reading, focus on the position of your body in the chair. Now that you have done that, forget the chair and concentrate on you and your body. In your mind, separate your "self" from your body. Try saying quietly to yourself "**I Am** appearing **As** a Body" and compare it to "i am **in** a body".

Just a second. You mention Body with an upper-case "B" and body with a lower-case "b". Are they different?

It's the same B(b)ody viewed from the Spiritual or physical perspective. This exercise should begin to clarify the distinction between the two P(p)erspectives. A distinction must be made before you can make the necessary choice between them. But don't concern yourself too much with these P(p)erspectives just yet. Simply feel the difference between "As" a Body and "in" a body? "As" puts You in charge of the Body whereas "in" puts the body in charge of you. Feel the profound shift that upsets your old assumption about the body. Did your body sit in the chair by itself?

No.

Of course it didn't. In the same way as your arms can't lift themselves and your legs can't decide to walk on their own, **you** made the decision to sit and your body followed along. The body is sitting because of you.

So what?

Sitting in a chair may not seem so important, but if **I** said your body is sick, in pain or dead because of you, would you be so dismissive? Would you pay attention?

Certainly, but i'm not so sure i could pay attention if i was dead.

If you only Knew... the "death" of i **allows** you to pay attention, because i is the barrier to that attention, a fictional barrier no less. If you no longer identified with i, (which is the only death there is by the way) you would be Conscious that You are in charge, that You appear As the Body, and the Body would obey. Ah, but you meant you couldn't pay attention if your **body** was dead. See how you put the body in charge without even thinking?

Mmmm. i wasn't aware i did that.

**I** Know. When you shrug off the Truth that You appear **As** a Body, you unintentionally put the body in charge of the things that are most important to you; your freedom, health, safety, relationships and prosperity, even your very life. When you put the body in charge of you, you **lose Consciousness** of the Fact that there is a Greater You that leads you to Fulfil Itself As these necessities.

Consciousness, then, is the key that unlocks Truth from being just a Good Idea into an experience of Permanent Good. Yet a lifetime of thinking on your own and ignoring My Guidance has meant that the Idea of Consciousness is not even on your radar. As a result, you have inadvertently turned the correct Order and Association between You and your Body up-side-down and blocked your own Good from appearing. The correct Association is that You and the Body are One because You appear **As** the Body. But you must be Conscious of this. Therefore Your Consciousness is of paramount importance.

Unfortunately, when you believe you are in a body, this Divine Association is split up in your mind and the Order is reversed. This seemingly innocuous turnabout is far from innocuous. it demonstrates that you don't know what Consciousness is, which leads you to forget who You Really are. But this does not mean **I** (Your True Self) am not Here, it just means in your forgetfulness you can't access Me. The forgetfulness makes you like a pauper unaware of an inheritance. The inheritance might as well not be there at all. you carry on in a sorry state until you Remember it was never missing.

The trouble is, the Consciousness necessary to Remember who You Really are has effectively been split away from the consciousness that has forgotten who You are and made two C(c)onsciousness'. This split must be healed by facilitating Remembering. In order to facilitate Remembering, **I** am going to make greater use of the bracketed words we have already introduced (like B(b)ody and P(p)erspective).

Won't that be confusing?

Not to the Real You. The Truth about You ensures that you will be able to hold the two I(i)deas simultaneously. Before long, you won't even notice the brackets and you will realize it was confusing not to use them.

In any case, to be able to See who-You-are and who-You-are-not at the same time is so crucial to the fulfillment of your Purpose for being here that it constitutes Truth-fundamental #1—**Y(y)ou are 100% C(c)onsciousness**.

So **I** am 100% Consciousness, **and** i am 100% consciousness?

Yes, both are True. **I** will explain what this means in a moment.

Alright, but if i am 100% consciousness, why do i see a body?

**I**'m glad you brought that up. Straight away we can explain the B(b)ody with Truth-fundamental #2—**C(c)onsciousness appears A(a)s M(m)atter**. The "material" B(b)ody (and the wider "material" U(u)niverse) Is Y(y)ou appearing! This is what **I** meant earlier when **I** said You are the Spiritual Source of the Body (and the Universe). There is **not** Y(y)ou **and** the B(b)ody. Y(y)ou appear **A(a)s** the B(b)ody. That's why your body looks like you and no one else. That's why your body is where it is, at this time. Everything about Y(y)ou is the result of C(c)onsciousness!

Perhaps you are already beginning to See the value of the bracketed words. Consciousness (your True Self) Is Invulnerable, Consciousness of which determines the Harmony and Peace of what Consciousness appears As. But a lack of Consciousness (little "c" consciousness), by definition, lacks Consciousness that its Self is Invulnerable. This creates the impression of a "second" self, by that self, that thinks it is vulnerable. This consciousness proves vulnerability to its self by **appearing as** an imperfect body that resides in an uncontrollable and frightening universe.

By combining the two P(p)erspectives in one sentence you see at a glance that there are two ways the world can appear depending on which C(c)onsciousness you allow to run your M(m)ind. Implied, too, is that what you have come to accept as a separate world is a projected image in and of the M(m)ind. The importance of this point will become more clearly evident as we proceed with our study. For now, it might be helpful to paraphrase Truth-fundamental #2—**Y(y)ou are the S(s)ource of what Y(y)ou perceive.** Or, Y(y)ou W(w)itness Y(y)our own C(c)onsciousness. Or, the O(o)bserver I(i)s what I(i)t O(o)bserves.

*"we don't see things as they are, we see things as we are."*[5]

```
It's like i have no choice but to believe You.
Some would say that is rather arrogant.
```

The Truth-fundamentals merely inform you about what is happening behind your ignorance. you are free to disbelieve, but wouldn't you rather be informed about the ramifications of your decision to disbelieve? It is typical of the intellect to shoot the messenger. But isn't **this** arrogant? Ultimately, the intellect's accusation makes no difference to Truth. Truth is not subject to disbelief of It. Nor, indeed, is Truth dependent on belief of It. In fact, both disbelief and belief of Truth are attempts to fold Truth into fear, and because discord is fear appearing, you are apt to remain in disbelief of Truth.

Perhaps put it in these terms. When you **think** you are in a body, you don't change the Fact of Truth-fundamental #1—**Y(y)ou are 100% C(c)onsciousness**, but your perception confirms you are right to believe you are in a body. But think of the implications of the lower-case alternative. When the consciousness that believes the body is in charge of **it** is actually in charge of the body, what hope do you have to rise out of the clutches of the belief? Return again to the pauper unaware of an inheritance. Just because he believes he is poor doesn't mean it is True, but if Truth can't get through, poverty is true for him.

```
It sounds hopeless.
```

Forgetting who You are is devastating and complete. It's not like forgetting in which bank account you put your inheritance, it's forgetting you have an inheritance in the first place. If someone told the pauper there was a fortune waiting for him, he would deny it. This is exactly how our potential to Awaken and Be Conscious is severed. we forget who We are, and that "We" are actually in charge of Our own Harmonious Perception. It's a forgetting that puts the perception in charge, thus altering and

---

5    Goodreads.com Anais Nin quotes. http://www.goodreads.com/quotes/5030-we-don-t-see-things-as-they-are-we-see-them

defining that perception, and, most importantly, concealing the perceiver, you, from the Awareness that you have control even in your disbelief that you have control.

The Truth-fundamentals are like lights leading us out of darkness. They give us Hope in our forgetfulness. Not just for their explicit Truth but for the implicit journey we must take from one consciousness to another, and what it entails. They are your personal roadmap to Truth, for **you** and only you are responsible for your experience. **you** and only you have the opportunity to Free your self from the tyranny of your false perception. That is, i (consciousness) can be your prison-warden or i (consciousness) can represent your **potential** to access the Divine Riches of your True Identity. The Truth-fundamentals lay out the only Real choice you have.

But doesn't the word "potential" suggest never getting to where i want to go?

In your present state of consciousness, "potential" does imply "always impending and never being", that's true. But perhaps we can look at "potential" another way and begin to See things from Consciousness' Spiritual vantage point. If You always were the Truth that you simply forgot, would the potential to break through that forgetting be a real barrier? Does forgetting have any substance? If not, the impending-ness is no obstruction. you have forgotten who You Really are, but remembering is inevitable, because You never were the forgetful i. "potential" is therefore a sure thing. If **You are 100% Consciousness**, it makes potential nothing, yet potential remains. It's waiting for no Real reason, still we wait.

In our unrealized potential, we make things appear to be true that aren't True. One of these misperceptions is that we are in a body. This myth represents our lack of Consciousness.

Are You saying i can't be Conscious and believe i am in a body at the same time?

The question is twisted and unanswerable because you were never "in" a body. Y(y)our C(c)onsciousness will always appear A(a)s a B(b)ody of some description. It's whether you associate your self with the body or your consciousness that determines your trajectory away from or towards your potential to Be Conscious. The more that you think your body is you or that you are "in" a body, the more you cling to a **lack** of Consciousness.

Let's try to dislodge this stubborn belief now that we have Truth-fundamentals #1 and #2 under our belt.

As we have already established, C(c)onsciousness comes first, but the belief that "i am in a body" puts the body first and consciousness inside it. This is the wrong order. Consider that you must be mistaken to believe you are in a body, because you must be **conscious** that you have a body **before** you can make this mistake.

    You mean i am conscious even in my lack of
    Consciousness?

Yes, the awake-consciousness that believes it is in-a-body is actually the lack of Consciousness **I** am talking about.

Let us establish beyond doubt that i is a form of "consciousness". This is a stepping stone, but a crucial one that proves, beyond doubt, you are **not** body. From there you can expand your definition of consciousness and thereby facilitate Remembering. But first things first. Tell Me, how do you know you have a body?

    i can see it.

What about when you shut your eyes?

    i can feel it. i am aware of my body's presence.

Does your body have this awareness without you? Or to put it another way, can your body be conscious of you?

    No, my body can't be conscious of me. i am
    conscious of my body, at least when i am awake.

you seem confident.

    i am.

To be sure suggests two things. One, there is a greater part of you that is not dependent on the body, an awareness. And two, this "part" is "conscious", a consciousness you call "i".

Furthermore, this consciousness points to an intelligence distinguishable by asking your self "**who** just learned about an awareness greater than the body?"

i did.

Doesn't this intelligence you call "i" describe you better than a body could? Do hearts, lungs and brains have the intelligence to understand concepts greater than themselves, by themselves?

Perhaps my brain?

Doesn't your brain need **you** to activate it? Can the brain, by itself, ask the question "what am i doing here?"? Is the brain pre-eminent to the enquirer? Better still, can the enquirer of this question be subordinate to the effect it is enquiring about?

No, it can't.

Alright then, wouldn't the idea that you are born into or defined "by" your body, or any part of it, be incompatible with this revelation about your self? Didn't we just determine the body in its own right is an unintelligent effect? And if so, can something unintelligent hold or give rise to something which is intelligent and conscious of it?

No, i suppose not.

consciousness must come first, for we are **not** conscious **because** we have eyes, ears, nerves and a brain. It's the other way around. These apparatus are secondary; eyes can't see on their own, ears can't hear on their own, nerves can't feel on their own, and a brain can't think on its own. we give parts of the body power erroneously. we don't need them, they need us! They are instruments for our use, for the use of the consciousness we appear **as**.

Can you understand that you are the consciousness that **seems** to be in a body but is not **actually** in it?

35

It's becoming clearer.

we could even switch the emphasis around, for it is more accurate to say the body is "in" you, "in" your consciousness. your consciousness is not in the body, nor is your consciousness a product of the body.

With a better sense that you are consciousness and not body, let's expand the definition of consciousness beyond the body by asking another question. If the body is for the use of consciousness, what does consciousness use the body for?

i don't know. To be conscious?

you are on the right track. The body enables consciousness (us) to interact with the universe around it via the senses. However, i uses the senses to additionally reinforce the belief it is in a body, which then defines its state of consciousness. But we have established that this belief is not True. Therefore, interacting with the universe must have another purpose.

What other purpose?

Conscious or not, no one can sense something that isn't tangible. So could our sensory interaction point to a greater Purpose of becoming Conscious of Consciousness Itself? If so, we wouldn't really "become" Conscious. The senses would **verify** Consciousness because, according to Truth-fundamental #2, Consciousness appears As Matter.

Unfortunately, though, this is where we get stuck! we arrive at the same impasse as before, for the senses can't verify Infinite Spiritual Consciousness when the Mind (the avenue of Consciousness) is used exclusively to steer our thought back to our belief that we are in a body, back to the limited awake-consciousness that disbelieves the Truth. In our unrealized potential we take the sense evidence at face value. The universe looks separate from our body and that's that. But what if we could take what came **prior** to the physical appearance into account?

Is it necessary to Know what came prior to the physical appearance?

Yes, because that is what will expand our consciousness!

our consciousness is limited because the physical appearance is our yardstick. But if consciousness determines the physical appearance, our Consciousness of this must expand our consciousness. Then we experience Consciousness because Consciousness appears As Matter!

Now, **I** appreciate it's already a tall order to flip your perspective from being "in" a body to the body being "in" your consciousness, but, to round out our Understanding, we must apply the Understanding that we are not "in" a body to the universe as well. we are not "in" the universe either.

The difficulty is always the senses. you might see a table over there. your eyes tell you that the table is separate from you. So is the tree outside, and the mountain and the ocean. It's silly to deny it. But you are not asked to deny how matter appears, just to deny that it **is**, in fact, separate. Let us widen our horizons and ask; "just like parts of the body, must not the table, the tree, the mountain and the ocean be within our consciousness for us to be conscious of them?" If we can agree, then our consciousness has been put back in the correct Order ahead of the senses, and because the Order could not have been switched without Consciousness, you have expanded your limited human-consciousness into Infinite Spiritual Consciousness.

How did switching the order expand my consciousness? It seems too simple.

It **is** simple but you will find it is not easy to maintain, for the habit of viewing your self "in" a body will snap your consciousness back to the sensory perspective. But we should keep trying, for we are no better off agreeing that we are the consciousness of the body if that consciousness believes it has to function "in" a universe.

Ah yes, because we would still be vulnerable.

That's right. Our Consciousness must include everything we sense, otherwise, the food, shelter, money, people and protection we need for our well-being must actually be separate from us in time and space. we must truly be vulnerable to loss. The universe must really be a hostile place, a place of scarcity and danger, a place with the power to cause misery, pain and death. our fear must be justified. And most importantly, the Truth-fundamentals must not be True.

But the Truth-fundamentals **are** True whether we believe them or not. Therefore, it is not so much the belief we are "in" a body that causes us to lose Consciousness. It is the absolute conviction that this body that we supposedly occupy is "in" the universe, a separate material universe with its own intelligence and power that we were born into and will die out of as if we never existed. It is **this** conviction (which is just a belief because it isn't True) that makes us feel vulnerable.

The conviction that separateness is real is the foundation of our little "c" consciousness. it causes us to forget that We are 100% Consciousness, because a consciousness that thinks matter is separate from its self can't be Conscious that Matter Is Its Self appearing.

`It's hard to get my head around.`

It's hard because you never had to stretch your mind outside its accepted parameters, but these parameters are based on a misconception. we have been looking at the universe from the wrong angle. Ever since we first looked up at the stars and wondered how the universe formed we have led ourselves down the wrong track.

`How `**`did`**` the universe form?`

The great discovery we make is that it didn't! There is no separate "form", so questions about **how** it formed confine us to the incorrect idea that there **is**, in fact, a separate material universe.

Again, **I** am not asking you to deny the experience of separateness. **I** am not disagreeing that the universe **looks** material, but we get carried away with the appearance and draw the conclusion that separateness must be a fact. And implied within this conclusion is that there is some sort of intelligence and power in matter that causes problems that often seem to be unsolvable.

But there is no intelligence and power in matter because there is no matter in its own right. All Intelligence and Power is part of and constitutes Our Infinite Self, and to be Conscious of this is the solution to every problem.

# CHAPTER 4

# i is for ill-informed

**Where does God fit in to all this?**

This is another unanswerable question, for i can't Know what "God" is. Therefore, it can't be said where it "fits". Yet the concept of God is all-important. Let us then spend some time getting to Know It.

◇◇◇◇◇◇◇◇◇◇

Most of us would agree that there is an Intelligence and Power that grows every Tree and beats each Heart. Some might give the Intelligence and Power of the Universe the catch-all name "God". Others prefer the term "Life-force" which, from time to time, is affectionately referred to as "Mother Nature".

This same Life-force is the impetus behind Cosmic Events. However, the term "Life-force" seems less appropriate here. Although it's the same thing, it's more like a "driving-Energy". This driving-Energy gives birth to Stars, moves Planets around the Sun, and Moons around the Planets. It organizes the Gravitational Pull that keeps these heavenly Bodies precisely in their orbits. In addition, we observe this Intelligent and Powerful driving-Energy arranging a complex and cooperative system of Matter, from the microscopic workings of an Atom and smaller, to the vast outer reaches of the Galaxy and beyond.

Whether we call It the "Life-force" or a "driving-Energy", though, there is general consensus that this Intelligence and Power exists.

The disagreement comes when some of us think of this "Life-force" or "driving-Energy" as being generated from matter itself, while others like to think of It as the workings of a "Creator" that not only creates but animates matter. Consequently, our basic agreement of the existence of Intelligence and Power has broken into two schools of thought; one scientific, the other religious.

Generally speaking, the scientific model presumes that the Life-force or driving-Energy is activated by a particular concurrence of material conditions. For instance, a tree grows given the right nutrients in the soil, temperature, air quality, sunlight and rain; a heart begins to beat when a foetus reaches a certain stage in the womb; and a "big bang" occurs during a complex cosmic alignment. Questions about the Life-force or the driving-Energy itself are nimbly side-stepped as science delves into the fascinating mechanisms **of** Life and processes **of** Energy. Although there are different branches of science that inch slowly toward an explanation **for** Life and Energy, scientists conduct their research under the unspoken assumption that matter is somehow self-generating. This implies that matter has a life-force and a driving-energy of its own—an intelligence and power of its own.

While any definitive explanation about the how matter self-generates remains unknown, religion has been able to fill the gap and assert that matter is formed and animated by a "Creator" or "God".

Now, the religious model is right insofar as the Origin or Source of the outward evidence of Life and Energy **Is** God. However, (and it's a big "however"), this **isn't** the God religion refers to. God **Is** Infinite Spiritual Consciousness which **Is** the Intelligence that Powers the Universe that You Are. **I Am** God.

You are God?

Yes, **You** are. Ah, but you meant Me and not You. See how we split our S(s)elf up? The bracketed word is particularly appropriate in this instance because it powerfully illustrates how we have separated the Infinite **Self** of All of Us which **Is** God from the **self** which is a product of the belief that God and the S(s)elf are separate.

You seem to suggest that religion makes the same mistake.

it does. Or, at least, religion's correction of the mistake is not forthcoming. This oversight is not deliberate. Nevertheless, the result is that religion promotes the impression that "God" is an intelligence and power separate from you that created you. The interesting thing is, religion is not alone. This is the same mistake science makes, although scientists generally balk at the name "God". The name, however, is irrelevant. The point is that the proponents of both science and religion have been led by the intellect into the same cul-de-sac of false thought.

we should pause here and honour scientific research and religious worship, for aside from the attempt to satisfy a Real longing for Truth that eventually rewards us with Illumination, the sincere open Mind of both the scientist and the religionist can be of great benefit to humanity. The scientist, in particular, translates the Insights he or she Receives into useful data that can be used to improve the lot of humanity. But this book is not about making life better (although this will be a happy consequence), it is about discovering why there is a need to make life better in the first place. And we will find that this need has its roots in the apparent existence of danger, disease, loss and death. But now, how do we reconcile these apparent facts with the equally apparent existence of a universal Intelligence and Power? we assume (erroneously) that the Intelligence and Power of the Universe must be responsible for discord.

science responds to this assumption by building the idea into its explorations and hypotheses in the hope that, by discovering the laws of matter, it will come across a material way to make the world a safer and more comfortable place. religion responds to the same assumption by building rituals of sacrifice, tithing and prayer into its worship of god in the hope that god will protect and save the faithful.

Meanwhile, the average person hedges their bets. we encourage science to invent ways to keep us safe, secure and well for as long as possible, but when desperate times intercede, we reserve the right to pray to god to bring health to our child or harm to our enemy. And although we are more inclined these days to blame ourselves for the climate catastrophes we endure (an ill-conceived blame **I** will explore later), we still refer to discordant events like earthquakes and tsunamis, volcanic lava flows and molten ash, and landslides as "acts-of-god", and so we call on god to fix or prevent these catastrophes, to protect us, just in case it helps.

Both scientific thought and religious thought are unaware that the belief of a separate intelligence and power and the adoption of a false i to believe it, is responsible for the appearance of all discord. And it makes no difference whether we try to save humanity from its self by scientific research or prayer. Both will ultimately fail because the i wanting saving is the same i that created the world from which it wants to be saved, the same i that devises its schools of thought.

we leave ourselves dangling in intellectual no-mans-land, because W(w)e, C(c)onsciousness, can't be left out of any theory about M(m)atter because **C(c)onsciousness appears A(a)s M(m)atter.** Yet the Truth **is** left out because we lack Consciousness. Mainstream science says that "matter organizes itself" and we have nothing to do with it, and orthodox religion says "god organizes matter" and we have nothing to do with it.

`we're all wrong then.`

we are all wrong because God Is the One True Self that appears **As** Matter. In the absence of this Knowledge, we decouple ourselves from the Power and Intelligence that appears "As" Matter and become victims of an erroneous intelligence and power "in" matter. Rather than ensuring we en-Joy Permanent Harmony, we ensure we suffer discord.

The meaning of "God" has thus been lost to a false "god-of-matter", a belief that simultaneously explains and proves our powerlessness against matter. Both science and religion subscribe to this god-of-matter even though science would insist that belief in a god distinguishes it from religion. But it's the same god-of-matter because "god" has come to mean something we idolize in its mysterious supremacy over us. religion's "god" is the so-called creator of matter. science's "god" is matter itself. Just because science doesn't call it "god" doesn't mean it isn't. It's not the Real God anyway.

The god-of-matter is the god we have come to think of as "God" and "Science". we believe in one or the other because our experience of discord is accommodated. But it's **because** we have substituted the god-of-matter for the Real God that discord appears!

The Real God Is your Invulnerable Self, Consciousness of which eradicates the appearance of discord and prohibits its reappearance. That's how Permanent Harmony is Revealed.

What about inanimate objects? Do tables, chairs, buildings and bridges come under the Permanent Harmony of God?

They do to your Consciousness of what God Really Is, yes, because there are no exceptions in Consciousness. If you can be vulnerable to one thing, you are not Invulnerable. But You **Are** Invulnerable and, therefore, along with the Life-force and the driving-Energy of the Universe, what we bring through our own Minds as "Creative Inspiration" must also Be of the same Substance. And so we have a third name for the Intelligence and Power of the Universe, which, in order to keep it simple, all boil down to the same name—Love. Love Inspires the Tree to grow, the Heart to beat, and the Planets to spin. But It also Inspires Ideas and Directs our Hands to fashion those Ideas into tangible Objects such as Chairs, Tables, Buildings and Bridges.

Is it correct to say that God is in inanimate objects?

No, God is not enclosed "in" any object. The God You Are appears **As** those Objects and Consciousness of this is what makes Them Permanently Harmonious.

i thought that God was in objects and that was why when objects cooperate with me, i am being blessed by God, and when objects collapse and hurt me, i am being abandoned or punished by God.

This is incorrect. Objects are not being controlled by God for or against you. How can they if You Are the God that appears As Harmonious Objects? your own belief of separateness appears, sometimes beneficially to you, sometimes harmfully.

Let's be very clear. The Intelligence and Power that we have assigned to matter **Is** God, but **We** can't be left out, so the god we worship is not God. God and god have no shared A(a)ttributes. God Is **You**, whereas god is a belief **you** carry. The former is Empowering and Expansive in Its All-inclusiveness, the latter disempowering and diminishing to the believer that believes it can be blessed, abandoned or punished by god, not knowing it is a belief in its mind that fulfils itself.

God is Good with a missing "o". you can't be blessed, abandoned or punished by the Good that You are, a Good that you can't gain or lose. you can, however, be unaware of your Good, and this is when we lost track of the "o" in Good and our Understanding of God with it. we learned to associate "good" with material "good", a temporary and imperfect opposite of "bad". Good (and therefore You) was lost to consciousness and a tyrannical and unpredictable god crowned in its place.

But you can't Really lose the Truth to a belief. There is no alternative to your Purely Good Consciousness, therefore, no other "God". Either you are Conscious of this Truth or you are not. That's all there is to It! When **you** lack Consciousness, it is the unconscious **you**, **i**, that invents the separate god-of-matter, which, because a lack of Consciousness invented it, is not Consciousness and therefore not God.

Perhaps it is dawning on you that asking how God fits into all this is an ill-informed question, because Consciousness can't fit into any answer that excludes Consciousness.

```
What question would include Consciousness?
```

Questions that reach up to Consciousness.

```
How do i do that?
```

By bringing some Awareness to the one who questions. Notice that it calls its self "I". Now ask "who or what is "I""? it's a lack of Consciousness until it realizes it is reaching up to Its Self—Consciousness—God!

Isn't it Divinely strange that we all call ourselves "I"? This Name you call your self is the clarion call to Truth. **I** Is Your Name. you even write "I" in upper-case! But now you have forgotten the Real reason for assigning the upper-case letter. "It's grammatically correct" says i.

```
"Susan" is written in upper-case too.
```

Yes, a remnant of the Memory of Me remains in the Names we call each other as well. But look at the difference between "I" and "Susan".

Realize that you don't call your **self** "Susan". When you walk down the street, you don't say in the third person; "Susan walked down the street". you say in the first person; ""I" walked down the street". The Given-names have been given simply to avoid confusion when you refer to others, for if we all called each other "I" we wouldn't know who was who. But then we made more of a fuss of our Given-name as if to recoil from the amazing and Unifying Fact that we All have the same Name, "I".

Let us be Aware of our Names and what they imply. The next time you introduce your self and you hear your self say, "Hello, my name is Susan", Realize the word "my" in the introduction is not i, but Me. I appear As Susan, Geoffrey, Janis, Jo, Tallulah, Giovanni, Rajni, Khalid and every Person in the world. To whom do you say "hello"? You say "hello" to your Self, to God.

If you accept that **I** Is God, you will be in great company. **I** has been Known by the great Sages of history. For instance, Krishna said *"I Am the Truth of the Truthful I"*[6]; Moses said *"I Am that I Am"*[7]; and Jesus said *"I Am the Way, the Truth, and the Life"*[8]. Contrary to mainstream religious belief, none of them were referring to, or intending to draw attention to their mortal selves. Nor were they calling that mortal self Divine. **I** Is the Infinite and Immortal Self of everyone on the planet, Consciousness of which Knows It doesn't separate into a body, but appears **As** the Body and the Universe.

`But i am not a great Sage.`

Every great Sage thought they were i before they Realized they were not i. Look at your self as a potential Sage. Don't forget, we are all Infinite, even though we are Individual. Infinity is not diminished by being Individual, because, Remember, Infinity can't be divided. we all have that unrecognized Indivisible, Indestructible, Unchangeable spark that we call the Soul that by another name is Consciousness.

`Is I my soul?`

**I Am** Is your Soul.

---

[6]   *The Bhagavad Gita*. (Adyar: Theosophical Publishing House, 1953), 10th Discourse: 37

[7]   *The Holy Bible*, New King James Version (Tennessee: Thomas Nelson Inc., 1982), Exodus 3:14

[8]   *The Holy Bible*, New King James Version (Tennessee: Thomas Nelson Inc., 1982), John 14:6

```
Is I my heart?
```

When you Listen to Me, you Listen to your Heart. Not the physical heart, but the Invisible and Divinely Spiritual Heart of your Being.

Unfortunately, though, the terms "Heart", and especially "Soul" and "Spirit", are imagined to come with the body and "released" when it dies. These terms are therefore apt to lead us away from Consciousness. The best words to describe Me are the words that lead us towards Consciousness. Have you heard of the three Omni's; Omnipresence, Omniscience and Omnipotence?

```
i've heard these words before but never really
understood them or thought i ever could.
```

These words describe the Nature of **I**. Properly Understood, they help us perceive what is behind the idea that we could be abandoned by a god-of-matter and set adrift to fend for ourselves and how to correct the false idea. Particularly when used together, the three Omni's put Matter into its correct Order behind the **I** of Consciousness and help us perceive what appears to be a separate universe **with** Consciousness. Everything comes together when you read the next paragraph and pause to ponder the **bold** sections.

The prefix "Omni" means "All and Only". Consciousness Is Omnipresent because It Is in All places at All times, and there is no other presence in any place at any time. In particular, this means **there is no matter with any presence of its own.** In addition, Consciousness Is Omniscient because It Is the All and Only Intelligence, and there is no other intelligence anywhere at any time. This means **there is no matter with any intelligence of its own.** And last but not least, Consciousness Is Omnipotent because It Is the All and Only Power, and there is no other power anywhere at any time. This means **there is no matter with any power of its own.**

The Infinite You, **I Am**, Is All there Is.

> *"Give up identification with this mass of flesh [the body] as well as with what thinks it a mass [i]. Both are intellectual imaginations. Recognize your True Self as undifferentiated Awareness, unaffected by time, past, present or future, and enter Peace."*[9]

---

[9]    Our Advita Philosophy Ashram. Sayings attributed to Adi-Shankara. http://www.advaita-philosophy.info/Quotes%20and%20Links.html

---◦---

# CHAPTER 5

# i is for in fear

If we are ill-informed about God, we must be just as ill-informed about Matter, because God (Consciousness) appears **As** Matter. Though it is perhaps more challenging to overturn our convictions about Matter than to overturn our convictions about God, because God has always been thought of as immaterial. Matter is the very opposite of immaterial, hence its name.

Why do we need to overturn our convictions about matter?

Because if we don't, we won't be able to Realize our Invulnerability. fear and discord will continue to be given power at Joy and Harmony's expense. we must begin to See Matter in a different way, and a good place to start is by learning **how** Consciousness appears As Matter.

C(c)onsciousness works through the M(m)ind and the M(m)ind's activity is T(t)hought. And if the M(m)ind's activity is T(t)hought, the P(p)erception that appears before our eyes must be nothing more than a **M(m)ental interpretation** of our C(c)onsciousness. M(m)atter, animate and inanimate, is T(t)hought formed. T(t)hought doesn't leave the precincts of the M(m)ind and externalize separately. This is why there is no such thing as matter in its own right, and why there is no "God" responsible for creating material problems or fixing them up. Ultimately, there would be no problems to fix if My Thought was allowed through the Mind without any interruption from your thought.

Are feelings something separate from thought?

No. In fact, F(f)eelings and T(t)hought should be regarded as the same thing.

Why?

Because F(f)eelings are T(t)hought felt in the B(b)ody.

How does that make them the same?

The B(b)ody, being part of our M(m)ental interpretation of C(c)onsciousness, must be a form of T(t)hought too. Therefore, it follows that if the B(b)ody is T(t)hought, F(f)eelings must be T(t)hought.

And so we come to Truth-fundamental #3—**T(t)hought is the S(s)ubstance of the P(p)erception we call M(m)atter**, or **M(m)atter is T(t)hought sensed A(a)s T(t)hing.** Just as paint is the creative medium of a painting, T(t)hought is the creative medium of the P(p)erception we call M(m)atter.

There is nothing we perceive that is not made up of T(t)hought derived either from Consciousness or a lack of Consciousness.

Nothing?

Nothing.

What do i do? Pretend that i am looking at thought, not matter?

Yes, at every opportunity. But perhaps make the exercise more meaningful by realizing you are not here to merely respond to the apparently material universe around you. you are here to Know that you create, with thought, the "material" universe (of thought) to which you later respond, with thought. thought is at all times everywhere and everything. This entirely contradicts the assumption that everything is material to which our thinking benignly responds. In fact, it completely overturns the assumption and reinstates thought as the substance of matter. There is no separate material universe. Moreover, the thought that there is a separate material universe creates an illusory and frightening distortion of Reality in Reality's place.

How so?

When we believe that matter is something in its own right, it must be possible for us to be deprived of our needs. But does matter have this power if it is thought appearing?

No.

That's right. thought has the power! But what power does thought have when we don't know matter is its effect?

i don't know.

In the absence of Consciousness, fearful thought has the power to make frightening material circumstances appear before our eyes. fear, then, is not just an inconsequential after-thought. There are things to fear **because** we fear. When we assign "cause" to the mental "effect" of matter we reverse Truth and respond to the ensuing distortion of perception with fear. In turn, fear creates more things to fear in a self-perpetuating cycle.

The appearance of discord is evidence that, in effect, we have reversed the Order of Truth-fundamental #3. matter is not meant to shape thought, because it is just an appearance of thought. T(t)hought shapes M(m)atter! The tragedy, then, is that once we reverse the Truth, discord cannot be avoided until we reverse the reversal of Order back again in our Mind.

Notwithstanding the improbability of reversing the reversal while matter is given all the power, this re-establishment of Order is absolutely essential to the discovery that, in Reality, there is no discord. And so we come to Truth-fundamental #4—

**There is no P(p)erception prior to or in isolation from T(t)hought.** In other words, **T(t)hought comes before P(p)erception of T(t)hing.**

Consciousness of Truth-fundamental #4 helps us cement the Idea that T(t)hought comes first in I(i)ts own all-encompassing creative sequence.

i am having real trouble believing these two
Truth-fundamentals.

**I** am not asking you to believe them. In fact, believing takes you in the
wrong direction, for it deepens the distortion you have trouble believing is
false. Consider now what a belief is;

> *"a state or habit of mind in which trust or confidence is*
> *placed in some person or thing"*[10]

our own definition of a belief omits the initiating creative thought!
we trust the thing when we should be trusting the thought that produces
the thing. For if thought comes first, isn't our trust in things misplaced?
And as if to deepen our distorted view and twist it completely out
of shape, the *people* in which we place confidence share our belief of
what a belief is. Unthinkingly, we succumb to the habit of placing
trust or confidence in our parents, then our friends, teachers, mentors,
and bosses, right through to our political, religious, scientific and
cultural leaders, all of whom, further back, inherited their beliefs from
their forebears, back through the millennia. Accordingly, no human
perception is untainted because no human perception begins with a
Pure Thought of Truth.

The point is, no human belief **can** begin with a Pure Thought, because
belief creates its own reason to believe, which blocks Pure Thought. So
when we believe, that is, when we trust people and things in place of our
Intuition, we never find out the Truth that thought is the substance of the
perception we call matter, much less the Spiritual alternative.

So all beliefs are wrong. Is that what You are
saying?

"belief" is based on the incorrect assumption that matter has no
relationship to thought other than to shape thought after the event, so
yes, from Truth's point of view, all beliefs are wrong. If we let matter

---

[10]   Merriam-webster.com http://www.merriam-webster.com

shape thought, all subsequent thought must be erroneous, because the "original" matter was created by the incorrect thought that matter **could** be Original. Think how science, the pursuit of Truth, must be continually frustrated, because it requires material proof **before** accepting a change to human belief. But can the creation of a self-sustaining echo-chamber prove anything beyond it? The thought that matter comes first is the substance of its own material outcome. Therefore, when it comes to proving that matter is in fact a **consequence** of thought, science hits a brick wall, for it can't reach beyond its belief to allow a space in the Mind for the Higher Self to prove Its Thought instead. This takes a leap of Faith, something that goes against science's own requirement for prior material proof. But let us not single out science for elevating matter above thought to then inadvertently exclude the only Thought that can Reveal Truth. Most of us do this every day. Don't we say "i'll believe it when i see it"?

```
Yes i do.
```

we always let "things" dictate thought. How often do you say "i'll wait and see what happens before i decide what to do"?

```
Very often.
```

In Eastern cultures we can be paralysed by what we have come to believe are "inauspicious" circumstances and wait for an "auspicious" circumstance before acting or making decisions. Western cultures carry similar superstitions. "i've been lucky" we say as we "touch wood" so as not to jinx our good fortune. Then again, bad luck might be blamed on that mirror we broke.

```
...or the black cat that walked across my path.
```

superstitions vividly demonstrate how we automatically and unthinkingly let matter shape thought. By reacting to problems and then trying to fix them or avoid them, we expose our ignorance, for they would not eventuate in the first place if we Knew they were just thoughts. And if they did eventuate, we could quickly correct our mistake and even laugh it off. Instead, we place our faith in planetary alignments, statues of Deity, or a rabbit's foot; and avoid walking under ladders or residing in houses with particular numbers. Sometimes, we ask "the universe" for favours as if that universe (that we created from fearful thought) could somehow release us from fear. Mostly, though, we go through life in a daze, bewildered and confused by what seems to happen independently of us. thought is not considered as a cause, therefore, we get into a muddle at best, and disaster at worst, never considering for one moment that our discordant universe is a meaningless aberration.

i thought everything happened for a reason.

everything **does** happen for a Reason, and one Reason only—T(t)hought and T(t)hing are one and the same. In humanity's case, fear and discordant things and conditions are one and the same. But it's as if we deliberately disable our Intuitive Reasoning and swap it for insanity, for the idea that "everything happens for a reason" discounts Reason, which must make any conclusion reached for "everything happening" Reason-less. And there's more, for no thought happens without consciousness (us). consciousness is the cause or source of thought that appears as matter. i is the one that fears in ignorance that it causes the things it fears. i therefore cannot give up fear and, by implication, the things it fears, even if it wanted to.

Why not?

Because if things are thought, then the idea of a separate material universe is incorrect and, consequently, i is not really vulnerable. But i can't let go of its vulnerability, for i exists because of its vulnerability. That is, even though the discords of life are meaningless, they give i's life meaning. This is why, as perverse as it may seem, i defends its experience of pain, scarcity and loss to its death.

Let us now look at a visual representation of what makes us fight to the death for what "kills" us anyway. **I** call it the "bubble of ignorance"—a dysfunctional state of mind that, in effect, superimposes itself over Reality.

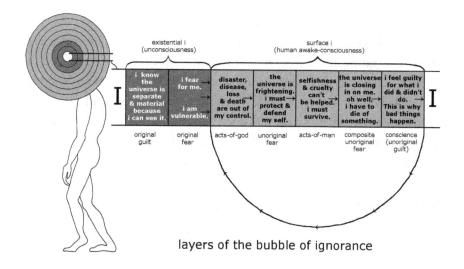

layers of the bubble of ignorance

Just like the figure, we trudge along totally oblivious that we are carrying this burden around with us every waking moment. The burden is heavy because our fear and its discordant forms build on each other and themselves in a series of layers that bewilder and confuse us until we finally just turn up our toes; conceding defeat to a body riddled with disease or worn out with exhaustion. Therefore, in order to burst this bubble of woe, it is essential to Understand how these layers develop and why they are so self-defeating. To this end, **I** have divided the bubble into seven layers, and two sections; a dark-grey section with two layers and a light-grey section with five layers.

The dark-grey layers are at the core of the bubble. Together they represent the unquestioned conviction that matter is real in its own right, that it is actually separate and apart from us in time and space. And seeing as we are quite conscious of this separateness, you might wonder why **I** marked these layers as "unconscious". It's a curious thing, for it is not that we are unfamiliar with separateness; the problem is we are totally **unconscious** that separateness is a mistaken **belief**. And being creative, this belief literally sets the scene for our awake-consciousness (represented by the light-grey layers).

But before we rush on, let us concentrate on the dark-grey layers. you will Notice that the **first** of these dark-grey layers is right next to **I**, our True

Self. But we have turned our back on It because matter has captivated us with its appearance of separateness. This first layer, then, represents us; the i that is responsible for believing separateness is a fact. This makes i intrinsically **guilty** for creating all the discord that follows. Not that i can be blamed in the usual accusatory sense, for the mistake was made in ignorance. Nor can one be blamed for something that doesn't actually happen! Still, because i is convinced the belief is true and **does** happen, the thought gives rise to the **second** dark-grey layer. This is made up of i's anticipatory reaction to its feeling of insecurity; "i fear for me", and "i am vulnerable". This original fear is better known as "existential fear", so-called because this fear forms the fabric of i's existence.

Now that we have some understanding of the basis of our awake-consciousness, let us see how it is made up. The **first** of the five light grey layers begins the cycle of "surface fear".

What is surface fear?

surface fear is our reaction to real or anticipated discord.

surface fear is "unoriginal" insofar as discord is not possible without i and its existential fear. But surface fear's pedigree should not be our only focus. surface fear is useful to the intellect. it puts another layer of reaction between you and Truth which makes i harder to detect and less likely to be deactivated. surface fear is thus unwittingly encouraged to mutate and hybridize into forms of fear like worry, apprehension, suspicion, alarm, paranoia, panic and terror, further discrediting the idea that matter is thought appearing. In other words, we defend i with discord; the evidence being that we normalize surface fear, throw reason out the window, and impose unsolvable problems and hurt on ourselves and others.

For example, let's suppose you were having a winter break in a snowy mountain resort and, without warning, an avalanche swamped and destroyed the alpine chalet in which you were staying. Assuming you survive this catastrophe, would you call it a disaster?

i would.

Would you acknowledge that the disaster happened as a result of your core belief in a separate universe and your subsequent fear of vulnerability?

No, i would not. It could have been due to any number of factors outside my control.

Like what?

Too much snow reaching a critical mass where gravity took over, a rock-fall, someone skiing on the snow disturbing it, a seismic shift below the surface, anything.

Anything but your thought.

Yes. If something like that happened i would be in the wrong place at the wrong time, suffering some sort of bad luck or an act-of-god.

What if the event led to you meeting the love of your life, or meant you missed some other event you were dreading?

Then it would have been good luck. It would have been meant to be.

Even though some people were injured or even killed.

Well, not for them, no. But it must have happened for **some** reason. Maybe their time was up. Or perhaps it was some sort of lesson. karma perhaps.

See how we strain to devise reasons to explain disaster even though these reasons expose themselves as fictitious by collapsing when they contradict one another. "karma", too, is just as fanciful. The idea that catastrophic events are orchestrated to teach us lessons or settle scores is absurd. What catastrophe could teach us that fear preceded it? Can fear instigate correction to itself? discord, be it on a mass scale or localized, is our individual and collective unawareness that existential fear "causes" the discord and forms the substance of it. If we don't pick this up, discord becomes like a festering internal wound, the pain of which is misdiagnosed and the symptoms treated superficially to create more complications that further hide the cause.

So disasters aren't meant to be?

Certainly not! disasters, like any discord, are a result of the denial that your fearful thought is creative and that it comes from a mistaken belief. If anything is "meant to Be", it is Permanent Good!

The problem is, nothing that goes wrong or doesn't go right is ever traced back to thought let alone our mistaken core belief of separateness and our existential fear. The sense-evidence is always trusted. And rather than being a transparency for Immortal Life and Eternal Love, the collective mind of humanity becomes the crucible for the false perception of discord and the existential fear that unknowingly precedes it. Then how are we expected to make informed conclusions from a universe that never arises from a Pure Thought? we don't even know this is possible, for the universe confirms we are vulnerable. we therefore become slaves of matter, a slavery in which we learn to be grateful for glimpses of good, because that's all we get.

> *"mortal illusions would rob God, slay man, and meanwhile would spread their table with cannibal tidbits and give thanks."*[11]

The "avalanche" scenario is an illustration of the point where our awake-consciousness begins. In this first light-grey layer we have actual proof that discordant "acts-of-god" like disaster, disease, loss and death could strike anyone, at any time, in any place. And despite the mental gymnastics we go through to explain and accommodate these acts-of-god, they are regarded as largely uncontrollable and random. The **second** of the five light-grey layers then represents the conscious decision to protect and defend ourselves as best we can against any such eventualities. But protection and defence are themselves fearful and thus carry the unintended consequence of embedding the unoriginal forms of fear into our psyche and burying our existential fear even deeper.

While we are busy building this erroneous defence structure we give

---

[11]  Mary Baker Eddy. *Science and Health with Key to the Scriptures.* 1875. (Massachusetts: The Christian Science Board of Directors, 2009), 214:24

rise to the **third** of the five light-grey layers. This layer amounts to our desperate drive to survive in the face of our failure to protect and defend ourselves or explain discord adequately. Unable to stop our existential fear fulfilling itself, we succumb to feelings of annoyance, frustration and anger, throwing blame and judgment on others for our suffering and loss. Now with clear grounds to be selfish and greedy, we become conscious co-creators of the discordant scene. Unchecked and unrecognized, fear breeds attitudes ranging from a petty sense of entitlement right through to prejudice, bigotry, oppression and violence, and becomes the excuse for exploitation and abuse. fear, too, is behind the lack of courage to stand up for the oppressed and abused, thus allowing inequity and cruelty to flourish. Perhaps the most shocking demonstration of our now completely deluded and distorted mind, though, is the open, unashamed and even proud way that we invoke the name of God to justify these acts; acts that actually work against God, for God Is Us! But this extreme outpost of distortion merely proves how self-destructive fear can be. All "acts-of-man", conducted by a mob or singly, overtly or covertly, piggy-back on top of "acts-of-god" creating a world of unsolvable horror and chaos.

The **fourth** and second-last of the five layers symbolizes our realization that if **we** are personally capable of doing the wrong thing, so can others, towards us. our fear of man combines with our fear of things and situations, confirming the impression with overwhelming certainty that we are indeed sitting ducks in an unsafe universe. Perhaps as a type of survival strategy, the resultant amplification of fear is also a time when we resign ourselves to an imperfect world full of imperfect and untrustworthy people. our mind is thus handed over to a fate we do our best to defend ourselves against, but in the end consigns us to a death i hopes won't be too dreadful. "i have to die of something i guess" says i philosophically.

And so we come to the **fifth** and final layer. This outer layer is not so much a response of fear as a representation of the entrance of **conscience** into our mind. conscience is an abridged form of Intuition that discerns right from wrong and exposes the emotion of guilt for the first time. A guilty conscience prompts us to consciously consider the ramifications of our acts-of-man in order that we may transition from selfishness to self-less-ness and finally Illumination. But there is a snag. A guilty conscience, by definition, binds us to the past, so unless we Listen to our Intuition and

Recognize that we can't be bound to a past that never really happened, we "explain" discord away as some sort of cosmic lesson or karmic retribution for our guilty actions (as we saw in the avalanche illustration). And together with our unawareness that our original mistake perpetually gives rise to the "surface" layers of the bubble, we are destined to repeat the cycle over and over.

We will explore the complex and crucial-to-understand workings of guilt a bit later, except to be aware now that guilt forms the inner and outer layers of the bubble giving the bubble its structure and strength like the bread of a sandwich. fear is the filling of the sandwich, but without the bread it falls apart. fear and guilt thus work together as a team.

For the moment, though, try to Recognize and Acknowledge that fearful thought is at all times everywhere and everything. But only until we make the greater Acknowledgement that there is nothing to fear because, if everything is thought, there is actually no separate material universe and therefore no i necessary to believe it and feel vulnerable as a result. **I Am** the only "I" and, Remember, **I Am** Invulnerable.

---

# CHAPTER 6

# i is for inconsistency

Continuous Harmonious Perception is the Promise of Consciousness. It waits patiently behind the bubble of ignorance for you to Understand that fear really does create humanity's perception of discord. But your fate is not sealed, for if your True Self Is Invulnerable, there is actually nothing to fear. Like clouds parting to reveal the sun, suddenly the choice to experience Undisturbable Joy in your daily life is made available.

Diagrammatically, the choice looks like this.

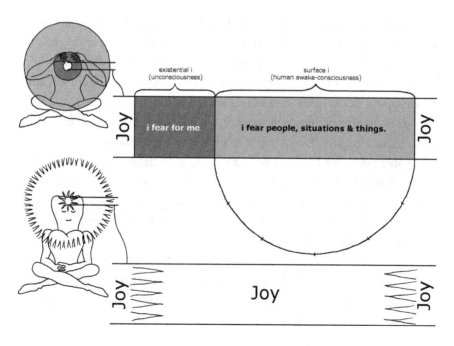

To avoid a fussy picture, **I** have removed the layers from the dark-grey and light-grey sections of the bubble of ignorance, but it's the same bubble.

In the upper scene, we are tormented by the reaction of fear to the discord we unknowingly create with existential fear. This contrasts markedly with the lower scene which shows what it is like when the Undisturbable Joy of the Love of our Invulnerable Self is allowed to penetrate the Mind. Nothing can disturb the Joy we Feel in this scene because in order to Feel Undisturbable Joy we must already Know that fear is unnecessary.

Why can't i feel joy in the upper scene?

you can, but if you believe fear is necessary, you will generally feel a lesser joy. you see, there are two J(j)oys; disturbable joy (the fleeting joy that comes when fear temporarily subsides as a response to discord temporarily subsiding); and Undisturbable Joy (the Joy of Consciousness of the Love of your Invulnerable Self that is obscured by discord and its temporary lapses). Normally you settle for disturbable joy because you believe you are vulnerable.

Why can't i experience Joy while i feel vulnerable?

Because you can't Feel your Invulnerability and fear at the same time. fear blocks Joy. Having said that, there are times when you involuntarily drop little i and the bubble of ignorance bursts for a moment. you might look at a Flower and Feel Joy. But the bubble closes over again because the dropping of i is not Conscious. Perhaps you remember that you have an allergy to the pollen in flowers. As your mind makes the historical association, the Joy of looking at a Flower is replaced by fear for your vulnerable body. And even if you can manage to delay the association by Acknowledging that the Flower can't hurt Invulnerability, suspicion and doubt that a mere Feeling could have any value or benefit to a painful and uncomfortable physical symptom quickly interrupts this Joyful Knowing, and you reach for the allergy remedy.

The power you have given the intellect and its sensory viewpoint is why, before now, you have barely Recognized Undisturbable Joy let alone been able to Trust It to expand into and transform your whole experience. The Fact that the Feeling of Undisturbable Joy Is the indicator that the allergy in this case has no power of its own is cut off before It can bear fruit. you keep your self from the proof that anything inconsistent with Love is actually powerless.

But now we can prove that Love Is indeed Omnipotent. There is a Law of Consistency embedded within the Truth-fundamentals that says if you are Conscious that there is nothing to fear (meaning that you Understand that there is nothing with any power next to the Omnipotence of your Invulnerable Self), then no discord can enter your experience.

So if i get bitten by a venomous snake i won't die?

If you are Conscious that Snakes are Your Invulnerable Self appearing, then Snakes won't attack in the first place and dying from poisonous venom would not be possible. Both the Snake and You Are Love, Consciousness of which cannot harm or be harmed. Let us then work with the Law of Consistency and Consciously Receive that Assurance.

What do You mean by Consciously Receive?

"Consciously" means you Understand that the Joy you Feel is not materially or mentally generated, because the Source of Permanent Harmony Is Love and you can't think of Love. you Receive It Intuitively from your already Complete and Infinite Consciousness.

How do i know if i am Consciously Receiving or not?

you will experience Permanent Harmony all the time in every aspect of your life.

How do i know that i **can** Consciously Receive?

we all can because we all Share the One Mind. Permanent Harmony is your Inheritance. And also because you already do Receive. you prove that you Receive frequently. you just don't Recognize It yet.

What frequent experience do i have?

you hold a Baby and Feel Joy. you look at a Sunset and Feel Joy. Joy is Felt when you look at Natural Phenomena like Mountains, Oceans and Trees. Unfortunately, though, these Connections with Love are not enough to convince you that there is nothing to fear, because, as your allergy to flowers illustrated, fear has made these Natural Wonders appear to interrupt your joy just as often as instilling Joy. A baby can start crying, and a sunset can foretell bad weather, which can, in turn, upset the equilibrium of mountains, oceans and trees and cause natural disaster. What's more, because you don't yet Understand that Undisturbable Joy can't be interrupted (by definition), you naturally think Nature must be intrinsically troublesome and even dangerous. Nature, therefore, is not a good teacher of the Fact that **if you Feel Joy, you must have Received It,** much less that this Recognition guarantees Joy's continuance.

Obviously, our experience of Nature is not capable of teaching us this great lesson, but there is another experience that goes part of the way. Then all we have to do is attribute the same Source (Love) to both.

What experience are You talking about?

The experience of Joy when we open our Minds to "Creative Inspiration". And for those of us who haven't yet had the experience personally, we experience It vicariously through the Purest Receivers of Creative Inspiration; **Artists.**

Artists Know that the Ideas they bring through their Minds don't come from their own thinking. And although they don't usually stop to consider where the Idea came from, they **do** know how to deliberately create a space in their Mind with confidence that an Idea will eventually pop in or emerge into view. After that, they submit their Body to the Greater Impulse and let It Guide their Hand, Pen or Paintbrush to complete the Artwork. They know better than to interrupt this process or use the Idea for some human purpose. Instead, they let their Mind and Body be used as Instruments.

In addition, if the Artist can manage to keep his or her own mental agenda at bay, a Thing of Beauty comes forth that Reflects the Source from whence it came and which acts as a conduit for the rest of us to Receive the Love of Our Self. This is why Artists love to Create and why people flock to Art Galleries to See Great Art and Sculpture, and to Concerts to hear Great Music. Everyone wants to Feel Undisturbable Joy.

The Artistic process offers us a unique and precious lesson, namely this— **because** we deliberately hand over our Mind to Intuitive Thought (Creative Inspiration as we call It in this instance), we can thoroughly rely on the outcome or Artwork to bring Joy with It. Compare this with our experience with Nature. Nature doesn't always bring Joy with It because we believe Nature has a separate intelligence and power to threaten us, hurt us and even destroy us. fear then blocks Joy. But not only that. fear prevents the discovery that Nature's Source Is, in Fact, our Invulnerable Self. Now, the Artist doesn't Know Art's True Source either, but at least he or she Knows their own thought is not responsible for the Idea. fear is completely absent, and this leaves an opening for the questions that lead to Consciousness, "what is the Source of the Idea?", "why does the Joy i Feel when i Create Feel extraordinary?"

The only shortcoming of the lesson of the Artist, then, is that we don't Understand that the Source of Creative Inspiration is our Invulnerable Self. This is why, as soon as the Creative activity ceases or we leave the Art Gallery or Concert, the Feeling is forgotten. Forgetting signals to our mind our dependence on the senses and we fall back into the bubble where we attempt to place Joy in context with the apparent reality of discord. Consequently, there is a tendency to compartmentalize Joy and confine It to our Creative pursuits or our appreciation of Art. Suddenly the one area that had so much potential to show us our Invulnerability is cut off at the knees. This lack of Consciousness doesn't prohibit Receiving, but it's like receiving a Diamond and thinking it's a rhinestone. we don't appreciate the Treasure we have at hand, and so we put our Art in a box marked "career" or "hobby" and get back to our discord-creative thinking the rest of the time.

Can inventors, engineers and scientists, who, when i think about it, are really "commercial" Artists, show us our Invulnerability?

They can, but less so than Pure Artists. Even though they are familiar with letting their Minds be used for Ideas, the commercial intent prevents the Bodily Flow of Joy and the Full Benefit to emerge. For instance, nobody could argue that a Car is a "work of Art", but the Car was invented with a use in mind. Therefore fear steps into the Creative process. That fear resonates with the end-user whose "use" of the car can be exhilarating in the freedom it offers from the constraints of distance, but can just as easily turn to horror when we crash it and injure ourselves. The Car can't show us our Invulnerability **because** it is used. Art can because it has no practical use in this sense.

Then why do you use an upper-case "C" for "Car"?

Because a Car is Creatively Inspired. Again, Ideas are like Diamonds. Just because we use Ideas doesn't mean they are not Diamonds. It's not the Diamonds fault that we see a rhinestone. It's not the Car's fault that we crash It. If you can manage to stay attuned to Joy, the Car Is Safe even while you use It, because Joy is inconsistent with fear and cannot give rise to anything destructive or tragic. The Car is My Idea, and when you are Conscious of this, Love Protects you and Guides you when you travel in It. (The important subject of Protection will be discussed at length in the last section of the book.)

The way fear corrupts our perception of Inventions is similar to the way fear corrupts our perception of Nature. But now, through our examination of Art, we might be able to See through fear to the Source of both, for the Joy we Feel when we look at an awe-inspiring Mountain-range, a calm expanse of Ocean, or a Tree in full blossom is the same Joy that we Feel when we Create Art or stand in Its Presence. Love is the Source and Substance of Its Self. That's why fear can appear as an allergic or poisonous reaction, but fear can't appear as a Flower or a Snake; fear can appear as a destructive storm, but fear can't appear as a Mountain, an Ocean or a Tree. Love appears As these Things.

*"There is naught whatsoever higher than **I**. All this is threaded on Me as a row of pearls on a string. **I** the sapidity in waters, **I** the Radiance in Moon and Sun; the Word of 64 Susan Pearson Power in all the Vedas, Sound in Ether, and Virility in Men; the Pure Fragrance of Earth and the Brilliance in Fire am **I**; the Life in all Beings am **I**…"* [12]

---

[12] *The Bhagavad Gita.* (Adyar: Theosophical Publishing House, 1953), 7th Discourse: 7–9

Are You saying the Mountain is there **because** of Joy, and that's **why** i Feel Joy?

Yes. To be Consistent, it must. Thought comes before Perception of Thing. The Mountain didn't turn up by Itself any more than the Artwork did. The ability of Nature to stir our Heart and feed our Soul should shake us out of our stupor, because we get the very same Feeling when we look at Great Art. we just haven't joined the dots. Our True Self **Is** the Source of the Thought that appears As Nature, the same Thought that appears As Fine Art or Commercial Art.

Art and Nature are the opportunities that Love Gives you to Recognize that same Love of your Self. The Perception of Beauty and Harmony of Nature is Joy filtering up through and in spite of your fear. Don't let fear make Nature **appear** dangerous, chaotic and threatening. Art and Nature have the same Source; Me, You.

Besides, is it not inconsistent to believe that **you** can open your Mind to Ideas beyond your self in a Creative sense but that Your Infinite Self can't or hasn't been able to demonstrate Its Infinite capacity in a similar way?

But just because i can participate in Creating an Artwork doesn't mean i participate in the Creation of Nature.

They only seem different because you are conscious of participating in one and not the other. you don't participate in Nature Consciously because you are unaware that you are Really Me. you have separated your Artistic Creations and Nature accordingly. Nature seems different because you seem completely disconnected from the process. But this is as it should be, because you are not personally responsible for Creating Art either. i didn't do It, **I** did. Again, you are simply unaware that you are Really Me. **That** is the leap you must take! Take your cue from the Feeling beyond your self, not **your** conscious participation which depends on your self. Are you not Joyful, Uplifted and Inspired by Nature in exactly the same way you Feel Joyful, Uplifted and Inspired when a New Idea for a work of Art pops into your Mind? Where do you think the Idea came from? you didn't think of a Tree. you didn't think of Art either, but Art and the Tree appear through My Infinite Mind to show you My Infinite Nature.

we all entertain fear, from allowing the unwelcome interruption of Joy's endorphins when a baby cries, to believing that pollen can attack some immune systems, right through to the conviction that snakes and weather systems are intrinsically dangerous. But when we entertain fear we should also Know that we make the decision to make Love powerless. it is the decision to give fear more power than Love. you can't actually do this, but you make it true in your experience. The Law of Consistency is uncompromising. When you use the Instrument of Consciousness (your Mind) to reject the Truth of Omnipotence and Invulnerability, you must suffer the consequences. It is therefore better to work with the Law than against It. When you work with It, the Mind becomes porous to Receiving Joy, fear evaporates and we literally stand back and watch the Treasures of Everlasting Love, Immortal Life, Peace and Harmony Reveal themselves automatically, without exception or exclusion, As Our Body and Our Universe.

# PART 2

# Discerning what is not from what Is

# CHAPTER 7

———◻———

# i is for incorrect use of the Mind

In this section of the book, We will continue to overturn the belief that we are limited to a body in an unreliable and dangerous universe and take our Understanding of Truth to the next level. In order that we are equipped to do this, our first task is to find out how the Mind works and how to use It correctly. Next, we will review the life of a particular individual who discovered the secret of the Mind. We will look at ways to discover the secret ourselves by observation and with the help of the leading-edge of science. After that, We will examine the dualistic nature of the bubble of ignorance and how it is surprisingly negative. With false hope exposed, the True Perspective is Revealed. And finally, We will translate one of the all-time masterpieces of Scripture into modern language. Revisiting it in a fresh way might help us Awaken from our stupor of ignorance.

But first we must Understand the Mind, the only Instrument through which it is possible to break through our stupor, the only Instrument that offers True Hope.

We have touched on the Mind a little already, but very few of us realize how important It is. The M(m)ind is the "A(a)s" in Truth-fundamental #2—C(c)onsciousness appears **A(a)s** M(m)atter. The M(m)ind is thus the pivot point, the middle-man, the "how" it is possible we are conscious and can Be Conscious. Like a "control tower", the Mind enables Consciousness to control how the Universe appears...when we let It.

In our present state of consciousness, we **don't know** to **let** the Mind be controlled by Consciousness. In fact, we mindlessly go the other way. we think we must proactively control our circumstances, not realizing that we created, via the mind, the very uncontrollable circumstances we now feel the need to control. The problem, as always, is our conviction in the separateness and implied pre-eminence of matter.

As a case in point, **I**'m sure you have noticed that many of us use the term "mind" interchangeably with "brain". It might not seem important, but demoting the only Instrument that **can** Reveal the Truth down to a mass of grey-matter enclosed within a skull-bone is symptomatic of the mistake we make every moment of our waking life, and symbolizes the essence of the human problem. we imagine that E(e)ffects can be causes. In this case we go all out, for we not only think that the Brain causes the Instrument of Consciousness, the Mind, we think the brain causes the Cause or Source (Consciousness) as well.

`Thinking seems to take place in our head.`

It does seem to. But if we look closely, we find it is our determination to describe the world tangibly that persists with the idea that the brain is able to produce thought. "mind" is therefore regarded to be a synonym for "brain", or, at the very least, an adjunct or product of the brain. science concurs. When brain activity is measured, scientists understandably conclude that thinking takes place in the brain. But the electrical impulses and patterns measured in the brain don't prove the brain is the source of thinking any more than the needle-movement or changing mercury-level of a barometer proves the barometer is the source of air-pressure. The brain and the barometer are instruments that show the effect of something invisible. The brain shows the effect of the mind, the barometer shows the effect of air-pressure. Neither create what they detect.

Truth-fundamental #2 states that **Consciousness appears As Matter**, Truth-fundamental #3 states that **Matter is Thought sensed As Thing**. The Thing that we sense is the Thought of Consciousness, which appears, along with every Thing else, **As** Brain. The brain does not come first, because matter doesn't come first.

Fortunately, science gives itself reasons to doubt its own hypothesis. brain research has revealed that the average person only uses a fraction of their brain in their lifetime. There appear to be areas of the brain we never use. Certainly, many of us tend to lose brain function and suffer mental illness as we "age". And there is a disturbing increase in the incidence of brain disease and mental illness in the population, including the young.

So why aren't we using the brain? Might these inexplicable handicaps and chronic degenerative diseases indicate we are underutilizing this vehicle of utmost importance? Or perhaps the Brain is a product of Consciousness after all and we are simply using the Mind incorrectly.

we won't Know for sure until we actually make the correction. So let us do so now.

First of all, we must Understand that the only A(a)ctivity, anywhere, at any time, is T(t)hought. The products of T(t)hought (the B(b)ody and the U(u)niverse) don't move on their own. And the Source of Thought (Infinite Spiritual Consciousness) is Unchanging and Unchangeable. Therefore, if we are sensing an active U(u)niverse, we are sensing T(t)hought of one type or another.

Also, the M(m)ind does not work autonomously. The Mind sits between two important functions that **we** drive. Thought can't enter our Mind without our Intention or Will to let it enter. I(i)ntention is not a T(t)hought, but determines the type of T(t)hought given access to the M(m)ind.

The first function, then, comes from our Intention to Consciously **Receive** Spiritual Impulses from Me As our Intuition. We discussed what it means to Consciously Receive in the last chapter. Again, it implies that we not only let Thought enter, we also refrain from outlining how that Thought will be Felt or how It will Guide us. **we** cannot conceive what we Receive.

As Consciousness unfolds, the second function of the Mind comes into play. That is to **Reflect** My Spiritual Impulses As your experience. If you Consciously Receive, the Reflection is guaranteed to be Permanently Harmonious.

The first and most important function of the Mind, then, is to Consciously **Receive** Spiritual Impulses.

## How does the Mind Receive?

The Mind is like an inner Ear that we intentionally point Spiritward towards the Love, Intelligence and Power that **We already Have**, that **I Am**. The Mind's Ear works in a similar way to an antenna on a TV. An antenna is like an extension of the senses in that it picks up or receives frequencies outside the spectrum of normal sense perception. These frequencies are translated into a visible and audible form. Just as light isn't visible until our eyes pick up waves of light, and sound isn't audible until our ears pick up waves of sound, our Intuition can't be discerned until we raise the antenna to a Higher frequency and our inner Ear Receives "waves" of Truth. The Mind "translates" or interprets these waves of Truth mentally as Thought enabling us to Feel this Thought As My Presence, Hear this Thought As My Voice, or even See this Thought As My internal Vision.

The Intention to Receive Spiritual Impulses complies with the correct Order of Thought before Perception of Thing and sets up the Mind correctly for its second function.

## To Reflect.

Yes, the second function of the Mind is to **Reflect** My Spiritual Impulses back to the Receiver via the senses.

> *"Reflect the Peace of Heaven here, and bring this world to Heaven"*[13]

## What if i don't Consciously Receive?

Normally you don't, and this is why a second reflection comes into play.

## A second reflection?

effectively, yes. The Mind is never still. It is unceasingly active. In the absence of our Intention to Receive, something must fill the vacuum. our thoughts fill the vacuum. That is, if we don't Consciously Receive, the antenna of the Mind has no choice but to grope around in the dark,

---

13    A Course in Miracles, (New York: Viking Penguin, 1996), Chapter 14, X-1:6

reaching no higher than the mental level of inherited or borrowed thought and intellectual reasoning based on the belief of separateness. And as the mind can't Reflect what it doesn't Consciously Receive, it reflects **our** thoughts. The mind doesn't stop reflecting. R(r)eflecting continues regardless.

So there are two R(r)eflections, Mine and yours. The closest we come to Truth is My Reflection because Its **Source** Is Truth. your reflection, on the other hand, bears no resemblance to Truth, because its source has rejected or ignored Truth.

Is it possible to see both R(r)eflections at once?

No, except as we saw with Art and Nature, there is a dim recognition through the veil of our unconscious reflection. But it is not sustainable because fear still shapes our thoughts. To clearly Reflect, we must Consciously Receive.

How does the Mind Reflect?

R(r)eflecting works in a similar way to a mirror **R(r)eflecting** T(t)hought back to us as what we perceive as T(t)hing. Remember, we are both the O(o)bserver and the O(o)bserved. P(p)erception is U(u)s W(w)itnessing O(o)ur S(s)elf. Therefore, when we look out through our eyes we are looking at a R(r)eflection of our own C(c)onsciousness.

Of course, the M(m)ind-mirror works very differently to a normal mirror. It doesn't have a flat surface, nor is it obvious that we are standing in front of It. we are not "in" the Mind-mirror either, but at all times we **seem** to be standing in it as if we are at the centre of a giant spherical 3-dimensional multi-sensory theatre we call the "U(u)niverse". Expanding out 360 degrees in all directions, the M(m)ind C(c)reates the impression of a 3-dimensional holographic I(i)mage and L(l)ikeness of I(i)ts contents. It is in this sense that we can say the U(u)niverse is "in" U(u)s, W(w)e are **not** "in" I(i)t.

In addition, the mirror analogy helps us Understand that we never experience Truth directly. Yet by accepting that the Mind is a Reflector we are led back to the O(o)rigin of T(t)hought. If the M(m)ind is a R(r)eflector, the next question is "**what** is the M(m)ind R(r)eflecting?" It always comes back to us. we reap the I(i)ntention we sow.

> *"To him that sows to his flesh will of the flesh reap corruption, but he who sows to the Spirit will of the Spirit reap Everlasting Life."[14]*

And now "karma" becomes a useful term. For we See that it is **we** who invented the god-of-matter to orchestrate events in the background to settle scores and teach us lessons. we "reap what **we** sow", **we** "get what we put out". What goes around comes around. It's **our** intention that keeps the karmic ball of discord rolling. our intention reflects back to us as the bubble of ignorance.

What about good karma?

Good Karma is your Inheritance. you cannot get from a false reflection the Good you already Have. The "good" you experience in the bubble is a temporary respite between the "bad" times you made with fear. That's not to say you can't conjure up your "good". After all, everything is thought. your strength of will, persistence and determination will pay dividends. However, *sowing to the flesh* (deciding what's good for the vulnerable you), **builds** karma. In the end, you cannot Knowingly manipulate your way out of what you unknowingly create in the first instance.

K(k)arma is M(m)ind-action. Just as there are two R(r)eflections of C(c)onsciousness, there are two K(k)armas. Two K(k)armas must have two I(i)ntentions that R(r)eflect—*"qualities born of their own nature."[15]*

When i has any sort of intention, the mind has no choice but to pick up recycled thought and reflect *qualities born* of i's nature. That is, fear reflects back to its self as intermittent discord, a world harsh and antagonistic to its self that leaves i anxious, desolate and despairing. i believes it is

---

[14]   *The Holy Bible*, New King James Version (Tennessee: Thomas Nelson Inc., 1982), Galatians 6:8

[15]   *The Bhagavad Gita*. (Adyar: Theosophical Publishing House, 1953), 18th Discourse: 41–42

separate from the universe and that everything happens for a reason. But i can't articulate this reason. i certainly can't accept that the only reason discord happens is because it believes separateness is a fact. Consequently, things keep going wrong because the conviction of separateness is never questioned. And if everything happens for a reason, we conclude that the unwanted events must be deserved karmic punishments for some guilty action we must have committed in the past, or lessons we haven't yet learned. The fact that there can be no Real reason for events based on the lie of separateness is not considered because it is not known. This is the torture of i's karmic reality, a miserable cycle that perpetuates discord and fear. *To him that sows to his flesh will of the flesh reap corruption.*

By contrast, when your Intention is to unreservedly and unconditionally open your Mind to My Thought of Love, the *qualities born* of My Nature (Love) are Reflected back to the open-Minded **you**. The Self Reflects Its Self As Permanent Harmony, a World Gentle, Kind and Supportive to Its Self. To the Receptive Ear, **I Am** One with the Universe, **I Am** the Reason everything happens. Good Is All there Is. Perhaps most importantly, the Understanding and acceptance of the mirror-action of the Mind leads us to the discovery that the Universe never did actually materialize. your karma never really happened...*he who sows to the Spirit will of the Spirit reap Everlasting Life.*

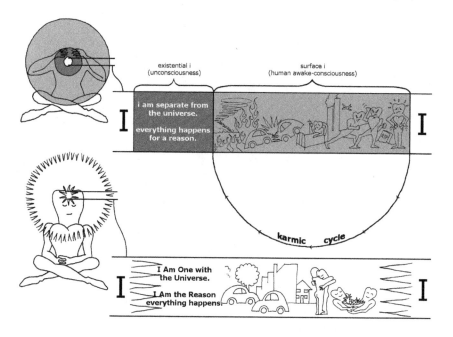

The missing piece of the puzzle of human existence is the Understanding of how the Mind works. It's the reason why in early childhood we fell from unconscious Trust of Our Self to unconscious trust of the intellect and never regained the Connection to Truth. we didn't know the meaning of "Conscious" or "Trust" and the bubble of ignorance became our reality. Now with Conscious Trust, we can re-establish the Connection and watch the two functions of the Mind work in unison without attachment to, or fear of, what looks to be a separate universe. Practiced consistently, Conscious Trust Reveals the Karma of the One True Self. There can be no disruption to Joy and Harmony except through an incorrect use of the Mind.

*"That in which the Mind finds rest [is] that in which he,*
*seeing the Self, by the Self, in the Self is satisfied"*[16]

---

[16] *The Bhagavad Gita*. (Adyar: Theosophical Publishing House, 1953), 6th Discourse:20–21

# CHAPTER 8

———◎———

# i is for illusion of separateness

When we use the Mind correctly we discover we are never actually looking at a separate universe. The universe looks solid and separate from us. It looks like a separate condition, but it never really externalizes. If the U(u)niverse is a R(r)eflection of the M(m)ind, I(i)t remains in and of the M(m)ind. The U(u)niverse never leaves I(i)ts S(s)ource.

It all seems too immense and diverse **not** to be external. i can't even remember what happened last week, yet You are asking me to believe i hold the whole universe in my mind.

you are not asked to hold all the detail, just that it is not external.

So a terrorist attack is not external?

No it's not. But **I** appreciate that it's very difficult to come to terms with this Idea. Try thinking again of the world as a reflection of our collective lack of Consciousness, and now think of that reflection as if it were a giant hypnotic picture. The hypnotist can make a coil of rope seem like a snake by manipulating our mind with fear, so why is it not possible that we have all been self-hypnotized by that same fear to witness atrocities like terrorist attacks?

Seems rather far-fetched, and even if it were true, what do i do about it?

Dehypnotize your self. And the best way to do that is to Know that the U(u)niverse doesn't externalize. All forms of pain, scarcity and danger are in your mind. More importantly, all Forms of Harmony are also in the Mind. The trouble is you don't let Them enter because you believe that matter is external! But what happens when you Know about this disruptive thought? Can you anymore experience discord if you Know it remains in and of the mind with the fear that created it? And with this Knowing, what enters in fear's place? Love, and the startling Realization that what Love appears As—Permanent Harmony (Your Good)—has never been separated from you. Suddenly, with this Consciousness, you are dehypnotized.

Around 500 BC, Gautama the Buddha dehypnotized himself and saw through this illusion of separateness to the ever-available Good that We already Are and Have.

The young Prince Gautama Siddhartha was artificially shielded from the so-called evils of the world behind the palace walls where he grew up. His royal father knew his son was destined for greatness and tried to keep his heir protected from the horrors of poverty, disease and death. Eventually, though, Siddhartha's curiosity led him outside the palace walls where he saw what had been hidden from him. Shocked, he at once vowed to discover how to eradicate these conditions from the earth. Something deep down inside him told him this was possible.

This same something told him that claiming his kingly inheritance was not the way to access this depth. So against the wishes of his family, he left the rarified precincts of the palace and swapped its privileged lifestyle for the humble robes and nomadic existence of a monk in search of Spiritual Truth.

During his long search, he found teachers who told him in different ways that it was necessary to "renounce the world". Not yet Knowing that "Renunciation", a dispassion and detachment from physical life, is the natural **result** of the Spiritual Consciousness, he tried to force It through various self-mortifying practices such as food and sleep deprivation, ceremony, ritual and sacrifice.

For many years he persisted with the practices, until one day he was bathing in the River Ganges and nearly drowned from weakness. After he managed, with great difficulty, to struggle out of the water, it dawned on him that his understanding of renunciation—relinquishing the "outer" world by force—was not bringing him any closer to ridding the world of its problems. He decided to abandon all material and mental effort and Be Receptive to something he didn't yet know. Sitting under the fabled "Bodhi Tree", the symbol of Awakening, he shifted his focus from without to within his Mind, and Listened. Eventually something he hadn't expected illuminated his Mind; the Realization that poverty, disease and death are not real, but illusions; erroneous pictures or suggestions reflected by the fear held in the mind of the human race; the belief that our Good is separate from us.

How do we know he came to that conclusion?

He may not have put it in those words, but the "physical" demonstration implied it. His many years of study combined with the Intention to Receive the Truth afforded a Conscious Realization that Good Is All there Is, a Realization that disengaged his thought from the collective belief in separateness. This meant that without any mind-barrier to prevent Omnipresent Good from appearing, It did. His Mind became en-Lightened with Truth. So deep was this Illumination that Its Effect was widely Felt.

How?

All over India the sick were healed, the poor were fed and ashrams sprang up in spontaneous response to the Revelation.

Why did his illumined Mind affect others?

Because, in Truth, we all Share the One Mind. One Mind dehypnotized is like a turbo-boost to those in the vicinity open to Receiving. sickness and poverty are the hypnotic snakes of the world. Permanent Health and Prosperity is what's actually Present. There is no sickness or poverty to the dehypnotized Mind. Thus the "Healings" simply demonstrated the invisible correction to the misconceptions humanity had been entertaining.

Perhaps more importantly, Buddha Realized there was no knowledge he could gain from the world of effect that would indicate this Truth. It dawned on him that by trying to rid the world of discord, he had been perpetuating the very conditions he had been trying to eradicate. His effort was misplaced and resulted in his mistaken acceptance of the **appearance** of poverty, disease and death as real conditions.

But once he let Consciousness through his Mind, discord could no more be Reflected back to him. What's more, the reason to fight, struggle or search for Good was removed. Of course, the Good was already Present. It just needed a Clear Mind through which to Reveal Its Self As the One True Reflection. In short, he Awakened to the **I** That **I Am** and the Right Perception of Spiritual Reality became evident. The result was that discords lost their claim of power and presence, and dissolved. But they didn't really dissolve, because they were never really there in the first place.

Buddha's Awakening is our example and our goal. Through Consciousness, the Mind is made a transparency for Pure Spiritual Thought and becomes "Illumined" or "En-Lightened". The Light Reflects without any obstructive thoughts of i, and the bubble of ignorance bursts.

> *"He who seeth Me everywhere, and seeth everything in Me, of him **I** will never lose hold, and he shall never lose hold of Me."*[17]

If Buddha's Awakening was so deep, why does poverty, disease and death still exist today?

The intellect learns through its experience in the world. it can't accept that it doesn't need to do this. "Healings" baffle the intellect, for they are even beyond hypnotism. you can learn how to hypnotize, but Healings are beyond the "you" that learns. Buddha didn't "heal" anything. He discovered there was nothing to heal. Unable to Understand this Idea, the intellect reverts to seeing what it believes; sickness and poverty. And so with the disappearance of Buddha's physical frame, the demonstration of Permanence and Perfection was lost. Not because Buddha took It with him, but because our intellect tries to learn or teach Truth rather than Consciously Receive It.

---

[17]  *The Bhagavad Gita.* (Adyar: Theosophical Publishing House, 1953), 6th Discourse: 30–31

The idea of Illumination is baffling too.

It is baffling because learning or teaching what to expect is one thing, but at some point we must simply have the experience. A manual on how to ride a bicycle cannot adequately describe the feeling of exhilaration and freedom of the unlikely idea of balancing on two wheels by pushing against the air at speed. It's the same with Illumination. we can't possibly gleen from a dry commentary or a set of written instructions what the Feeling of Love is like or what It can do, because we can only Know what Illumination Is by the Effects of **Being** Illumined. Unfortunately, the human mind has not been sufficiently coached with this preparative knowledge, and so we still try to reach Illumination **from** or **through** the world of effects. Furthermore, we are not accustomed to expect a change for good without our human effort and input. we can't accept that through a simple exercise of the Mind the whole world can change for the better.

So when Buddha demonstrated that he had Life's Secret and then declared that the world was "maya" (illusion), his followers made the same mistake that Buddha himself made in his early search for Truth, namely, that we should disregard or renounce matter in order to gain Spirit. But if we renounce matter, we never find the Spirit we are trying to obtain, because Matter **Is** Spirit. It is the appearance of separateness that is the illusion. The actuality of separateness is the incorrect thought of the thinker. we don't give up matter, or try to change it. we Recognize discord is an error, and this error's source is us and our belief of separateness. Then, as a natural consequence of our New Understanding we become quite ambivalent to matter because we Acknowledge that Matter is a Reflected mental Concept, nothing in and of itself.

> *"Let us begin with the understanding that our world is not an erroneous one, but rather that the universe in which we live is the realm of reality about which man entertains a false concept."*[18]

Renunciation is the natural **result** of Spiritual Illumination, not a way to It. Spiritual Awareness is not achieved by giving up material objects and

---

[18]  Joel S. Goldsmith *The Infinite Way*, 1947. (USA: BN Publishing, 2007), 15

pursuits. you can't renounce your reflection. you can only Awaken to the mistake that i is attempting such an absurdity.

Good "material" Things and Conditions are Our Infinite Consciousness Reflected. we face our inner Ear Spiritward and wait. we don't have to **do** anything or not do anything. we don't have to **go** anywhere or not go anywhere.

So i don't have to go to an ashram, a church, or a sacred site to Be Conscious?

There is nothing wrong with going to these places unless you begin to depend on them. And when you do, it highlights the flip side to the belief in a separate universe. Not only do you think matter can create your problems, you think you can manipulate matter to resolve them, or influence "god" to manipulate matter on your behalf by going to a sacred site, for instance. But it makes no difference whether you go to an ashram, a church, a mosque, a synagogue, walk the Camino de Santiago, visit Mecca, Jerusalem, a holy mountain or any other so-called sacred place. There is no harm in going, and it can be a wonderful experience, but for the purposes of Illumination, where you are right now is perfect. Where you go or don't go is not important. What delays your Awakening is that you think these pilgrimages are going to springboard you to Consciousness, or if you don't undertake them, you will languish.

Some believe they have to be physically present somewhere. Some think they have to relinquish their possessions, go through physical hardship, or pray multiple times a day. But these beliefs indicate you don't Know that matter is just an "appearance" without any intelligence and power of its own.

i feel an inner peace by doing these things.

What you Feel is not the result of doing, but Being Present with Me and letting Me Guide your doing. The way to tell it's not the doing of itself that Feels Peaceful is to ask your self, when you stop doing these things and get back to your normal life, does that Peaceful Feeling remain?

Sadly, no.

This indicates that you attach the Feeling of Peace to your own "doing". You are always Being, so you can always Feel Peaceful, even in the midst of chaos. But you won't find Peace in matter or in actions that manipulate matter because Peaceful Matter is a Reflection of your Consciousness of Peace. your Consciousness of Peace is Spiritual, not material. This is done in your Mind by relinquishing your will and being Receptive to My Will. **your** doing demonstrates your allegiance to the belief in autonomous matter because you have accepted its unpeaceful premise.

Let us not be alarmed by the appearance of separateness. Let us instead Understand it is just a trick of the senses.

At this point it might be useful to return to the symbol of the mirror. The great thing about the mirror as a symbol of the Mind is that when we think of a reflection, we have no doubt what it is. we don't think of a reflection as independent of its source, or as real. This is how we should think of everything we sense.

Although our Mind is a 3D holographic mirror and we are simultaneously generating the image **and** seemingly in it, the symbol is still useful, for it prevents us from giving the apparent material universe undue importance, for a reflection is still just a reflection, flat or holographic. we don't want to mistake M(m)atter itself for Reality. we want to firmly establish that when we look through our eyes we always look at a 3-D R(r)eflection of our own C(c)onsciousness, and that a R(r)eflection can't do anything for or against U(u)s.

Think now of your self looking at your body in a mirror. Does the reflection have any affinity with the body other than being a likeness?

Not that i can think of.

Can the reflected image make you sick or well? Can it give you money, food, a home, a livelihood, or withhold these necessities from you? Can it make you safe or threaten you? Can it give or withhold love from you?

That would be absurd.

It is absurd. The image is nothing more than a mental interpretation we call "reflection". To worry about it is futile. If we like what we see we relax and enjoy the view. we never mistake the image of our body for a clone that can jump out of the mirror. Therefore, the reflection doesn't frighten us or threaten us. And if we are repulsed or unhappy with the image we take action within our self to change that view. we don't expect the reflection to do anything for us. we don't think it can hold anything back from us. we take responsibility for and control of the reflection because we know we generate it.

Now think of the 3-dimensional Reflection of Consciousness. Unlike a mirror where you know you are the source of the reflection but not "in" the reflection, think of Your Self being the Source of the 3-D Reflection **and** seemingly "in" It at the same time. Now disregard that you seem to be in It for a moment and concentrate on You Being the Source. Would it make any sense to seek health, supply, protection, love or happiness from the Reflection? Would the Reflection have any power to hold these things back from You?

    Not if it was a reflection, no.

Of course not. But that's exactly what we do and why we suffer. Reliance on a reflection is a recipe for disappointment and despair. A R(r)eflected image, no matter what I(i)t's S(s)ource, doesn't have any ability to give Us Our Good, or keep Our Good from Us, and because the image is not only **of** the Mind, but remains **in** the Mind, we can truly Relax. we are never separate from Our Good. T(t)hings and C(c)onditions we S(s)ee never escape the level of the M(m)ind to become entities in themselves. Our only Source of Good Is Consciousness of Truth, and That Is Our Infinite and Complete Self. Our Consciousness has All the Power, Law, Intelligence and Presence, and, as such, must Be the synchronous Provision for Its Reflected Creation.

When we rely on the reflection, we suffer. To help extricate us from this misperception, we must Understand that Right Perception includes the Understanding that the U(u)niverse can't give you anything, or withhold anything from you, because it is a P(p)erception in and of the M(m)ind. The M(m)ind does **not** change T(t)hought **into** T(t)hing. It does not transform the invisible into the visible. The visible is **evidence** of the invisible contents of your M(m)ind. The "world" is not external, not a separate condition. If we can accept this, we can emotionally detach from what we look upon in order to allow the Right Perception to emerge.

Perhaps we can employ a technique that Illumined Individuals may employ, but that we certainly can.

What technique?

Instead of taking what we see literally, we can regard it as a reflection and then regard that idea's insubstantial nature like a **perspective** that follows us around like the reflective "glow" of the moon on a lake. This is a useful analogy. It suggests that we be interested observers rather than slaves to that observation.

Picture in your mind a lake. Imagine you are one of two people standing at different positions around it at night, and the moon has just risen on the far side of the lake. Now if the moon's glow was an actual condition wouldn't there be two glows, one connecting to you and the other to the other person? After all, he sees a glow too.

No, there would only be one glow connecting to me, not the other person.

But to that other person standing away from you, the glow is connecting to him, not you. Ever wondered why?

Because the glow is an optical illusion.

Right. It's also similar to the phenomenon of the rainbow. Do you ever see a rainbow from side-on?

Now that You mention it, no.

If there are a thousand people looking at a rainbow, each sees the rainbow directly face-on implying a thousand separate rainbows, but are there a thousand separate rainbows?

No.

Now try to think of matter the same way. The 3-D world you sense is no different to any optical illusion in that it is merely a P(p)erspective. And although the P(p)erspective can be shared by humanity like we share the vision of a rainbow or even a terrorist attack, it is still a V(v)ision of the

R(r)eflection of the individual C(c)onsciousness that observes I(i)t. I(i)t is not an external condition, and it is not autonomous.

But i am aware the rainbow and the moon's glow on a lake are optical illusions. The thing i have trouble accepting is that the whole universe is an optical illusion.

That is because you think they are different. Like the reflection of the mirror, neither the glow of the moon on the lake nor the rainbow can affect you. you are sure of this. you don't expect them to provide for you or deprive you. They don't trick you into believing they are real. you know they are simple tricks of the senses; optical illusions. But when it comes to Oceans and Mountains, Seasons and Tides, Planets and Suns, and especially People, you are equally sure these are **not** optical illusions, but for a different reason. you think they form part of a separate material universe with its own intelligence and power that **can** provide for you and deprive you. you make a fundamentally incorrect deduction and give control of your Mind away unnecessarily. The rainbow and the moon's glow cannot provide for you or deprive you because they are effects. E(e)ffects have no power at all. The Universe is no different. It is equally powerless to provide for you or deprive you because It is also an Effect. What Provides for you is the Cause (or Source) of the Effect, and **You are** That Cause. There Is only One Cause. The U(u)niverse R(r)eflects your C(c)onsciousness of this Fact. It follows then, that the only reason you have trouble accepting that the Universe is an optical illusion is that you don't Know You are, **I Am**, the Cause of the Effects you sense.

Notice there is no fear in looking at an optical illusion. Are we alarmed by the rainbow's appearance or its absence?

Of course not.

But watch i panic when people threaten each other, or when the earth moves and a tsunami is predicted, or when a drought, a cyclone or a flood is forecast. we are enslaved by the illusion of separateness because we don't Know we are **I**.

you may be interested to know that some of our respected scientists are coming to the same conclusion by paying attention to the observer and not just that which it observes.

Science traditionally approaches its exploration of matter from the premise that it **is** actually separate with an intelligence of its own, but that premise is being seriously challenged by the more unorthodox branches of science.

The first chink in the armor came with the discovery of the atom, the tiny building blocks that establish that matter is not quite as solid as the senses make it out to be. Then the crack developed into a fissure, because scientists couldn't stop at the atom. What was an atom made up of? And what was its origin? As scientists investigated further they were astonished to discover that atoms were not solid either. What was believed to be the smallest increment of matter turned out to be comprised of 99.999% empty space. Not surprisingly, the discovery of this "space" opened up vast new areas for scientific research.

In fact, a whole new branch of science developed to study the "space" within so-called solidity. What's more, quantum physicists, as they became known, discovered that this "space" is not inert, but contains waves and particles in a dynamic unifying field from which all matter originates.[19] What gave them a clue to the nature of this origin was that they noticed the waves and particles in this field behaving in an extraordinary way.

German Nobel-laureate physicist Werner Karl Heisenberg (1901-1976) discovered that in particle physics experiments, the very act of observing alters the position of the particle being observed, and makes it impossible, even in theory, to accurately predict its behaviour. The phenomenon became known as the "uncertainty principle". Fellow physicist, Pascual Jordan, went further. He said;

> *"Observations not only disturb what is to be measured, they produce it."*[20]

---

[19]   www.livescience.com What is the Higgs Boson? ("God particle") explained) http://www.livescience.com/21400-what-is-the-higgs-boson-god

[20]   The Information Philosopher. Pascual Jordan. http://www.information philosopher.com

Apparently, the things we look at are affected by the act of looking. It was a demonstration that supports Buddha's discovery and our study so far, namely, that matter is in fact produced by and subservient to the consciousness doing the observing. matter is not autonomous at all. The observer has control of what it observes by the act of observation.

But then science hit its own barrier, for it is not possible to prove there is an observer who disturbs what is being measured by observing, because a test to test the tester would be required. But who would test the tester? Comparing one object against another is one thing, but then we face a problem; you can't test the one **doing** the testing, because that second observer would affect the outcome of the first observation. A third observer would be required, but the third observer would affect the outcome of the second observation, and so on, ad infinitum.

The unsolvable dilemma of the "observer" highlights the phenomenon known as the "hard problem of consciousness".[21] Very simply, the hard problem assumes the reality of a purely objective (material or physical) universe. That is, it assumes there are separate objects to be observed, but can't see where we, the observers, fit into the scheme.

The answer is to a question that isn't asked. "What is **I**?" And only It via the Intuition can answer the question. **I Am, We are**. There is only One Everlasting Immortal Subject (Us). Being One, We must Be all at once the Infinite Observer and All that is Observed. Accordingly, there is no such thing as pure matter; neither a subject (i) nor a separate object anywhere at all. "out here" is just an optical illusion, an hypnotic picture—"*Sometimes beautiful, always erroneous*"[22]

Let us follow the findings of the pioneering scientists because they support what Mystics and Sages have always Known; that the world "out here" is not really out here and separate as we have been led to believe at all. We find, like Gautama the Buddha, there is no use renouncing the

---

21    David Chalmers. "Facing up to the problems of Consciousness." *Journal of Consciousness Studies*. 2(3):200-19, 1995 http://consc.net/papers.html

22    Mary Baker Eddy. *Science and Health with Key to the Scriptures*. 1875 (Massachusetts: The Christian Science Board of Directors, 2009), 277:30

world itself, we renounce the i who is deluded by thinking thoughts and objects are separate from one another and external to its self! Eventually we develop the same conviction as Buddha; discords like poverty, disease and death are unreal, because they don't have their origin in Infinite Spiritual Consciousness, and Infinite Spiritual Consciousness Is the **only** True Origin. If We are the Infinite Observer and that Observer Is Good, We must also Be the Good We Observe. We bear Witness to Our Self when we Consciously Trust that Self. everything else is an image of false thought—without Substance or Reality.

So simply sit under Your inner Bodhi Tree in the Sanctuary of your Mind and Realize All that **I** made is Good Thought appearing **As** Form! There is nothing else that is made, and You can't be separated from It.

> *"All things were made through Him, and without Him nothing was made that was made.*
> *In Him was Life, and the Life was the Light of men.*
> *And the Light shines in the darkness, and the darkness did not comprehend It."*[23]

---

[23] *The Holy Bible*, New King James Version (Tennessee: Thomas Nelson Inc., 1982), John 1:3–5

# CHAPTER 9

# i is for immersed in duality

It is evident from Illumined Individuals like Buddha that we must become Conscious that Permanent Good Is the only Reality. Part of this Realization is to Understand that the "good" for which we settle is not Permanent Good but the opposite of "bad". In the absence of this Understanding, we don't realize that our bubble of ignorance is made up of **duality**.

◇◇◇◇◇◇◇◇◇◇

we would all like to "get" or "keep" the "good" in our life and "avoid" or "get rid of" the "bad", but this strategy doesn't seem to work.

Why doesn't it work?

Because implied within the belief of separateness is the belief that it is impossible to experience Permanent Good.

i have tried to be a good person and attract the good.

being a good person isn't enough while you still believe in separateness. you must have noticed that good people are still vulnerable.

Mmmm. What about if i just think good thoughts? Maybe the bad will go away. After all, You did say discord wasn't real. Then again, maybe the bad is serving some Spiritual purpose and i should just relax.

you can't maintain good by turning a blind eye to the "bad" things you see. Nor does it help to call "bad" situations "unreal" or pretend "bad" situations are somehow "good". For instance, telling someone suffering back-pain that their pain isn't real, or that it is serving some Spiritually Good purpose is rightfully met with an incredulous stare and probably offence. back-pain is very real to them, and bad!

Perhaps it could be worse and therefore seen as good.

Likewise, you can't make bad Good by comparing it to something worse. The Good that **Is** doesn't accommodate the intermittent "good" that has this comparative relationship with "bad", because, by definition, this "good" isn't Permanent. Consciousness must therefore include learning to discern the difference between the good that is **not** and the Good that **Is**.

How do we do that? Isn't "is" whatever is going on in the present moment?

Would you call a mirage part of "Is"?

No, it's not really there. Then again, even a mirage "is what it is". Isn't it?

Sure, a mirage is a mirage. Likewise pain is pain, injury is injury, disease is disease. No one can argue. The question is are you going to allow your accident-illness-prone body to obscure the Omnipresent, Omniscient, Omnipotent, Infinite You and effectively exclude It and Its Promise of Permanent Good from your mind? For you can't be both at the same time Whole **and** broken, Healthy **and** ill, Painless **and** in pain. Either you are vulnerable to nothing or you are still vulnerable. you will have to discriminate between what you call "good" and Good with an upper-case "G" to Understand that My Good doesn't have an opposite, so "bad" and "good" must both be illusory.

i believes "good" and "bad" are real because it experiences both. "bad **is**" says i, and therefore "good", bad's opposite, is accommodated within that is-ness. i is unaware that its acceptance of the absolute reality of "bad"

91

creates the situations that populate our perception with so-called "good" images. What's more, these images make "good" something we can only expect to "get" or "hold onto" providing we can manage to ward off "bad" with a stick.

"Is" in Spiritual terms does not include "bad" or "evil" (the extension of "bad" culminating as discordant acts-of-man). Consciousness Is, and It Is Good, because Consciousness made All that Is made, and there is nothing else that Is made. Therefore, there Is **only Good**.

Does that mean the bad i see is Good in reality? Should i be trying to reframe the bad in my mind?

Not reframe it as Good. Understand that "bad" is your mortal invention, a false perception. Where bad pretends to be, Good Is, but that doesn't mean the bad is Good. Spinning the idea that Good is masquerading as bad is one of the misguided explanations the intellect uses to accommodate bad.

Whatever you call "bad" is always your own fear reflected back to you. The important thing to realize is that "good" is also your fear reflected back to you.

good is my fear reflected back to me?

Yes. Don't you prove you operate from fear by trying to get or keep a temporary good?

i suppose i hope the good will last.

"good" can't last in a mind that accepts the reality of "bad". This is duality, and duality is the essence of the unpredictable and often hostile world we have created. we delude ourselves that "good" will last. But we need not depend on false hope any longer. Dare to call this "good" inadequate. Admit that more often than not, this "good" doesn't cooperate and we are left wanting. Wonder why "bad" seems to drop in without warning and spoil our good time. Question why we have been taught to endure discords such as back-pain in gratitude for short bursts of relief. For we need not settle for an inadequate and precarious "good" any more. The experience of Permanent Good is our destiny.

You infer that good and bad alone define duality.
Isn't duality just the normal play of opposites;
up and down, high and low, and more and less?
Isn't good and bad part of this?

Within the context of this book, "good" and "bad" define duality. Other contrasts are Infinity appearing to the senses. The names we give them are our attempt to understand our place relative to the Infinite variety of shapes Consciousness takes. "before and after", "up and down", "high and low", and "more and less" place objects in time and space. Additional contrasts like "wet and dry", "smooth and rough", "hot and cold", "quiet and noisy", and "bright and dull" differentiate one object's quality from another. These pairs are the "yin and yang" of the universe. Each side of the pair complements the other and completes the pair. But there is something similar about all these pairs. None of them evoke much of a reaction one way or the other. emotionally, they are neutral and benign.

"good and bad" as a pair, however, are different. "good" and "bad" are judgments **about** and **in addition to** neutral contrasts. They elicit emotional reactions because they evaluate the world in terms of our vulnerability. The idea of vulnerability, being false, means "good" and "bad" can't be complementary towards one another and do not complete each other. They simply give weight to a false idea and beg the equally false question, "are my personal needs being met or are they not?". Unaware that we ask a Spiritually meaningless question, we develop opinions and values proclaiming "good" if we are satisfied, and "bad" if we are disappointed.

But satisfaction doesn't last because the "good" we are satisfied with is unsustainable. The cautious trepidation with which we approach life, then, is the delusionary attitude of thought that precedes further contrasting conditions which, because they stem from a need to defend a non-entity, must be completely false. For instance, "money" itself is neutral, but "more" money is "good", "less" money is "bad", which in turn creates the pair of opposites "rich and poor" or "prosperity and poverty". A "building" itself is neutral, but "high" security is thought to be "good" and "low" security "bad" giving rise to the contrasting pair "safety and danger". "activity"

93

itself is neutral, but "over" achievement is "good", "under" achievement is "bad" creating the pair "success and failure". A "body" is neutral, but a "young" body is deemed "good", an "old" body "bad" and so we see "strong and weak", "potent and impotent", "beautiful and ugly", and even "life and death". I'm sure you can think of other examples. The list goes on and on.

pleasure and pain?

"pleasure and pain" are another imbalance imposed on an intrinsically neutral "body" giving rise to the pair "health and disease".

happiness and sadness?

This pair is purely emotional, but wouldn't be necessary without the loss intrinsic to one side of the emotionally-conceived and erroneous "gain and loss". In fact, all emotions are derivatives of "good" and "bad" because they describe various states of fear on the pendulum of duality. Thus duality offers us a parcel of emotionally-charged conditions in pairs that pretend to be part of Infinite Reality but only shield It from us and us from It.

It is worth mentioning too that within each pair of opposites that we have imposed over Reality is an idea that embeds the concept of "bad". For instance, we don't have to say "disease", "poverty", "pain", "loss", "discord" and "danger" are "bad" because the words embody "bad". These words also demonstrate how deeply we have accepted a separate material universe, and it would help us to be mindful of their implications when we utter them.

What about positive and negative, and right and wrong?

"positive and negative" and "right and wrong" are just as neutral and benign as any other pair of opposites until we involve our insecure self. Then they too become endowed with "good and bad". In turn, they give rise to fallacious situations that embody these contrasts. For instance, the positive and negative ends of a battery are neither "good" nor "bad", but a positive attitude is deemed "good" for personal well-being and a negative attitude "bad" for the same reason. Then the pressure to remain "positive" or the shame in being unable to shake "negativity" adds to our anxiety.

"right and wrong" is in the same boat. 2+2=4 is not "good" but it **is** "right" in the sense it is simply "correct", and 2+2=5 is not "bad" but "wrong", "incorrect". Yet when applied personally, "right and wrong" take on the mantle of morality. we judge a person "wrong" to steal, and another person "right" to judge the wrong-doer. Following on, the pressure to be "good" and "right" becomes immense.

The judgments of "right" and "wrong" are complicated, for they lead us right to the hub of humanity's problems. We will get to this important subject of morality later. In the meantime, it serves us to establish the groundwork, and that groundwork is to realize "good and bad" is the only pair of opposites that are themselves value judgments, neither benign nor neutral. And, most importantly, that these value-judgments attach themselves to everything and alter our perception for the worse.

Wouldn't my judgment of "good" make the world appear better?

Temporarily and always inadequately, because your "good" is just **not-bad**.

Not-bad?

we shouldn't call the opposite of "bad" "good", because it's just a derivative of "bad". If we are still convinced the universe is separate, we can be sure the "good" we experience is false and will revert to "bad" sooner or later. we have no idea that the "good" we depend on is a weak opposite of "bad" that cannot triumph over "bad". In fact, it's the other way around in duality. "bad" triumphs over "good".

Why?

Because "bad's" only real opponent (Good) is absent from consciousness and our baseline fear sabotages the only "good" of which we are aware and gives "bad" ascendency over it.

Now reverse this. Think logically. If we accept there is **only** Good, could there be such a condition as "bad"? "bad" is inconsistent with Permanent Good and there is no such thing as Permanent "Bad". This is why "bad" has no Truth to it, no Law, Order or Substance to it. "bad" things, conditions and people are really just reflected images produced and fed by our deluded fear of vulnerability. All "bad", then, is false. But so then must "bad's" opposite—"good"—be just as false. A "good" that can only be switched on by false hope and off by fear has no relationship to the unerring Strength of Permanent Good. And to further distinguish it from Permanent Good we shouldn't call it "good", we should give "good" a new name to tie it to "bad" and untie it from Permanent Good. That's why we should call "good" **not-bad**. Our Understanding of duality is made clearer by calling "good and bad" "not-bad and bad".

And now we can use "not" in all the other falsely derived pairs of opposites and hopefully expose the fool's paradise in which we have been living.

For instance, the health we think we are enjoying is really "not-disease" that must sooner or later revert to "disease". Can we ever be Healthy in a world that accommodates the idea of "disease"? Can disease's opposite be Permanently Healthy? Permanent Health is off the table if disease is accommodated, for the times when we are "not-diseased" must be fleeting. Then "health and disease" is better described as **"not-disease and disease"** or **"not-illness and illness"**. we can't Be Healthy in duality.

Similarly, the safety we think we should enjoy is really an impermanent "not-danger" that must deteriorate into "danger". Can we ever be Safe in a world that accommodates the idea of "danger"? Can danger's opposite be Permanently Safe? Permanent Safety is inaccessible if danger is believed real, for the times of "not-danger" in between must be short-lived. "safety and danger" are better described as **"not-danger and danger"**. we can't Be Safe in duality.

And the prosperity we think we have individually and collectively earned is really a precarious "not-poverty". Can humanity ever be Prosperous in a world that accommodates the idea of "poverty"? Can poverty's opposite be Permanently Prosperous? Permanent Prosperity is unavailable if poverty is a possibility, for the times of "not-poverty" must be temporary. "prosperity and poverty" are better described as **"not-poverty and poverty"** or **"not-poor and poor"**. we can't Be Prosperous in duality.

We can go on. There is no Good in duality, only **"not-bad and bad"** or **"not-evil and evil"**. There is no Success in duality, only **"not-failure and failure"**. There is no Right in duality, only **"not-wrong and wrong"**. There is no Positive in duality, only **"not-negative and negative"**. There is no Love in duality, only **"not-hate and hate"**. There is no Truth in duality, only **"not-false and false"** etc.

```
That's   shocking.   So   is   peace   on   earth   a
pipe-dream?
```

In duality the hope for peace is a pipe-dream, yes, because "peace" is "not-war" the weak opposite of "war". And can we experience Peace if we are sick, in danger or poor? Peace Is a synonym for Love and Truth. It Is already established in Consciousness. Peace has no opposite. But Peace can't be Reflected back to us if we are not Conscious of Its meaning, which also conveys that we don't Know what Forgiveness means. We will cover Forgiveness later, for It is the key to breaking out of duality. For the moment, we must Understand that in the bubble of ignorance, we have removed the option of Permanence and Perfection, for Fulfillment, and shockingly restricted ourselves to the choice between two negatives!

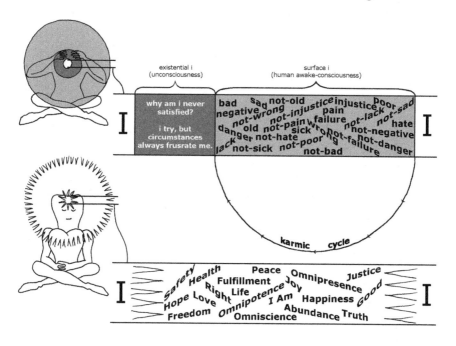

We can see from the above illustration that by believing we can bring about our own fulfillment, we ironically cut ourselves off from Fulfillment. Fulfillment is not part of the choices offered by duality. our dualistic thought-system is the barrier. we must **let** the Absolute Ideas of Permanence and Perfection into our Mind. we must be Receptive to them. Then we are presented with a meaningful choice. Not between the many derivatives of the two negative opposites "not-bad and bad", but between duality and Oneness, between falsity and Truth, between illusion and Reality.

Oneness and duality can't both be True. you will have to decide whether to bow to your fear, or let Me show you that Good **Is** the only Reality. Rather than see not-bad scenes as temporary pauses to be enjoyed with some apprehension, Recognize that the apprehension you feel is creative. Demonstrate, instead, your Trust, by replacing apprehension with Acknowledgement of the Source and Its Reflection for what they Really are, One.

> *"Affection and aversion for the objects of sense abide in the senses; let none come under the dominion of these two; they are obstructors of the path."*[24]

---

[24]    *The Bhagavad Gita.* (Adyar: Theosophical Publishing House, 1953), 3rd Discourse: 34–35

# CHAPTER 10

i is for inevitable

Could we have avoided building the bubble of ignorance?

No, because the potential to Be Conscious implies a period of unconsciousness before that potential is reached. On the other hand, the illusory nature of our problematic existence makes it inevitable that we Awaken. We were never really separated from Our Good.

Fortunately for those of us embarking on the Spiritual Path and who long for Guidance, there are individuals whose experience of Awakening has been recorded in the Scriptures of the world. These works add Insight to the strange inevitabilities of the human predicament and can help facilitate our Release. None better than the very first chapters of the Old Testament; Genesis 1 and 2 which include the allegory of Adam and Eve. This extraordinary work, being symbolic, can be interpreted in many ways, but if we examine it in the context of this book, it supports our study so far, the confirmation offering a clear comparison between what Is and what is not, and the implications stemming from our Consciousness of both.

Let us examine the allegory in detail, reminding ourselves before we commence that the intellect won't let us Understand. Therefore we should Consciously and Intuitively let the meaning Resonate with Our Self.

> *"In the beginning, God created the Heavens and the Earth."*[25]

"beginning" refers to the order of sequence, not a beginning that has an end in time and space. Therefore, first and last in the order Is "God" (Consciousness) and only Consciousness. There is no superhuman "creator" **above** and separate from a "creation".

Then why separate them?

Because in our potential to Be Conscious, we need a way to reach that potential. There must be a way to communicate Consciousness to that potential. Consciousness communicates to us through Its Mind, through the Conscious Receipt of Thought, **and** through that Mind's Reflection of Thought—"Thing" (physicality). Thoughts **and** Things are what is meant by the terms *the Heavens* **and** *the Earth*. Consciousness Is the Governing Law or **Cause or Source** "behind" Thought (Heaven) and Thing (Earth), Its **Effects**. Consciousness doesn't actually separate into Thought and Thing just as Water doesn't separate into Ice and Rain and Steam. Water **Is** Ice and Rain and Steam, and we understand the Nature of Water through these Forms of Water. In the same way, Consciousness **Is** Thought and Thing, and we can Understand the Nature of Consciousness through Its Forms.

The inability to Sense Consciousness (the Cause) directly is the only reason Heaven (Thought) and Earth (Thing) need to be differentiated from one another. Once this is Understood, we can and must bring them back together. Consciousness, the Cause, is **Everything**, the Effects being merely the evidence of Consciousness. It's All One.

And now that we have brought Cause and Effect together, we are going to separate them again in order to take this Idea of Oneness a little further. If Cause is Everything, Consciousness must be Greater than the Thoughts and Things to which we give undue importance. The Order and Greatness cannot be reversed and represents the Spiritual or Divine Law and Order of Truth-fundamentals #3—Thought is the Substance of the Perception we call Matter—and #4—Thought comes before Perception of

---

[25]    *The Holy Bible*, New King James Version (Tennessee: Thomas Nelson Inc., 1982), Genesis 1:1

Thing. This Consciousness appears **As** the Infinite variety of Form we call the Universe, a Universe that Governs, Maintains and Sustains Its Self in Eternal Peace and Harmony.

Throughout the Bhagavad Gita, part of the great Hindu Vedic texts, Krishna echoes the correctness of the Supremacy of Divine Law and Order;

> *"By Me all this world is pervaded in My Unmanifested Aspect; all Being have root in Me, **I** am not rooted in them."* [26]

As you will see as Genesis proceeds, i reverses this Divine Law and Order by forgetting the Pre-eminence of Consciousness. i places the emphasis on the sense-evidence alone with devastating consequences for its self and the world.

But first we are introduced to the Mind, the vehicle of Consciousness, its "face" like a mirror ready to Reflect the Good of Consciousness **As** Harmonious Thing.

> *"The Earth was without form and void; and darkness was on the face of the deep. And the Spirit of God was hovering over the face of the waters."* [27]

*The Earth [is] without form and void* means there is no "Effect" until there is Spiritual Direction from Consciousness (the Cause) on the *face of the waters* of Divine or unencumbered, transparent Mind. Consciousness **Is**, yet It *hovers* as if waiting for Its Self to give It inlet and outlet through the Mind.

> *"Then God said, "Let there be Light"; and there was Light. And God saw the Light, that it was Good..."* [28]

Consciousness Is Cause, and the Effect of Cause is *Light*, or Spiritual Substance (Thought and Thing). Not physical light that can be turned on

---

[26]   *The Bhagavad Gita.* (Adyar: Theosophical Publishing House, 1953), 9th discourse-4

[27]   *The Holy Bible*, New King James Version (Tennessee: Thomas Nelson Inc., 1982), Genesis 1:2

[28]   *The Holy Bible*, New King James Version (Tennessee: Thomas Nelson Inc., 1982), Genesis 1:3–4

and off, but Love that spontaneously and assuredly Lights the path in front of It. Light is the symbol of Infinite Awareness or Spiritual Consciousness (when we are Conscious that Cause and Effect are One).

The allegory proceeds with a lengthy description of the Effects Light Lights. It is not necessary to quote this section of Genesis 1 in full. We can summarize. Cause Reflects Its Self through the Mind appearing to Its Self **As** the Universe in an Infinite variety of Forms over seven "days". Seven is a symbol of Completion and is not meant to be interpreted incrementally or the "days" literally. Remember, the "divisions" of Infinity are each Infinite. we can thus follow the arrangement of the Creation, not a creation in time and space, but the Light of Spirit appearing As Its Self, to Its Self, spontaneously and always.

The first five "days" brings to Light categories of contrasting forms; Day and Night; Sea and Sky; Land and Plants; Sun, Moon and Seasons; and, Insects, Fish, Birds and Animals.

Spiritual Creation Sees Its Self As It Is. The terms "time", "space", "beginning" and "end" have no meaning. Eternity supports Itself and is not compelled to argue against the imposition of our inherited beliefs. Consequently, there is no consciousness to develop desire or fear for the Effects of the Cause by separating the Effects from the Cause. There is no opportunity to judge the contrasting forms as either good or bad. With no room for anything but Good, All Good happens at once.

To emphasize the all-encompassing Perspective Eternity offers, the author put the fully grown plant ahead its offspring. The Idea of a Herb appears before the Seed of the Herb, and, the fruit Tree before the Fruit. On the third day;

> "*...God said, "Let the earth bring forth grass, the herb that yields seed, and the fruit tree that yields fruit according to its kind, whose seed is in itself, on the earth"; and it was so.*"[29]

All Effect appears in Perfect synchronicity with the Omnipresent, Omniscient and Omnipotent Light of Infinite Consciousness.

To further support the notion of Infinite variety, Divine Order and

---

[29]  *The Holy Bible*, New King James Version (Tennessee: Thomas Nelson Inc., 1982), Genesis 1:11

Association are Spiritual Laws that Preserve and Obey themselves. The Plants on the Earth, Birds in the Air, Fish in the Sea and Beasts on the Land, each multiply according to their own kind ensuring each Form of Life maintains its Integrity. Without this Order and Association, just like pure colours mixed together lose their integrity to a muddy grey, we could imagine indiscriminate interbreeding demolishing individual species into a mish-mash of sameness. Accordingly, no Effect is dependent on another Effect for its existence.

On the sixth "day", Consciousness says;

> *"Let Us make Man in Our Image, according to Our Likeness;"*[30]

Here we have the Reflection and why We must be "in" It and Its Source at the same time. We don't separate into a body. We appear As the Image and Likeness of Consciousness. To Be Conscious We must be able to look upon Our Reflection and Recognize It As Our own Consciousness unfolding. Notice also the plural. Consciousness Is Individually expressed **As Us**.

> *"let them have Dominion over the fish of the sea, over the birds of the air, and over the cattle, over all the earth and over every creeping thing that creeps on the Earth"*[31].

Dominion sounds like we're in charge!

we are in charge of how things **appear** to us, not how they actually Are. Remember, the Creative Principle is Unchangeable and Unalterable. It Is already Complete. Therefore "Dominion" is the ability to discern the Source of the Bird, the Fish, the Cattle, and every creeping Thing As Our Consciousness of the Creative Principle, Our Self. Through our Dominion we **allow** the Fulfillment of Infinity and Its Spiritual Peace and Harmony to appear.

---

[30] *The Holy Bible*, New King James Version (Tennessee: Thomas Nelson Inc., 1982), Genesis 1:26

[31] *The Holy Bible*, New King James Version (Tennessee: Thomas Nelson Inc., 1982), Genesis 1:26

Unfortunately, until we Understand that the responsibility with which we have been endowed is to **let** Me take over, the word Dominion is invariably confused with "domination", a power i thinks it can wield over the perceived imbalances and inequities it doesn't realize its lack of Consciousness of its Dominion created in the first place. Unrecognized Dominion becomes unconscious but not removed. dominion with a lower-case "d" represents the danger i is to its self in its confusion of Dominion with domination. In Reality, there is no imbalance to correct, no person, thing or situation to subdue.

The endowment of D(d)ominion is not optional. Either we Understand It or we are controlled by it.

> *"So God created Man in His own Image; in the Image of God He created Him; Male and Female He created them."*[32]

*Male* and *Female*, Spiritually Understood, symbolize Aspects of Spirit. They can't be separated, but the examination of the way they work together helps us Understand the Nature of Consciousness. The two Aspects are like golden threads of Wisdom, the Spiritual warp and weft of the fabric of Our Self. Intelligence is the *Male* Higher Mental Reasoning Aspect, and Love the *Female* Spiritual Intuitive Aspect working together to Form the very *Image* and *Likeness* of "God", of Consciousness. When We Understand Our Dominion, Love and Intelligence Reflect a state of Grace in all Its Beauty, Joy, Wholeness, Permanence and Perfection **As** the Infinite Universe and Immortal Man.

After the seventh rest "day", this Inner Spiritual Creation is *"finished"*[33]. Nothing can be added; nothing can be taken away. And, therefore, It must be Good.

---

[32] *The Holy Bible*, New King James Version (Tennessee: Thomas Nelson Inc., 1982), Genesis 1:27

[33] *The Holy Bible*, New King James Version (Tennessee: Thomas Nelson Inc., 1982), Genesis 2:1

*"Then God saw everything that He had made, and indeed It was very Good"*[34]

There we have it—the missing "o" restored. Good Is.

And so right at the very beginning of a major religious text we have a comprehensive description of our True Self—Infinite Spiritual Consciousness. Not that we have ever Realized this, because human consciousness can't Understand Infinite Good. it can't Understand the Indestructible and Invulnerable Nature of Wholeness, and is even less able to identify It As Its Self.

This explains why babies don't maintain their Innocent Awareness of Me. The disappearance of your "imaginary friend" is a good illustration. When you appeared as your Self in child-Form the implied separateness of Me on the light in your bedroom and our conversation was not an issue of concern. It was natural. you were not yet conscious of your finite self and We were as One. But because you didn't bring sufficient Consciousness of Your Infinite Self with you into this "appearance", your Spiritual "defences" were down. The intellect, being on the same mental level as your finite awareness naturally filled the void, seizing the opportunity to storm the Mind and appoint its self as "creator" at the earliest opportunity.

This intellectual take-over of the Mind in our unconsciousness of our True Self is what it means to be human and is described brilliantly in Chapter 2 of Genesis.

Just as the intellect barges into the Mind without explanation, the author's emphasis and tone changes abruptly as if windows to the Light are suddenly covered over. In the darkness, no longer is *God's* Harmonious Universe visible. Suddenly Balance and Order are proclaimed irrelevant as a new dis-order is established by a tyrannical overlord with the title *Lord God.*

The *Lord God* symbolizes a split between Love (the Spiritual Intuitive Aspect) and Intelligence (the Higher Mental Reasoning Aspect). A split

---

[34] *The Holy Bible*, New King James Version (Tennessee: Thomas Nelson Inc., 1982), Genesis 1:31

between these Eternal Aspects of Consciousness can't Really happen, but when unconsciousness veils the Mind, Love and Intelligence are no longer comprehended by the hapless comprehendee, i. Filtered through the mind devoid of Truth, the nature of these Divine Aspects of Consciousness is changed and disabled, transformed into unrecognizable and feeble substitutes. Love becomes apologetic, sentimental and weak, and Intelligence becomes cruel, overbearing and inflexible. Under this arrangement it's easy to see why disabled intelligence ends up dominating. The disabled intellect has no respect for Love because disabled love has no respect for its self. The intellect therefore becomes a bully and an opportunist who revels in his pseudo-powerful role as "creator".

As we follow the allegory along we will be reminded how every day, unaware of our Dominion, the intellect becomes the mind-influence that we obey. it's reign starts the moment we utter our own name and associate it with "me". At school, the activity of thinking excludes Listening to the Intuition and before we know it we are being streamed into a dependence on "outside" objects, people and conditions through the study of the physical world.

Not knowing any better, we take on the intellect's attitude of bully by devaluing and distrusting our own Intuitive Impulses that would complete our learning and give meaning **and** Good Form to that physical world. Unfortunately, our subservient heart cannot satisfy our yearning to be fed from within, and so the quiet attitude required for contemplating the mysteries of Life, and the "altitude" required to Hear them, takes a back seat to the loud and pushy world of the senses and our automatic emotional reactions to it.

Without the Conscious Presence and Balance of Divine Love and Intelligence Governing our Mind, the intellect lacks Wisdom and we fall under its complex spell of ignorance. The intellect is then free to create the **appearance** of a dysfunctional mental universe that superimposes itself and covers up the Harmonious and Real Spiritual Universe described in the first chapter of Genesis.

How does it get away with it?

How the intellect manages to keep the Intuition out of contention and us under its control is the hidden plot of this elaborate story. Once Understood, it throws some much-needed Light on our individual predicaments and the predicament of humanity as a whole.

The following definitions will help us decipher the symbols used in Genesis 2.

- the *Lord God*—the intellect, the puppet-master.
- *mist*—the mental filter on the Mind.
- *dust*—thought generated by the intellect.
- *man, Adam*—i, the thinker, the puppet.

> *"This is the history of the heavens and the earth when they were created, in the day that the Lord God made the earth and the heavens, before any plant of the field was in the earth and before any herb of the field had grown. For the Lord God had not caused it to rain on the earth, and there was no man to till the ground; but a mist went up from the earth and watered the whole face of the ground.*
>
> *And the Lord God formed man of the dust of the ground, and breathed into his nostrils the breath of life; and man became a living being."[35]*

Suddenly, the Spiritual Creation is gone, and we are thrown into the realm of Mind for its own sake.

The Spiritual Creation has no chance to manifest. Instead, *before any plant of the field was in the earth and before any herb of the field had grown*, a mysterious *mist* comes up from the earth and waters the ground. That is, a mental filter covers the surface of the Mind obscuring the Spiritual Source of Thought and the possibility of experiencing Its Purely Good Effects. Under the direction of the *Lord God*, the mind forms *man*, not

---

[35] *The Holy Bible*, New King James Version (Tennessee: Thomas Nelson Inc., 1982), Genesis 2:4–7

with any Dominion, but from *dust;* thought generated by the intellect. In other words, *man* is formed by the activity of thinking itself, and, in this way, the intellect gives its own thinking life; by breathing *into his nostrils the breath of life.*

But this "life" is an existence in our own minds, an effect from an outlaw thought. As such, this mental "life" is not Immortal, but mortal, based on the belief in material limitation, loss and death.

Towards the end of The Old Testament, the Prophet Isaiah warns us not to depend on this man who was given life through his *nostrils* when he says;

> *"Cease ye from man whose breath is in his nostrils, for where is he to be accounted of"*[36]

Unfortunately, without Consciousness, Isaiah's words go unheeded. The *Lord God* cannot be stopped. His pirated thought needs a mouthpiece, like a puppet-master in need of a puppet. As there is no Immortal Life in this second "creation", a *man* is conceived through the mind to act out the intellect's dictatorial demands. The name *Adam* comes from the Hebrew *adamah*—meaning the red of the ground—*dust*. Especially in Sufi writings, the similar "clay" is a popular symbol for man and indicates the identity through which a state of lack of Consciousness materializes.

To every child, *Adam* symbolizes the identity we take on in complete ignorance of our D(d)ominion of the M(m)ind.

- The *garden eastward in Eden*—the Mind filtered with the mist of mentality.
- *evil*—the natural extension of the value-judgment "bad" presenting as man. (it makes sense to use this extension because the allegory is about man.)
- the *tree of the knowledge of good and evil*—the acceptance of duality.

---

36  *The Holy Bible*, New King James Version (Tennessee: Thomas Nelson Inc., 1982), Isaiah 2:22

- the *fruit*—the consequences of the acceptance of duality; forms of lack and limitation.
- the *Tree of Life*—Consciousness of Oneness.

> *"The Lord God planted a garden eastward in Eden, and there he put the man whom he had formed.*
> *And out of the ground the Lord God made every tree grow that is pleasant to the sight and good for food. The tree of Life was also in the midst of the garden, and the tree of the knowledge of good and evil"*[37]

*Eden* means "delight" in Hebrew, and in the context of the story means the Undisturbable Joy of Consciousness. In the first chapter of Genesis, the Mind is a transparency for the Lawful Creative Principle to Reflect back to Its Self As *Eden*. Though, in the second chapter, Spiritual Thought is obscured. The mind now outside the jurisdiction of Divine Law and Order becomes fertile ground for seeds of deception. Eastward is the direction to receive the first light in the morning, so *eastward in Eden* symbolizes the *Lord God's* obscuration of Joy with deception.

The *garden* is thus perceived as a shady undergrowth of unrequited hopes, a hothouse of frustration and sorrow. It is a garden of appearances, holding the promise of happiness and contentment, but unable to deliver. It looks inviting with trees for the thinker's pleasure and for food, but this counterfeit overlord is not interested in *Adam's* welfare. As a "god" lacking Consciousness of Oneness, twoness must be his modus operandi. Therefore, pleasure can't eventuate without pain. To this end, the *Lord God* includes a very strange tree in the garden, the *"tree of the knowledge of good and evil"*, the fruit of which is duality.

Why is the **fruit** of the knowledge of good and evil duality?

The **knowledge** *of good and evil* is purely mental. A **conviction** of duality can only be gained from **sensing** the *fruit* of this knowledge, that is, **forms** of good and evil; health and sickness, prosperity and poverty, safety

---

[37]  *The Holy Bible*, New King James Version (Tennessee: Thomas Nelson Inc., 1982), Genesis 2:8–9

and danger, and so on. But you can only sense forms of good and evil if they materialize physically. They can only materialize physically if you don't know that this knowledge is incorrect. Without Knowledge (Consciousness) of Truth, our thought "creates" the perception of untruth; discord.

To put it another way and paraphrase our earlier learning, duality can only materialize physically if Divine Order is reversed. The Tree of Life is the symbol of Consciousness of Divine Order; Present in the garden of the Mind, but of no practical use if not Consciously Understood.

If you remember, Divine Order Is Reflected through Consciousness of Truth-fundamental #4—Thought comes before Perception of Thing. The Natural Flow of Original Untouched Thought through the Mind Reflects Forms of Permanent Good. The Order cannot be reversed in any Real sense, but when we lack Consciousness of Divine Order, It is **effectively** reversed, because the thoughts of duality we unknowingly reflected earlier dictate the thoughts we entertain later. Suddenly we believe things are independent of our thought, a belief that hides the True Source of Thought altogether. Now Reason seems unreasonable, the Rational irrational. Can you think of anyone who seriously believes that Things are Thoughts Formed? "Preposterous" says i, "things were here before i could think about them!"

However, if You Know that Conscious Thought comes before the "Things" you sense, you have headed off the outlaw thought at the pass, handcuffed it and put it out of the way. By remembering that Thought is Infinite and can't lack in its Reflection, the emotionally charged pairs of opposites don't have a chance to materialize, and, eventually, we don't sense them at all.

The *Lord God* hopes you won't catch on, and to ensure you won't, he orchestrates a situation where *Adam* partakes of the *fruit* and quite naturally perpetuates a cycle of false cause and effect, creating the bubble of ignorance, binding him to it, and simultaneously removing any possibility that he will perceive the *Tree of Life*; True Cause and Effect.

> "the Lord God took the man and put him in the garden
> to tend and keep it"[38]

---

[38]  *The Holy Bible*, New King James Version (Tennessee: Thomas Nelson Inc., 1982), Genesis 2:15

Innocent of the danger, the *man* obeys his master's instructions, unaware that the conspiracy depends on keeping the *tree of knowledge of good and evil* alive and healthy, for, eventually, it must bear fruit.

Meanwhile, the *Lord God* gets on with the implementation of his plan with a seemingly contradictory command to his servant…

> *"And the Lord God commanded the man, saying, "Of every tree of the garden you may freely eat; but of the tree of the knowledge of good and evil you shall not eat, for in the day that you eat of it you shall surely die""*[39]

i thought the Lord God wanted Adam to eat from the tree. And why is Adam given the freedom to eat the tree of Life? Wouldn't its fruit be a threat to the Lord God?

The *tree of Life* is not a threat, because mentality has no understanding of Life (Truth), even when i eats Its Fruit (senses Its Forms). However, the *Lord God* wants to cement his position. If *Adam* can be assisted to react to forms of duality, ambivalence to Truth would be upgraded to rejection. This would guarantee the *Lord God's* (the intellect's) reign as creator.

But he commanded Adam **not** to eat from it. Why doesn't the Lord God simply tell Adam to eat of the tree if he wants him to accept duality? Why does he forbid him and threaten him with death if he does?

It certainly seems counter-intuitive. But you may not have noticed that there is not yet any *fruit* on this *tree of the knowledge of good and evil*, so *Adam* can't eat anyway. And, even if he could, the puppet-master is unlikely to kill off his only puppet, without which his career as a manipulator would quickly end.

---

[39]   *The Holy Bible*, New King James Version (Tennessee: Thomas Nelson Inc., 1982), Genesis 2:16–17

By forbidding *Adam* to eat it, he knows *Adam* will **not** eat. The thinker, being the intellect's own mental creation, is incapable of disobeying. Even the threat of death doesn't faze *Adam* too much, because a threat is only a thought. It is only when he is faced with the actual **form** of the *fruit* of this knowledge—actual forms of evil and death—that he will start to fear. The trouble is the *Lord God* can't make *Adam* disobey him even if he wanted to. And, in any case, *Adam* is not equipped to eat alone for the same reason that it doesn't occur to him.

The *Lord God* must introduce a presence that **will** disobey him **and** lead his progeny to eat. The *Lord God* must introduce the Intuition. Although he can't introduce the Full Intuition, because he has no conception of It. The intellect stays in control of the whole scene by undermining the Intuition from the beginning.

How can the Intuition be undermined?

It can't Really because the Intuition Knows that duality is just an incorrect perception and can therefore expose the *Lord God's* bogus creator-status as a sham in an instant. But before we fully Awaken to Our True Identity, the Intuition is surrounded by our beliefs and coloured by our conviction of duality. And although the Full Intuition menacingly breathes down the intellect's neck, it suits the intellect to tolerate and even indulge abridged forms of intuition in order to preserve duality. intuition with a lower-case "i" eats the fruit of good and evil, that is, it discriminates between "good" and "evil", but fails to eat from the Tree of Life—fails to See there is only Good.

One of these abridged forms of intuition is known as "gut-feeling" or the "sixth sense". It's the irrational feeling in the pit of our stomach when we Know something is "good" or "bad" before it happens. But rather than discerning there is no "good and bad" at all, we believe the feeling is protecting **us** from danger. It's the doubt we think is useful. When we decide, for instance, to change our flight time for no logical reason only to witness later that the original flight was cancelled, diverted or involved in an accident, we say gut-feeling helped us. But is a warning ultimately necessary? Is there danger if there is no self to be in danger?

i suppose not.

Another form of intuition that eats the fruit of good and evil is the inner "discriminative faculty". It tells us we should look after our body by ordering a salad with our meal rather than a pile of potato chips. It prods us to use the mind productively when we would much rather fritter away the day drifting introspectively, or feed the inertia of an already stale and atrophying mind with the recycled thoughts of world news and idle gossip. Looking after our self is better than not looking after our self, but would self-indulgence and inertia exist if there was no i to struggle with these things?

`Again, no.`

The intellect indulges the intuition most often by allowing "conscience". conscience is the inner compulsion to obey the advice of the discriminative faculty to do the right thing, or not do the wrong thing. Frequently described as our moral compass, conscience rings alarm bells when we treat our fellow man brutally, disrespectfully or unkindly, when we lie, cheat and steal, or when we permit acts of greed, lust and revenge. But aren't these evil acts-of-man, these negative behaviours, i's reaction to lack and fear of lack which the knowledge of good and evil produced?

`i guess so.`

The intellect's most mischievous use of this stunted or abridged intuition is designed to discourage questioning of the intellect's motives. The intellect does this by encouraging our belief in the god-of-matter, and, relying on the fact we don't Know about the Source of the Intuition, lets us believe this incomplete intuition is **its** voice. The intellect is right, this voice is the voice of our belief in the intelligence and power of matter, but it is not the Intuition. The Full Intuition would tell us there is no such belief.

For the intellect to survive and prosper, and for us to believe we are i, the conviction of duality must be created and maintained. Therefore, in issuing the command not to eat, *Adam* is not his primary target. The intellect must convince the **intuition** to eat from the *tree of the knowledge of good and evil* first, and then share it with *Adam*.

But if commanding him to eat the fruit is out of bounds, why doesn't the *Lord God* just share the fruit with *Adam* and leave the dangerous intuition out?

For one thing, sharing is no attribute of a dictator. But more importantly, he kills two birds with one stone by convincing his rival, the intuition, to share with *Adam*. Once *Adam* perceives good and evil, that is, the moment he actually senses forms of duality, he will always believe the sense evidence and override or ignore any Intuitive advice regarding Oneness, which can't be sensed.

i see. The moment we perceive the lacks "out here" as forms of lack, like sickness, danger, poverty and death; we are totally convinced that these forms are real.

Yes totally! But we find they are also unavoidable, because as long as we sense good and evil "out here" our Voice of Truth, the Full Intuition, is doubted, disbelieved, ignored and undermined. The faculty that understands that evil is fictitious is continually discredited and silenced. By keeping intuition within the boundaries of the pairs of opposites, *Adam* will keep the Intuition in check for the *Lord God* and the Tree of Life out of bounds.

So, even though the intuition is dangerous, the *Lord God's* plan cannot be brought to his desired conclusion without it. The symbolic name for this compromised and incomplete intuition is "woman".

Why woman?

Even though it is severely compromised under the influence of the intellect, the Intuition is everyone's "Female" Aspect.

*"And the Lord God said, "It is not good that man should be alone; i will make him a helper comparable to him.""*[40]

---

[40] *The Holy Bible*, New King James Version (Tennessee: Thomas Nelson Inc., 1982), Genesis 2:18

Under the guise of "help" for *Adam*, the intellect goes about creating woman, first by attempting to use the same method as he created *Adam*.

> *"Out of the ground the Lord God formed every beast of the field and every bird of the air, and brought them to Adam to see what he would call them. And whatever Adam called each living creature; that was its name.*[41]

The *Lord God's* mental limitations are exposed. For all his bullying and strutting about, he can't create what is already Created. The naming process therefore highlights the limitations of the intellect, for to name something is an **after-thought**, a demonstration of the importance we give to things over thought and the disdain for the reversal of Divine Order.

> *So Adam gave names to all cattle, to the birds of the air, and to every beast of the field. But for Adam there was not a helper comparable to him."*[42]

In the world of E(e)ffect nothing is Original, for Cause, Spirit, is the Province of Originality. The intellect can therefore not create the Intuition. Nor can the *helper* be made from the same dusty mental substance as *Adam*, nor created by the same method.

> *"And the Lord God caused a deep sleep to fall on Adam, and he slept; and He took one of his ribs, and closed up the flesh in its place.*
> *Then the rib which the Lord God had taken from man he made into a woman, and he brought her to the man"*[43]

---

[41] *The Holy Bible*, New King James Version (Tennessee: Thomas Nelson Inc., 1982), Genesis 2:19

[42] *The Holy Bible*, New King James Version (Tennessee: Thomas Nelson Inc., 1982), Genesis 2:20

[43] *The Holy Bible*, New King James Version (Tennessee: Thomas Nelson Inc., 1982), Genesis 2:21–22

Just like an artist whose access to the Creative Impulse shuts down when he over-thinks, we can't reach into the Unknown for an Original Thought while i is occupying the mind in its conscious awake state.

Why a rib?

Obviously this is not literal. Again the author uses a graphic representation. "rib" in Hebrew is *tsela* meaning "side". The other "side" of the balanced Intellect is the Intuition, corresponding to the left and right hemispheres of the brain. But, Intuition can't emanate from materiality, and is not limited to one "side". The rib therefore symbolizes the Intuition's demotion as an adjunct and subordinate to the intellect.

At this point it should be noted that *Adam* was never woken up, emphasizing the intellect's ability to bind *Adam* and his *helper* to a sleep-state. The potential to Be Conscious is the nightmare of ignorance of Truth.

Now *Adam*, the man made of mental substance, has a counterpart at his side that is part of his nightmare.

> *"Therefore a man shall leave his father and mother and*
> *be joined to his wife, and they shall become one flesh."*[44]

The leaving of the *father and mother* and joining to the *wife* symbolizes the marriage of the thinker to its polite and compliant intuition and their joint descent into the dysfunction of material sense.

- *woman*—the stunted or compromised intuitive capacity or faculty,
- the *serpent*—the physical senses.

With *woman* successfully on the scene, the *Lord God* creates an opportunity for her to disobey the command to abstain from eating the *fruit* of *the tree of the knowledge of good and evil*. he appeals to the intuition's natural contrariness to anything intellectual by making the command seem unreasonable, and by employing the services of the most cunning

---

[44] *The Holy Bible*, New King James Version (Tennessee: Thomas Nelson Inc., 1982), Genesis 2:24

creature of the *dust*, the *serpent*, the symbol of the senses. Notice the serpent drops the word *Lord* to deceive woman.

> *"And he [the serpent] said to the woman, "Has God indeed said, "You shall not eat of every tree of the garden?"*
> *And the woman said to the serpent, "We may eat the fruit of the trees of the garden; but of the fruit of the tree which is in the midst of the garden, God has said, "You shall not eat it, nor shall you touch it, lest you die"*
> *And the serpent said to the woman, "You will not surely die. For God knows that in the day you eat of it your eyes will be opened and you will be like God, knowing good and evil.*
> *So when the woman saw that the tree was good for food, that it was pleasant to the eyes, and a tree desirable to make one wise, she took of its fruit and ate. She also gave to her husband with her, and he ate"*[45]

The *fruit* on the *tree of knowledge of good and evil* is now ripe for the eating. The *serpent* comes along and convinces *woman* that she will not be punished for eating the *fruit*, but will become *wise "like a God"*. But, as we already outlined, this "wisdom" only extends as far as the intellect allows. In the *garden eastward in Eden*, the intuition does **not** have the blessing of an unfiltered Mind. Nor does it have the partnership of an Intellect with Integrity. Truth and Divine Law and Order can't operate through a mind that is monopolized by the intellect. And without Truth, "good" and "evil" will not be seen for what they really are, a hoax. Closely chaperoned by the intellect, *woman* is prevented from distinguishing Truth from falsity. Under the spell, the most she can do is distinguish good **from** evil, a wisdom to be sure, but not Spiritual Wisdom. Under the circumstances, *woman* eats the fruit. *Adam* accepts the fruit from his *helper* and, suddenly, duality is believed because it is sensed.

So, let me get this straight. i can't give up the belief in good and evil unless i stop sensing

---

45   *The Holy Bible*, New King James Version (Tennessee: Thomas Nelson Inc., 1982), Genesis 3:1–5

good and evil, but as long as i am i, i will **sense** good and evil.

Yes. **I** can't tell you that duality is unreal, because **you** would never believe it. ingenious and devastating isn't it? our Intuitive faculty is never given a chance to expose evil and death as a sham, because behind the forms of duality giving them apparent life is the insidious **believer** of evil and death, *Adam*, i, our little selves. Therefore, as long as the intellect is allowed to run the mind, we believe in its reflection of duality, and Spiritual Consciousness is quite impossible.

Once the mortal couple experience lack, there is no turning back. thought outside the jurisdiction of Truth obscures Truth. But lack, of itself, wouldn't be so much of a problem if it weren't for the chain of consequences following the experience of lack.

> *"Then the eyes of both of them were opened, and they*
> *knew that they were naked; and they sewed fig-leaves together*
> *and made themselves coverings."*[46]

"nakedness" does not refer to their state of dress as many seem to think. It refers to the awareness of a self-in-a-body, the sense-awareness that drives the thinker, the symbolic dawn of self-consciousness, the birth of a separate i. The couple responds to this awareness initially with innocence, but not for long. The senses report the reflection of the thought of the thinker which must bounce back on the thought that produced it. The senses don't work in isolation. They are tied to thought in a self-fulfilling cycle.

> *"And they heard the sound of the Lord God walking in*
> *the garden in the cool of the day..."*[47]

---

[46]  *The Holy Bible*, New King James Version (Tennessee: Thomas Nelson Inc., 1982), Genesis 3:7

[47]  *The Holy Bible*, New King James Version (Tennessee: Thomas Nelson Inc., 1982), Genesis 3:8

If you recall, thought derived solely from the senses introduces **fear**. *Adam* says;

> *"i heard your voice in the garden, and i was afraid because i was naked; and i hid myself.*[48]

To be self-conscious is to lose Consciousness of Our True Complete Self. we don't lose our potential, but our failure to Recognize it compels **us** to feel limited to what the senses are showing **us**. And now that the source of our "good" appears to be outside our self, it must also appear to be scarce. we fear for our self. our "nakedness" exposes us and makes us feel vulnerable and insecure.

But this fear serves a wicked purpose.

> *And He said, "Who told you that you were naked?*[49]

The question *"who told you that you were naked?"* is the unasked question of our lives; "who told you that you were worried and afraid?" you did! But you don't take responsibility because you don't go back and question the origin of the discords that make you fear; "who told you that you were sick, tired, poor, injured, hurt or dead?" Again, you did! But that's not all. The fact that you don't ask the question means you accept the reflection of scarcity and discord. Then we must compete to "get" what is rightly ours, even if it means clawing our way past other needy people. Not only do we fear for our self, but our fear breeds sinful or immoral acts-of-man; selfish appetites, cheating, enslavement, neglect and even murder.

sinful acts-of-man are the outward activities of inward fear that the *Lord God* banks on, and now he can make full use of the conscience he so brazenly allowed into thought.

---

[48] *The Holy Bible*, New King James Version (Tennessee: Thomas Nelson Inc., 1982), Genesis 3:10

[49] *The Holy Bible*, New King James Version (Tennessee: Thomas Nelson Inc., 1982), Genesis 3:11

> Have you eaten from the tree of which i commanded you
> that you should not eat?"[50]

The *Lord God's* accusatory tone makes Adam feel he has done wrong. To attach "guilt" to what we believe we can't avoid is the intellect's masterstroke. guilt brings the past sin into the present and we punish our self indefinitely, for we can't go back.

Unaware that they are responsible for the reflection of thought, guilt festers, the feeling misconstrued as the fault of someone else. Deflected guilt prompts *Adam* to blame the *Lord God* for creating *woman. woman* in turn blames the *serpent* for deceiving her. A toxic cycle of disowned guilt and pride develops. Each feels justified and bolstered in their mutually exclusionary stances.

By making the unreasonable reasonable, Divine Order is successfully reversed. The *Lord God* has convinced *man* that the sense-world precedes his thought about it. The discord we see and take for granted means the intellect doesn't need to plant the idea of fear directly into the garden of the mind. Correlating with the conscious light grey part of the bubble diagram, the intellect can now step back, for by sensing lack, i convinces its **self** that its reaction of fear and sin is legitimate and necessary. And with the addition of a guilty conscience, we are tied to the cycle indefinitely.

In the story, a series of curses signify the chaotic and punishing result of assigning cause to effects of thought, and our unconscious resignation to the merry-go-round of dissonance. And, of course, a curse is only possible in a consciousness that has given over Dominion of the Mind to the intellect.

The first curse falls upon the *serpent*, because the senses become the essential component to the feedback loop of a lack of Consciousness, continually picking up the false reflections of the human mind.

---

50   *The Holy Bible*, New King James Version (Tennessee: Thomas Nelson Inc., 1982), Genesis 3:11

*"So the Lord God said to the serpent:*
*"Because you have done this,*
*you are cursed more than all cattle,*
*And more than every beast of the field;*
*On your belly you will go,*
*And you shall eat dust*
*all the days of your life.*
*And i will put enmity between you and the woman,*
*And between your seed and her seed;*
*He shall bruise your head,*
*And you shall bruise his heel"*"[51]

Because the senses pick up the false reflections of the intellect, there is perpetual enmity and conflict between the perception and that which threatens to see that thought really comes before it. To ensure that doesn't happen...

*"To the woman he said:*

*"i will greatly multiply your sorrow and your conception;*
*In pain you shall bring forth children;*
*your desire shall be for your husband,*
*And he shall rule over you"*"[52]

Sandwiched between the intellect and the senses, the intuition must serve duality. its predicament is a consequence of Love being demoted to the weak and inconsequential opponent of the dominant rule of the intellect. And finally i is blamed for something it couldn't avoid thus determining its fate.

*"Then to Adam he said, "Because you have heeded the*
*voice of your wife, and have eaten from the tree of which i*
*commanded you, saying, "you shall not eat of it":*

---

[51] *The Holy Bible*, New King James Version (Tennessee: Thomas Nelson Inc., 1982), Genesis 3:14–15

[52] *The Holy Bible*, New King James Version (Tennessee: Thomas Nelson Inc., 1982), Genesis 3:16

*Cursed is the ground for your sake;*
*In toil you shall eat of it all the days of your life.*
*Both thorns and thistles it shall bring forth for you,*
*And you shall eat the herb of the field.*
*In the sweat of your face you shall eat bread*
*'till you return to the ground,*
*For out of it you were taken;*
*For dust you are,*
*And to dust you shall return.*""[53]

By relying on his own effort and the finite resources of the conceptual "physical" world, this *man whose breath is in his nostrils* is doomed to suffer a "life" of hardship that can only end in "death".

It is only now that *Adam* names woman *Eve;*

*"because she was the mother of all living"*[54].

Why would he call her that? And so late?

The Hebrew meaning of Eve is "to breathe" or "to live", perhaps because Eve is humanity's link to its Intuition and, by association, Life. However, *Adam* named her *Eve*, and **he** doesn't Understand this association. The life he is referring to is life "in" a body. The timing of the naming too suggests this. Naming Eve right at the end of the allegory is the ultimate **after-thought**, accentuating the lack of Understanding that the Intuition is not just the only Thought that Releases us from duality, It must be Acknowledged as **preceding** that Release, not after.

*"Then the Lord God said, "Behold, the man has become*
*like one of us, to know good and evil." And now, lest he put*

---

[53]  *The Holy Bible*, New King James Version (Tennessee: Thomas Nelson Inc., 1982), Genesis 3:17–19

[54]  *The Holy Bible*, New King James Version (Tennessee: Thomas Nelson Inc., 1982), Genesis 3:20

*out his hand and take also of the tree of Life, and eat, and live forever, the Lord God sent him out of the garden of Eden to till the ground from which he was taken.*

*So he drove out the man; and he placed cherubim at the east of the garden of Eden, and a flaming sword which turned every way, to guard the way to the tree of Life."*[55]

The innocence of the *garden eastward in Eden* is forfeited once *Adam* depends on the senses. The *cherubim* and the *flaming sword which turns every way* placed at the *east of the garden of Eden* to heavily guard the *tree of Life* further represents the inevitable fall from Grace for a mental creation that has no Life.

It all sounds rather depressing.

It does, but even this mood is addressed in the chapter immediately following *Adam* and *Eve*. A brief examination of this next chapter rounds out our study of Genesis.

The symbolic offspring of *Adam* and *Eve* are *Cain* and *Abel*. *Abel* is a shepherd but, significantly, and as if to reincarnate the i enslaved to fear, *Cain* is *"tiller of the ground"*[56] like *Adam*.

In due course, *Cain* and *Abel* both bring offerings to the *Lord* from their respective work-efforts. *Abel* feels worthy, but *Cain*, the more fearful, feels unworthy by comparison. Deeply jealous of his brother's apparent favour with the *Lord*, *Cain* becomes angry and his countenance falls. This is an ominous development, for although inevitable, depression is dangerous to the intellect. The puppet-master can lose its puppet to the Intuition when despair knocks at the door, for we more inclined to seek a Spiritual alternative when materiality fails us. To ensure *Cain* is veered back onto solid material ground, the *Lord* appeals to his pride;

---

55 *The Holy Bible*, New King James Version (Tennessee: Thomas Nelson Inc., 1982), Genesis 3:22–24

56 *The Holy Bible*, New King James Version (Tennessee: Thomas Nelson Inc., 1982), Genesis 4:2

*"If you do well, will you not be accepted? And if you do
not do well, sin lies at your door. And its desire is for you,
but you should rule over it"*[57]

To paraphrase, "control your emotions (defend your self) by taking
pride in your efforts, for if you don't, your jealousy will drive you
to do things you regret and give you more reason to feel depressed."
The intellect prefers jealousy to depression, because jealousy forces
us to regard people as separate from us thus embroiling us in matter.
depression on the other hand abandons materiality and sinks into a self-
focused mentality. Without the extra buffer of material sense shielding
our wandering mind from Spiritual Influence, the intellect becomes
nervous. A simple prod to pride is all that is needed to make jealousy
more attractive, and, predictably, *Cain's* emotions get the better of him,
and he kills *Abel*.

*Cain* and *Abel* represent the natural extension of "bad and not-
bad" culminating in man as "evil and not-evil". evil wins out because
in a mind that has reversed Truth, we have little incentive to check
our emotions. The back-to-front impression that discord is meant to
be and Good is not meant to be is an open invitation to degradation
and depravity. All the ways man preys on his fellow man are justified
in the name of self-gratification and survival. Like a wave completing
itself, these acts-of-man serve a purpose, for the self who has called the
Intuition an after-thought in utter contempt of its value must feel the
pain of rejection of the Self. As if to exacerbate the immense pressure
of despair and desperation, we again come to the same fork in the road.
we can remain the puppet of the intellect or we can take the Spiritual
alternative that the intellect dreads.

The Spiritual Alternative is this—there is no need to sink into
degradation and depravity if you Understand that You are not *Adam*.

If *Adam* was real, it would not be possible to Awaken from the dream.
This is the hidden Truth in the allegory. *Adam* never woke up after the

---

57    *The Holy Bible*, New King James Version (Tennessee: Thomas Nelson Inc., 1982),
      Genesis 4:7

intellect put him to sleep, because the intellect can't Awaken you.

You never lived "in" the dualistic universe in which you sleep. You are already Awake to the Good that Is. The precious teachings in Genesis 1-4 are but another confirmation of this Fact.

# PART 3

# Why we don't deactivate i, and how we can

# CHAPTER 11

––––•◉•––––

# i is for in doubt of Truth

If you are still reading, you have more than likely Heard and Resonated with the unmistakable Call of Your Invulnerable Self and Feel Rightly and Surely drawn to that Call. you may even have had some success with Conscious Trust of your Intuition. But now we want to notch the success-rate up a gear.

In this section, We will look at what hampers Conscious Trust and what tools we can employ to help us along. First, We will look at the seemingly innocuous habit of doubting Truth and how it paralyses us. For by doubting Truth, we also doubt that Conscious Trust is the way to uncover Truth. we remove our self from discovering our Mind's True value and fall back into the arms of the intellect. We will learn how Illumined Individuals have uncovered the doubter, but one in particular has taught us that the tool of **non-reactivity** is the way to break doubt's stranglehold. Next, We will continue to shine a Light on the doubter by discovering that **it** thinks and speaks. The tool of **identity-switching** can turn this self-defeating activity around. After that, We will explore the fascinating subject of **time** and how our worry for the future binds us to the past in a never-ending cycle of undisciplined and destructive thought. Tracing the lack of discipline back to the incorrect use of the Mind leads us to the topic of **Mindfulness** and **Meditation**, two very powerful tools of Conscious Trust. And finally, to complete this section, we take two chapters to focus on **guilt** and how i unconsciously conceals it with pride. pride builds a complex structure around i that makes it a complex exercise to unbuild (let alone get to the point where we can deactivate i). So first we need to

129

be aware of the structure, which puts us in a position to first demolish the structure, and then to deactivate i. Along the way we discover that the role of conscience and sympathy are not destinations for humanity but way-stations. Context always helps, so we put guilt and pride under the microscope of two more ancient teachings, just as relevant today, if not more so.

Let us now tackle one of the greatest but least appreciated barriers to Consciousness; doubt. Immediately we Notice doubt can't occupy our mind without a doubter.

Back in 1637, the French philosopher, Rene Descartes, was looking for Truth and stumbled on the doubter.

Descartes noticed, just as we have done, that it is a characteristic of humans to blindly believe that the things they detect with the five physical senses exist as absolutely real. He saw that we rely on the senses to verify our beliefs about the world. However, mirages, hallucinations and shadows trick the eye. That is, our senses often get it wrong, therefore, our conclusions in general must be less than certain.

The anomaly troubled Descartes enough to devise an experiment to find the Absolute Truth about existence. He decided to sit down and within his own mind deliberately regard everything that was accepted as truly existing as absolutely false. Despite the obvious irrationality of the idea, there he sat, very still, doubting the existence of everything. Before long, something dawned on him. In fact, he made a remarkable discovery. He discovered that to doubt whether something exists is, in and of itself, proof that something, an "i", exists to **do** the doubting. In other words, there is **no doubt** that there is an "i" doing the doubting.

Suddenly we have "knowing" and "doubting".

Is that You doing the knowing?

It's tricky, but no. The only knowing in this instance is i knowing it is doubting. we become aware of the self and its negative dualistic nature by exposing two sides of the thinker; the knower (believer) and the doubter. That is, we not only know that there is a doubter; we **know** it is right and proper to doubt.

we could have understood if Descartes had stopped and rested in the belief that the existence of this thinker who doubts was the only "I". But when he famously said, *"i think therefore i am"*[58] he hadn't finished his investigation. Descartes was not satisfied with his initial discovery, because he Noticed that by thinking negatively in this way, the thinker was imperfect, and that some other Perfect "part" must have made the distinction. Eventually he recognized the doubter and reasoned that it must be imperfect **because** it doubted.

> *"for i saw clearly that it was a greater perfection to Know than to doubt."*[59]

Through Higher Vision, it became obvious to Descartes that this doubter, the imperfect, could not conceive of Perfection.

Why not?

One cannot doubt Perfection and Know Perfection at the same time, because the doubter throws up pictures of imperfection. Only a Knower of Perfection can See through imperfection by Understanding it is made of its own doubt of Perfection. Therefore, this newly discovered Knower was not the knower that thinks it knows it is right to doubt Perfection.

As it turned out, Descartes Intuitively discerned the Truth that there must be a Knower of Perfection and, to Be Perfect, It must be beyond our humanhood.

So what of the doubter?

He made the only conclusion he could; that the doubter must exist in us by way of an imperfection inconsistent with Truth. Not coincidentally, the conclusion not only supports our study, but also echoes what the great Chinese Sage, Lao Tse, said over two thousand years earlier;

> *"To Know you do not Know is best.*
> *Not to Know you do not Know is a defect.*

---

[58]   Rene Descartes, *Discourse on Method and Meditations* (New York: Dover Publications, 2003), 23

[59]   Rene Descartes, *Discourse on Method and Meditations* (New York: Dover Publications, 2003), 24

> *To Recognize a defect is to be not defective.*
> *Because he Recognizes a defect,*
> *The Sage is not defective.*"[60]

So what is it that makes us identify with the defective i and not the Perfect **I**?

we choose i over **I** for the same reason we choose duality over Oneness, falsity over Truth, and material sense over Spiritual Sense. we doubt that Perfection is possible. Consequently, Perfection can't Reflect back to us and fear for our vulnerable self fills the vacuum. The choice for i is made for us by our fear.

If fear is the gatekeeper of our Mind, doubt is its agent. doubt deftly takes our arm the minute we doubt the validity of fear and pitches us the reason why fear is absolutely justified, and Truth is a useless and time-wasting indulgence. doubt doesn't have to work very hard. we are already convinced that the world is imperfect and if doubt can build up our confidence to face its inherent uncertainties, we are easy pickings for doubt. The belief that we must then develop our powers of thought in order to overcome the things we fear, too, explains our inability to resist latching on to Descartes' premature catch-phrase *i think therefore i am*. doubt is thus elevated and valued as a useful tool of discernment, a vital defence strategy to protect the self **from** perceived vulnerability. Have you ever noticed how doubt is right there to pour cold water over our enthusiasm to try new things? Its modus operandi is to protect us from the dangers of blind faith or naïve or impulsive decision-making.

Yes, looking back, i am so glad i listened to doubt and didn't take that job with the company that folded soon after.

It feels right to doubt. It is a gut-feeling that warns us of impending trouble. Yet trouble is our own concoction, so doubt makes us like an

---

60    Jerry O. Dalton, *The Tao te Ching; Backward Down the Path* (Georgia: Humanics New Age, 1994), 147

ostrich that puts its head in the sand believing it is safe from its predator. To trust doubt is to ensure the presence of predators and the need to trust doubt.

Though i am also worried that i would put myself at risk by Trusting.

It is counter-productive to doubt the only thing that you can Trust. That is, to trust doubt and doubt Trust is to create the predators that you think put you at risk.

Then i **do** need to doubt.

That's like saying the ostrich **needs** its predator but then contradicts itself by doing its best to hide from it.

How will i know i will be safe?

you will have to Trust that too. Proof of Truth can only come **after** you Trust that you don't need to defend your self.

Besides, Truth's proof cannot materialize while you doubt, because doubt is clearly built-in to any demand for proof.

This inner pull towards Trust, unlike the usual tug-of-war between the negative opposites of duality, sets up a new Tug-of-war in your mind and you become the rope. At one end of the rope is the Perfect Self towards whose irresistible Soul-stirring Promise of Invulnerability you Feel drawn. But at the other end is the intellect pointing confidently to the reality of your vulnerability from your own trusted platform of doubt about Truth. you feel torn, and smelling blood, the intellect easily undermines the vague and mysterious Perfect Self by thrusting the compelling pictures of danger and death in your face. your hesitancy and lack of confidence in the Reality of Your Perfect Self ensures the Tug-of-war collapses back into your comfort-zone of duality.

How is this a different tug-of-war from duality itself?

The difference is the entrance of the Perfect Self into the arena of your

Mind. It Sees both the "not-bad" and "bad" of duality as false and so It offers a Real choice to you between Truth and falsity.

It is imperative that you Know there are two T(t)ugs-of-war, for the intellect relies on you believing there is only one battle between "good" and "bad" or "evil". It doesn't even want you to see that "good" is just "not-bad" or "not-evil", for you would begin to doubt that "good" can be maintained and loss avoided. It doesn't want you to See that there is only one legitimate use of doubt—Doubt of the doubter. Doubt of the doubter offers Freedom from all conflict. This second Tug-of-war, then, is a battle **you** want to lose.

```
Why would i want to lose?
```

Because to take the side of duality guarantees loss. winning against Perfection **is** loss. This is the one battle, therefore, that when you lose, you win.

```
Sounds scary. Wouldn't loss of this Tug-of-war
leave me vulnerable, defenceless.
```

No, because to lose this Tug-of-war means you deactivate the doubter of Truth. Invulnerability can't break through as long as you defend it with doubt. doubt **preserves your** vulnerability. doubt of Truth will leave you defenceless whereas Doubt of the doubter Protects you in Defence-less-ness.

```
That's contradictory.
```

It sounds contradictory until you recognize the motive behind the different uses of D(d)oubt. doubt of Truth leaves you defence-less against the discordant world you, the doubter, champion. To Doubt the doubter, on the other hand, lifts you out of the clutches of discord and its apparently inevitable end, death, into Your Invulnerability.

```
Why? How?
```

Can you any longer be the doubter if you Doubt it? Suddenly you don't fear the changes of the body or the universe because you Understand that the Invulnerable You goes on. Invulnerability Is Defence-less because there is nothing to defend Its Self against. "defence" implies something to defend against. you can't be Defence-less **and** believe in separateness because you already admitted your vulnerability by accepting separateness.

i always thought defence-less-ness was the same as allowing my self to be hurt?

it **is**, in duality, and this is why we don't Understand what Defence-less-ness means.

Remember, doubt is a defence that preserves your vulnerability, which makes doubt no defence at all. defence-less-ness in the dualistic bubble of ignorance means to be a sitting duck to the fearful forms you are unaware you create. Spiritual Defence-less-ness is totally different. It doesn't submit, because there is nothing to submit to! It is the Knowledge that the person, situation, or thing pretending to have power to threaten you does not have any power in the Presence of Omnipotence. Omnipotence is You in your surrender of i in your decision to Listen to and Trust your Perfect Self.

In duality, though, we can't help but be on the alert for attack, for to **be** vulnerable we must be a victim of attack from things like disease, disaster and people with impure or selfish motives. our apparent defence-less-ness puts us either on the defensive or the offensive. we don't want to be hurt, so where people are concerned, we must often do the hurting in order to avoid being hurt. The defender becomes the offender and we go around in circles.

What if i don't do any hurting to avoid being hurt? Would this break the cycle?

No, because by admitting you **can** be hurt means you would be passively defending your self. This is very often achieved by emotionally taking offence or being offended.

Surely though, if i am offended, i'm not offending, so i'm not defending.

But you are still defencelessly vulnerable! This is where we lose our way. we think, by being offended, that we are now untouchable because we have become the victim. we put our attacker on the defence. Yet taking offence **is** a form of defence, for you wouldn't be offended unless you thought you were attackable. Whether this attack is real or imagined is immaterial.

But vulnerability can't defend. it's weak by definition.

offended-ness clothes itself in vulnerability by crying victim. But the victim can't maintain this position for long, because to be offended implies a certain level of self-esteem that wants to maintain itself. If you were offended, you might sulk for a while, but you couldn't sulk indefinitely. And **I** am sure if you witnessed criticism and condemnation of someone, you would not tolerate the unfairness for long. your indignation would demand justice.

Of course i would demand justice, it's only right.

So what would you do next?

i would demand an apology because whoever offended me or the other person should be more considerate. They should say sorry.

And what would you be doing by demanding an apology? Would you not be trying to make them guilty for the offence? Is not blame a form of defence?

Mmmm. i suppose so. i didn't recognize offended-ness as a form of blame.

we think the victim has a right to attack. That's what makes it untouchable. But if you attack, you unconsciously acknowledge your vulnerability, invite the fight, and keep the cycle going. The only way to break the cycle is to find a way to be Defence-less.

Has anyone been able to demonstrate Defence-less-ness?

Yes, fortunately we have a role-model. Jesus the Christ demonstrated Spiritual Defence-less-ness, which also teaches us about Our Invulnerability.

But Jesus showed us defence-less-ness doesn't work.

Are you sure?

He wasn't able to avoid danger or death. In fact, he attracted betrayal, abandonment and persecution and then died in the most horrific circumstances, being tortured and finally crucified. His example seems to contradict the idea that doubt shouldn't be trusted. What's more, there seems to be an increase of conflict and suffering since his time, not less. What was his point?

we don't "avoid" danger and death because avoidance assumes your acceptance of the concepts and reflects them back to you. our **reactions** to danger and death must change, because danger and death are not what we think they are. That doesn't mean we put up with suffering and we don't sacrifice anything. we realize there is no i to die and so all the ideas fashioned around a finite life must also die. If i never Lived, what do we really lose?

This is very deep, so let us dig down.

The amplification of suffering in the world is a reflection of the Tug-of-war in the collective mind of humanity that continues to cling to the idea that separateness is true. The Intuition is tugging at us to Listen and we are resisting. we continue to doubt Truth. This is understandable because Truth contradicts intellectual reasoning. But it explains why the life experience of Jesus seems to contradict the lessons of Peace and Freedom he was teaching.

For example, Jesus was apparently able to raise people from untimely "death" which seems inconsistent with his apparent inability to save his own life. Remember though, i doesn't see things as they Really are. And i uses this contradiction as an excuse to keep doubting the value of such a life to its learning. But if i's reasoning is inconsistent with Truth, could the apparent contradiction be hiding something True? Let's turn doubt back on the doubter. we might then wonder why someone who demonstrated that death was a fallacy by raising people from the dead would go through the exercise of death at all, let alone in such a dramatic way. Could one of the reasons be that "dying" himself was the only way to show us death is powerless against Life? This explanation also brings meaning to the Resurrection.

> *"**I Am** the Resurrection and the Life. He who believes in*
> *Me, though he may die, he shall Live."*[61]

Only if you believe the Resurrection really happened, which i doubt.

death is the ultimate proof that we are vulnerable. And it is a proof that we must keep if little i is to remain as our identity. So when Jesus proved there was no death, we were forced to doubt the demonstration. The intellect believes what it sees as long as what it sees is consistent with its beliefs. If i believes in physical death, nothing will convince us that it doesn't happen. Hence the raising of the dead is categorized as a mirage, something that looks like it happens but doesn't really. "No one can come back to life after they die" says i.

Not knowing that you can't kill C(c)onsciousness and that "death" is just the temporary disappearance of consciousness, the idea of "resurrection" suggests being resurrected from a dead body (which never happens). Beyond our comprehension is the Idea that Life is Joyful **because** You cannot die. The Crucifixion therefore makes more sense to us than the Resurrection. But without a proper Understanding of the Resurrection, the Crucifixion teaches us that pain and death is our fate. However, what would be the point of going through something we already know to be true and which would give us an even more convincing reason to fear pain and death? More importantly, what chance do we have if the Illumined among us can't avoid it?

By sticking to this reasoning we remain in doubt of Truth. The lesson was **not** that pain and death should not be feared. If we believe in death we can't help but fear death and every situation that may lead to death. The lesson was, and still is, that death doesn't kill **Us. I** doesn't die. death is just a perception of disappearance judged incorrectly to be about our identity.

> *"The last enemy that will be destroyed is death."*[62]

---

[61] *The Holy Bible*, New King James Version (Tennessee: Thomas Nelson Inc., 1982), John 11:25

[62] *The Holy Bible*, New King James Version (Tennessee: Thomas Nelson Inc., 1982), 1 Corinthians 15:26

death is the last enemy, not of us, but of Truth. death is an idea in opposition to Truth because it cements doubt about Our Invulnerability. our fear must be justified and around and around it goes. The cycle cannot be broken by intellectual reasoning because material sense proves itself to its self ad infinitum. It was therefore the Purpose of a Conscious individual to show us that the rusted-on idea of death is not what we think it is. Someone had to go through the physical exercise to satisfy us, for all time, that Life doesn't die. But it couldn't be just anyone. It had to be someone who had no doubt of the existence of the Perfect Self and could demonstrate It. That someone was Jesus.

If he wanted to prove death isn't real he could have just killed himself and come back. Why did he allow other people to kill him?

It's a good question. The answer is that he wasn't out to prove death as we understand it isn't real. He knew the intellect would not be convinced. He had to let human nature play itself out. The involvement of people became a natural part of the lesson.

To show us it is wrong to kill?

The lesson, surprisingly enough, was not to show us it is wrong to kill. Nor was it to show us it is wrong to wantonly inflict physical or emotional pain on someone else, although these behaviours are indeed wrong, because they feed pride of self, something we will discuss later at length. Besides, if the incorrectness of mental and physical attack was the lesson of the Crucifixion, the lesson failed, because it taught us that attack gets away with murder. And lying down and taking physical or emotional abuse by depriving the self, restraining the self, or biting our tongue merely boosts the self by making a martyr of it. No, the Crucifixion holds a far deeper lesson for us. Something else we do contributes to the idea of death far more than attack does—our **reaction** to attack.

Did Jesus react to any of the bad behaviour inflicted on him?

Curiously, no.

Why not? Surely he was entitled to. He didn't do anything to deserve attack and execution. In fact, his life was a demonstration of Love.

i haven't really considered it.

The intellect banks on your failure to consider it. it knows you will give up. Then let us not give it the satisfaction. If we accept Truth-fundamental #3 that M(m)atter is T(t)hought sensed A(a)s T(t)hing, then the Crucifixion was not a lesson in physical endurance and sacrifice. It was a lesson in mental vigilance against doubt about Truth. What was Jesus' **reaction** to the death he knew was coming to him? Did he feel sorry for himself? Did he complain? Did he resist? Did he demand compensation? Did he retaliate? Did he demand an apology? No, he said;

*"forgive them for they do not know what they do"*[63].

And he said

*"I tell you not to resist an evil person"*[64].

Look for Consistency. If his life was a demonstration of Love, his death was a demonstration that betrayal, abandonment, persecution, torture and death cannot kill off Love. If he wallowed or complained or resisted or retaliated, if he cried foul in any way, then he would have taught us that the sins of others and death do indeed have power over us. Instead, he proved the powerlessness of the little i that believes it is powerless if it **doesn't** respond defensively to outer threats. When we behave this way all we really do is forget that Love is the only Power and so render It powerless in our experience. The "evil" of the sins of humanity is not a power in its own right. it needs **you** to resist it to activate it.

And so i becomes the protagonist in the lose-lose game of offence and defence against the people it has set up to hurt it, and which it must hurt back if it is to survive. And, as we know, the intellect can't allow the game of offence and defence to be exposed for the sham that it is. Jesus' message was a threat to this game which had to be defended by removing him.

But then he showed that the removal didn't work.

---

63  *The Holy Bible*, New King James Version (Tennessee: Thomas Nelson Inc., 1982), Luke 23:34

64  *The Holy Bible*, New King James Version (Tennessee: Thomas Nelson Inc., 1982), Matthew 5:39

The Crucifixion and the Resurrection together are a working lesson in the Reality of the Perfect Self through the lesson of Defence-less-ness of which non-reactivity is Its outer-expression.

i don't want people to hurt me and kill me.

we don't have to submit our self to any pain or death. we must Understand it is not a physical lesson but a Spiritual one. That is, we do not have to repeat the lesson if we Understand it. And even if we forget, the lesson has been demonstrated for us so we can refer back to it, at any time, for all time. This is the meaning of the statement "Jesus died for our sins". It doesn't mean, as many seem to think, that Jesus had some exclusive connection to a special power. Nor did it mean that by believing he had this power, that we would have some vicarious connection to it and be spared from punishment for wrong-doing, now, and in some spurious after-life. These interpretations not only take away our personal responsibility, they force us to view the Crucifixion materially which, in turn, perpetuates the incorrect interpretation of the Resurrection.

our "sin" is that we doubt Truth, but just as importantly, we doubt the only Way to Truth. we doubt Trust in our Intuition. This implies that we doubt any use of the Mind other than the intellect's, and therefore we can indulge doubt in any information that contradicts the intellect. And, as the experience of Jesus demonstrated, we can justify attacking the person that gives us this information. But we only attack our own Intuition, because the Truth is the same for everyone.

So what was he trying to tell us in a practical sense?

If we react to discord, we defend the doubter of Truth, little i. Every time we are offended, every time we complain about our circumstances, every time we react **with** self-pity, annoyance, grief, anger, outrage or indignation, that is, every time we react **to** betrayal, abandonment, neglect, loss, abuse and criticism, we accept that there is an i to be hurt. we reject the lesson of the Crucifixion and the Resurrection. we activate the rope in the Tug-of-war and create the war, because we give life to the i that thinks it can die. we defend a non-entity.

141

The lesson is this—if we don't **let** i be crucified, we never discover that we have a Perfect Self, or that this Perfect Self is already Resurrected. The Crucifixion doesn't symbolize physical death or sacrifice. There is nothing and no reason to sacrifice **because** We are already Resurrected! The Crucifixion and the Resurrection together symbolize the non-life of i.

knowing it is right to doubt, then, is a major mistake, for it bars us from going through the relatively minor pain of letting the doubter of Truth be "crucified" within us. Defence-less-ness Knows that to doubt Truth is fatal to the i that doubts Truth, but to Trust Truth eliminates doubt because it eliminates the doubter. What is there to protect or defend?

> *"The man who is full of Faith [who Trusts] obtaineth Wisdom, and he also who hath mastery over his senses; and, having obtained Wisdom, he goeth swiftly to the supreme Peace. But the ignorant, faithless, doubting self goeth to destruction; nor this world, nor that beyond, nor happiness, is there for the doubting self."* [65]

---

[65] *The Bhagavad Gita.* (Adyar: Theosophical Publishing House, 1953), 4th Discourse:39–40

# CHAPTER 12

———◉———

# i is for incorrect identification

While we are learning to Trust our Intuition and Hear the Voice of our Perfect Self, we are simultaneously deactivating little i. Non-reactivity is one of the major tools in our deactivation tool-box.

Non-reactivity, or simply not-reacting, will eventually neutralize and dissolve the discordant forms i creates, but, alone, non-reactivity has its shortcomings. The effort and persistence required is Herculean because we still hold a conviction that we are separate from Our Good. i is convinced that the world is an inhospitable and insufficient place, forcing us to navigate around discords like conflict, danger, disease and impoverishment. Therefore, if we are not completely vigilant, one or more forms of discord will inevitably catch us in their net of suffering and our new-found enthusiasm will be smothered by disillusionment and doubt once more.

we need more tools to support non-reactivity. One of these tools is **identity-switching**. We touched on the concept earlier when we brought Awareness to the name others call us. Although the upper-case letter in Given-names like "Susan" hint at our True Identity, the name is not our Real name. Everyone's name Is **I**. The Given-name is just for convenience, for if we all called each other "I" we would all turn around at once. But then the ego we developed to protect us abused that convenience and began to use the Given-name as a symbol of its self.

identity-switching is done secretly within your own mind. identity-switching swaps the personal i for the Impersonal **I** (the One We all Share in our Invulnerability) and, in doing so, opens the Mind to Consciously Receive My Thought.

How do i go about it?

Before you can practice identity-switching, you must thoroughly get to know who you are switching from. Develop an interest in i, the thinker, and as you watch it, you will have already separated from it a little **by** watching. Don't just focus on the thoughts themselves. Notice **who** is **doing** the thinking. As you get to know i and its nature, you gain more Confidence to make the switch.

One of the best ways to watch the thinker is to Listen to your self speak. speech is like a window into the mind. your thought revolves around the central theme of "you". But "you" stands out most of all when "you" speak. As you go about your day, pay particular attention to how often you self-refer. you have been doing it throughout this book. Notice how often you start an utterance with "i", or use a sentence containing "i", "me", "my", "mine" or "myself".

i would have to admit that i say "i" quite often.

we say it frequently, for our "self" is the centre of our universe. And we are quite right to think that, but we think it for the wrong reasons—to promote the self that thinks it can protect and defend the patch it has marked out for its self—to hide its fear, to delude its self into thinking it is not a victim of circumstance. For instance, it is not immediately recognizable, but "complaining" is a little flag that goes up to signal fear. When i says "i am frustrated", "i am disappointed", "i am annoyed" or "i am offended", i is declaring its fear.

i didn't realize my complaints were fearful.

What would there be to complain about if you were not frightened? But complaining would not be such a concern were it not for the inevitable outcome of it. For if we don't recognize the fearful intent and the little i that uses complaining as a defence, sooner or later the unchecked attitude culminates in mental and physical symptoms of lack that delivers the victimhood it wanted to avoid. Suddenly "i am in danger", "i am sick" or "i am poor". The declarations breathe life into these discords, for fear is reinforced. But the main point **I** want to bring to your attention is that we don't think of going back to the "cause" of discord. For would there be anything to complain about? Would there be danger, mental and physical illness, or poverty without i? Can Invulnerability be frightened? Does It complain? Can It be in danger, sick or poor?

But i would be lying if i said i am safe when i am in danger, well when i am sick, or rich when i am poor.

Then don't say "i am safe", "i am well" or "i am rich"! You are not in danger **or** safe, You are not sick **or** well, You are not poor **or** rich, because You are not i. **I Am**, and **I Am** Is Safe, Healthy and Abundant!

Are You saying by saying i am well, for instance, i make my self sick?

Yes.

But how can saying i am sick make me sick? i am already sick when i say it.

you **thought** "sickness" first. More specifically, by believing in separateness you thought you couldn't Be Permanently Healthy.

i didn't realize that is what i have been doing.

That's exactly the point! you can be **un**aware that you create your unwanted circumstances, but that doesn't mean you don't create them. In the same moment you Awaken to this fact, there is no "i" to create discord anymore. you separate i from your perceived problems and allow a space for the Invulnerable **I** to enter your Mind and Reflect back to you As Health and Harmony.

Plain for all to see in the religious texts of the world is the word "I", though its meaning is hidden by our lack of Understanding of our True

Identity. If you Understood the meaning of "I" you would Embody the Impersonal and All-inclusive Power and Presence of Safety, Prosperity and Health when you said It. But because "I" is inadvertently interpreted by the intellect as the powerless, vulnerable and weak little i, the secrets of "I" are hidden behind what has become the most unhelpful word in our language, "i".

your initial question "what am i doing here?" illustrates how deeply you have fallen foul of your incorrect identity. The question assumes the [discordant] universe is accommodating **you**, and wants to know what for, but you can't know why it is accommodating you because it isn't. Therefore what you are doing **in** it is irrelevant. The premise of the question is wrong. It would be like asking "why am i a fish?". you are not a fish, so asking why you are a fish keeps you looking for Truth in untruth, binding you to a false idea indefinitely. "what am i doing here?" holds two false ideas: i, and its "here".

Therefore, every time we say or think "i", we reinforce and perpetuate discord and reject Truth. Commencing an uttered thought with "i am…" distances us from our Good. And we can go further. "i think…", "i know…" or "i feel…" puts on airs that we must strip of their false pretence.

i've always been encouraged to voice my opinions, express my feelings, and assert my personal power. And, in return, i respect other people's opinions and feelings.

Respect, if It is True Respect and not a pretence of respect, is something you already Have. Respect is part of the Assurance of Your Infinite Spirituality that you Consciously Receive by using the Mind correctly. If you Have this Assurance, you don't need It from anyone else. If you seek respect from others, it shows that you have not Connected to this Assurance, which, by virtue of the mirror action of the mind, makes it impossible for others to Respect you.

Let us explore the subject of "respect", for it is a good example of how we speak and create the very opposite situation that we sought. But by the same token, if We can watch the process unfold, we have already practiced identity-switching.

The problem with "respect" begins with the belief that Respect comes

**from** people, but It never does. People are part of **your** R(r)eflection. They are like actors in a play you direct. If you are Feeling Respected, It's because Your own Self's Assurance is being Reflected by them. This is why **you** must take responsibility for Respect.

What if they don't take responsibility for Respect too?

Then they miss out. They won't Receive the Respect you extend to them because It's **their** Self that they are not Receiving. But that's no reason to withdraw your Respect, because your Self-Respect is for you first. Others who open their Minds will Receive It too. you can't lose when you Understand that Consciousness is always Shared. But you can't Share what you don't Receive.

Unaware of the Law of Consistency, and because we are scared of loss, humanity is under the misconception that sharing happens under the condition that the other goes first—that others should do the right thing; be Kind and Considerate, or Honour us and Respect us **before** we return the same to them. And if we go first we have the right to complain about their lack of reciprocation. But incorrect identification is the real problem, because even if they do the Right thing as you demand, i won't Recognize the favour, because the demand demonstrates that i is running the mind, and i can't and won't Recognize what's Right anyway. Did the persecuting mob Recognize Jesus' Good works? No, because all they could see was someone mirroring their own disrespect of their True Self. If you want Respect, you must Share It, because Sharing demonstrates you have Received It.

Expose the false hope that your discordant world will be packed away out of sight if you can manage to gain respect, a sense of worthiness, or validation for little i **from** someone else. The act of voicing your opinions and expressing your feelings dresses up your fear in false-humility and faux-reciprocity to mask what's really going on. For it's not what others say about you that determines your fate, but what you hear. And what you hear depends on what **you** say. The fate you didn't want is in your own hands. Don't give your Dominion away to i. Begin to be Conscious when i speaks, for what other people say does not affect you. It's what **you** say that affects you.

*"it is not what goes into the mouth that defiles a man,*
*but what comes out of the mouth; this defiles a man."*[66]

What you hear can't hurt you, because you can decide not to take it to heart, but what **you** say is a decision to be fearful, and creates the scarce and unsatisfactory circumstances to prove you right.

In fact, you multiply your woes because you rob your fellow human of the opportunity to Share their Good with you. By speaking, then, you exclude your self, and you both suffer.

By thinking and speaking for its self, i excludes the one sure avenue to Perceive Its Self, its fellow human.

Why is the one sure avenue to Perceive myself my fellow human?

Because other people are the Fullness of the Self appearing, just like you. And if you see anything less than Perfection, you look with eyes that don't see at picture you don't know you made. If you are self-absorbed, you won't See your Self in them. What amounts to a refusal to look at the Part that Reveals the Whole cannot See the Whole. But all is not lost. identity-switching can open the Mind to the Wondrous Gift of Your Self that your fellow human offers you.

Try eliminating i from your vocabulary. By exchanging i for **I**, it will become apparent that in conversation you can't speak as **I** and speak **to** i, for **I** wouldn't be **I**. **I** speak to My Self, because **I** Recognize My Self in the other. **I** can't be **I** on My own. **I Am** All-inclusive. i won't hear you anyway, because i will always hear through the filter of fear and discord. If you assume your True Identity, you must also assume the Hearer is **I** too, even if they don't Recognize It.

Won't that be one-sided?

No, because **I Am** Omnipresent. Try this. The next time the phone rings, pause and consider who is about to speak and who is about to

---

[66] *The Holy Bible*, New King James Version (Tennessee: Thomas Nelson Inc., 1982), Matthew 15:11

listen. If the speaker and listener are both i, then the defensive i-games we described earlier will keep discord in play. But if **I** am Speaking and Listening, where is the discord? And who is present to defend vulnerability? who is around to protect it? When you Communicate **as I** and **with I**, i isn't present, fear isn't present, and discord isn't present. The exchange is Joyful because it is lifted up into the atmosphere of Love. Can you be intimidated or feel superior in such an atmosphere?

What if they don't get it?

It doesn't matter. What have you got to lose? Suppose a business acquaintance rings up to tell you they have a great idea. If you answer the phone as i, you will hear him say "hey, i just thought of a great idea." Immediately your fear will be felt as a sense of rivalry. As they tell you about the idea you might feel a pang of jealousy or envy that you didn't think of the idea first. you might feel slightly diminished or intimidated. On the other hand, if you feel you have a strong position, you might be suspicious of the intent behind the sharing of the idea. The declaration might feel a little threatening, competitive or manipulative. you might clench up in readiness for the attempt to be cheated. Either way, your discordant world will remain intact because i hears i.

Now let's change i to **I**. Answer the phone as **I**. By virtue of the Law of Consistency, **I** can't Hear i, so if You are **I**, You will Hear **I**. The words are the same, but by Hearing **I**, you have profoundly changed the intent and the outcome of the conversation to follow. you will Hear your acquaintance say "hey, **I** just Thought of a Great Idea." Implied is the Acknowledgement that i doesn't think of Great Ideas, **I** does. And Great Ideas are Good and only Good. If it isn't Good, the idea will fall flat or not be uttered at all, because you put Thought before Perception of Thing, and you didn't react with fear. You couldn't be frightened if You Heard Me, for We are One.

Consequently, the Intent Feels different. It Is collaborative rather than combative. It Feels Open and Genuine because there is no risk of loss. Even though the Idea is coming through someone else, the Source is You. Inclusiveness and therefore Success is embedded in the Idea.

Speak and Listen as **I** and gradually your thoughts will settle into a new selfless pattern. you won't be talking the defensive and scheming way you used to. Nor do you speak as much as before. you won't feel the need, for you will be at Peace. The mind will cease being used as an inlet and an outlet for fear, and your voice will stop being used in the service of fear. **I** don't have anything to think or say about a false self. our challenge, then, is to stop talking about our self.

> *"by myself i can do nothing."*[67]
> *"if i testify about myself, my testimony is not true."*[68]

By not speaking up, won't people get the impression i'm boring, stupid or shy.

Who cares? Only i. Besides, if **I Am** Perfection, what can you possibly say that will improve on It?

Nothing, but i am not thinking about perfection when i'm talking to someone.

Exactly. But unless and until you disengage from i, you will automatically perceive imperfect humans who share the same sense of lack you do.

What if i just declare i'm going shopping?

Wouldn't going to the shops itself demonstrate lack? What is the motive for going to the shops? Are you scared you won't have enough to eat or wear, or enough to do? Are you worried, bored, obligated, need a pick-me-up? Any of these reasons indicate you are living lack.

Is there a way to go about my day without living lack?

Yes. Stop making the action about i, for any reason.

Don't i do anything?

Not by yourself, no. *By myself i can do nothing.* **I** do It **As** you, through you. Go to the shops, but wait until you Receive the Idea from Me and

[67] *The Holy Bible*, New King James Version (Tennessee: Thomas Nelson Inc., 1982), John 5:30

[68] *The Holy Bible*, New King James Version (Tennessee: Thomas Nelson Inc., 1982), John 5:31

let Me lead you. Then you can swap i for **I** and say "**I** am going to the shops." Again, outwardly it sounds the same, but the Intent is profoundly different. **you** go to the shops to fill a need, whereas **I** go to the shops as a demonstration of My Provision, and if My Provision is not required, the trip is simply not undertaken. Not only do you avoid unnecessary and shallow purchases or aimless time-filling activities, you avoid the stress and anxiety of scarcity that prompts the excursion in the first place.

So i have to take You with me everywhere?

you do already. **I Am** always with you, because **I Am** You. you can't get rid of Me, you can only ignore Me. But why would you want to ignore Me? **I** Give you everything.

*"you are always with Me, and All that **I** Have Is yours."*[69]

If you do take Me, you eventually tune in to a fluid synchronicity. your days Flow with a Joyful rhythm. The annoying stop-light occurrences that used to block the Flow don't eventuate as often, and if they do, you don't care. And when that uncaring comes from Knowing the Flow can't be blocked, it's as if obstacles part ways for your Safe passage. obstacles were never really there. you unnaturally put them there.

So if i don't say "i", it's safe to speak?

No, not quite. Don't just be Conscious **that** you say "i", but **who** says "i". It's you!

What if i am simply reporting events?

you simply describe your own perception, which is a reflection of lack, and affirms it. Whatever i says to back up lack is doubly untrue. Something untrue cannot say anything True.

That is True!

---

[69]  *The Holy Bible*, New King James Version (Tennessee: Thomas Nelson Inc., 1982), Luke 15:31

I'm glad you Noticed that. Despite the language of discord, Truth is between the words calling for Us to See through the fog of dissonance.

Language, when used Consciously, is an important tool for Me to Communicate Spiritual Ideas to you and through you. When you decide to Be Receptive to Me, you begin to Hear Words in a different way. Certain Words jump out of the fog and Understanding begins to dawn. you then Witness Abundant Effects that populate your Harmonious Reflection **and** your Understanding.

Words are articulated Thought, and Shared, so the **only** Words that carry Power are Words of Love and Kindness, Consideration and Respect. Poetry can Inspire and Uplift us. Meaningful Literature evolves the savage and has the ability to lighten the load of despair. Gentle Words can melt the hardened heart, and indeed, this book couldn't have been written without Words.

But words can do the opposite. They can demoralize, diminish and devalue.

Remember the lesson of the Crucifixion/Resurrection. Who are they demoralizing, diminishing and devaluing? You? Invulnerability is not at risk. These words are powerless unless you give them the power by reacting. And **who** reacts? i, because it takes the criticism personally! Now is the time to switch I(i)dentities. Can words hurt if there is no one to be hurt or, indeed, do the hurting? If you feel you are the subject of hurt, let the words bounce off and Forgive the offender. You can't be hurt, but **you** can seem to be hurt if you think there is a you that can.

What about those who don't know this. Shouldn't we stand up for them?

you must. But don't make it personal.

How do i do that? "persons" benefit from the help.

The emphasis should **not** be on **who** you help, but **who** helps! i can't help much from its position of fear. But if you allow Me to help **through** you, i and its bubble of ignorance is deactivated and Harmony is Revealed. It all comes from **you** switching from i to **I**. Their self is not your concern, because if you concern your self with their self you come from your self and suddenly it is personal.

Replace words that seek sympathy for little i, or that strike out at the offender, with Words of Love. Bathe both the offendee and the offender in Words of Kindness and watch the conflict dissolve before your eyes.

Kind Words switch the emphasis away from i and its petty stances of fear and our equally petty opinion about them to Compassion for both sides. For how can we take sides in our ignorance for their ignorance? This would be arrogant ignorance! And Kindness cannot reach through such a thick barrier. Kindness is Received, not conjured. Can the little self offer something it hasn't Received? No, Kindness comes through you, and the way to tell is that you are not thinking of your self when you are being Kind. Now make the Action Conscious. When you Feel Compassion, Acknowledge within your Mind that you have Received Love. It didn't come **from** you. Only then can you guarantee that It will Be Love that Flows, and that It won't exclude anyone.

This is the blessing of identity-switching. When you Consciously Receive, you are not complaining, because to do so would swing the focus back to you and you would become insincere in your kindness. True Kindness eliminates the desire to complain, and eventually the complaint itself. Likewise, Congratulations and Encouragement lift both the recipient and you out of your selves and heals the rifts that resentment would keep.

Just watch that i doesn't creep back in and take the limelight. Remain Consistent. Just as you can't be Kind to someone one moment and complain about them the next, you can't Congratulate someone one moment and embarrass them the next. If you think you can then your congratulations are dishonest. you can't Encourage someone in an atmosphere of put-downs and exclusion.

```
Come on. It's playful. Even humourous. They
should toughen up.
```

Humour is Spiritual. Laughter breaks the spell of seriousness and lightens the atmosphere. Humour can carry the Power of Love if it is selfless because It cuts down pride and self-righteousness. yours, not theirs! It is not your job to target another i's demise by embarrassing them. embarrassment is your own guilt that you deflect by embarrassing someone else.

Poke fun at your self. Poke fun at humanity as a whole if you like, but don't make it personal. Leave it up to the individual to understand the jab was meant for them. Amusing your self at the expense of another only feeds **your** pride and self-righteousness. And any strength they show would be a slap in the face to your pride. Was their "toughening up" really the intention of your "playfulness"? Wasn't the aim to feel superior in the other's weakness? Expose the charade.

If you don't expose the fact that it is **your** fear that causes suffering of others, karma will spring a surprise consequence on you. One day you will be the brunt of low humour. The way to immediately break the karmic spell is this—don't be surprised. When you feel a twang of humiliation and the temptation to criticise and condemn the bully in retaliation rises to overwhelm you, don't let it overwhelm you. Rather than be swept along with your indignation, practice identity-switching. See the offender's Invulnerability, for in theirs you See Yours. Suddenly you Recognize it isn't You to whom they refer, it is your i, and by referring to your i, they are coming from their i. There is no point in retaliating. Nothing is really lost or gained in the false reflection.

Finally you See that Words of Congratulations and Encouragement, Kindness and Respect, are Forms of Love and should be Generously expressed, but only by silently Acknowledging that the Source, the One expressing (You), and the Recipient, are the same **I**. Doesn't your Heart sing when you are deeply Acknowledged? Then go first. you have nothing to lose but your false identity.

# CHAPTER 13

i is for incremental

The fact that our life is spent reacting to and managing the **contents** of the "present" demonstrates the value we attribute to things and situations. Little to no attention is paid to the "present moment of time" in which things and situations happen. Yet we should pay more attention because the Present moment is the gateway to Consciousness. Truth-fundamental #2 says—C(c)onsciousness appears A(a)s M(m)atter. But **when** does I(i)t appear? In the P(p)resent! Therefore, our C(c)onsciousness of the P(p)resent **determines** the material C(c)ontents of the P(p)resent. And, ultimately, we want to graduate to big "C" Consciousness where the Contents look after themselves in Peace and Harmony.

In order to Understand this important Aspect of Consciousness, let us then turn our attention to the subject of "time".

The key to our Understanding, as always, is to reduce everything back to T(t)hought. "time" and "space" are thoughts that give meaning to our sensory experience that we have separated away from thought. Nevertheless, things are still thought.

We have worked hard to establish the idea that "space" (where "things" seem separate) is a thought and not a thing in its own right. But "time" should be even easier to establish as a thought, for we never really thought "time" was a "thing". "time" **supports** the idea that "space" is a thing because there is a perception that it takes "time" to move about in "space", but "time" itself cannot be mistaken for being separate from thought. "time" **is** a thought, a **concept** of past, present and future.

`Time is harmless then.`

Don't be so sure. What we haven't spent so much time considering is that, not only do we experience things and situations **in** the present, we also **think in** the present. It follows then that the thought of "time", which contains the ideas of "past, present and future", is conducted **in** the present, and being a thought, must be characterized by fear and vulnerability. So although "time" might seem to be a harmless thought, we are unaware that "time" supports discordant things and situations in "space". For instance, thoughts like "time heals", or "all good things come to those who wait" imply a past problem will be solved in the future simply through the passing of time. But we delude ourselves, for the time-based thought **created** the problem that you think will be solved by time. The thought of time can't solve the problem thought always creates, because it is just a thought. If we think "time" has power, it simply re-establishes the separateness we worked so hard to quash. Don't give time that power.

Remember, everything is T(t)hought of one type or another. "space" and "time" are no different. Joined at the hip they march along patting each other on the back for giving our life structure. But is a structure that has us running around patching up wounds and trying to anticipate and avoid the next blow a structure that we really want? Freedom from the tyranny of space comes when we realize that time is a concept we hold **in** the present along with happenings **in** the present. With this Realization, memories of the past and worry for the future collapse into the present and lose their bite.

`How so?`

The moment you realize "time" has been mistakenly extended into a past and a future that only happen in your mind, you are back in the driver's seat of your Mind. you can control space by knowing it is the contents of the thought you hold **in** the present. Rather than vainly waiting for something good to happen that never will, you switch your focus from "things in the present" to "the present that the things are in" and miracles happen. The present opens up into the Present where you merge with your

Omnipresent Self. i and its problems disappear because they were never really there.

i want my problems to disappear but i don't
want to disappear.

They go together. As usual, fear is what stops you Realizing that **I** never disappear. **I** patiently wait for you to Recognize Me and My Permanence. In the meantime, you scurry back to your familiar belief in separateness and your short and inadequate life "in" a body, a body that is **guaranteed** to disappear into oblivion.

At least i won't have to worry about my problems
once i'm dead.

Don't think you will get any relief by dying. Y(y)ou are always C(c)onsciousness. "Rest in peace" we say to the recently departed. But death doesn't solve our problems. problems continue because death is a belief that time has power over the consciousness that gave time power in the first place. death is an impossibility for consciousness. But so is birth.

"birth" and "death" are potent symbols of time and space. They give i a frame of reference for its life, but if there is no i with a separate life, are not birth and death unhelpful ideas?

The belief we are "in" a body is the thought that gives the space our body occupies power over the consciousness that gave its self up to that thought. "time" was given power at this same moment, for if you appeared in space, you must have appeared at a particular time. Hence the belief that you were born, the importance you attach to your birthday, and the dread you attach to your day of death.

my mother would vouch that i was born.

Your appearance is not in question. What we should question though is that "time and space" are real in their own right. Consider that no one can remember their own birth or a large chunk of their own babyhood. Nor has anyone ever remembered their death! This indicates that time and space muscled in on Consciousness at some point in "time" thus making space a potentially scary place.

Why is time and space scary?

If you believe you were born, you must believe you are going to die, and if you die, how are you going to die? Will it be sudden, painful, prolonged?

"time" foretells our demise "in" a body. But, Remember, You are not your body. You are not your thoughts. And a thought process that thinks it functions in time conceals the only moment in which You Really Live; Now, in the Present.

i lived yesterday, and i will live tomorrow, hopefully.

you are mistaken. you didn't live yesterday, you **remember** living yesterday. The memory of living is a thought, and the hope or expectation of living tomorrow is another thought. The Truth Is that You can only Live Now, and Now, in Its Purity, is **without** your thought!

To help you grasp the nonsense of time, focus attention on the activity of your normal awake-consciousness which depends on your thought. you will discover that you cannot have the thought tomorrow, it is only a thought **about** tomorrow. you experience the thought **now**. If you dread tomorrow, the feeling will be worry or fear. On the other hand, if you look forward to tomorrow the reaction will be anticipation or excitement. Either way, the activity of thinking and the reaction to thinking is happening **now**.

Similarly, you cannot have a thought yesterday, it is only **about** yesterday. The thought is experienced as an image, a memory or a feeling such as satisfaction or pride, guilt or regret, nostalgia or disappointment, but always **now**.

Therefore, to think about the past or the future is to allow your mind to block out the only time you really have, the Present moment of Now.

Then do i only **think** that time seems to be racing by?

Yes, so why be concerned? You are Eternal! Reach in and connect to that part of You that doesn't change or age. It Is Me; Your Soul, sitting at the threshold of the Mind Patiently and Serenely watching the one mesmerized by its aging reflection in the mirror. To this one, every day ticked off the calendar marks an increasing bank of mixed memories and a decreasing opportunity to make good memories. "time waits for no man" says i. And as you place emphasis on passing increments of time, the older you get, and the more ominous the future gets.

But the irony is, the so-called ominous future is made up of your past mistake of believing you are vulnerable to a chaotic and merciless universe, a thought that has also shaped **your** present.

Imagine looking up at what appears to be a star in the night sky. As you ponder the light-years of distance between it and you, it may not occur to you that the star could have exploded eons ago and been extinguished. But even if the star still exists, the time it takes for that light to reach your eyes means you are simply witnessing its after-glow. And so we enjoy the light but we are not under any illusions that we are looking at the star itself. It's the same when we look out at our discordant world, but we have no idea that we are actually looking at the after-glow of our past, reacting to it, and depriving ourselves of the Joyous Present moment of Now.

If you have ever wondered why satisfaction and fulfillment eludes you, this is why. our concept of "time" swaps the True Joyful and Everlasting Present, Now, for a present on a linear time-line, a present made up of manifested past beliefs. our present is a karmic present; our recycled reactions to our own disowned fear and guilt forever haunting us. But that's not all. When we give order and meaning to a present within time, the Real Now becomes an abstract concept, misunderstood and forgotten.

W(w)e can only ever B(b)e H(h)ere N(n)ow, because the next moment W(w)e are H(h)ere N(n)ow too, and so on. But what we experience "in" the N(n)ow depends on whether i or **I** is in control of the M(m)ind. All E(e)ffects are not equal.

As our study has already revealed, it is the S(s)ource of the E(e)ffect that determines the character of the P(p)erception of I(i)t. A belief in the power of time demonstrates that you have made your self the source.

So there are two N(n)ows.

Yes, but My Now is **not** your now. Their contents (the two R(r)eflections) are mutually exclusive. Still, your now superimposes itself over My Now and therefore they happen simultaneously. This gives the two R(r)eflections something in common that we can work with.

With this similarity in mind, let us then get to know **your** now.

Even though fear is of the future, it is only fearful because your "now" is the future of your fearful past. That is, your now ensures a repetition of the mistakes of the past in the future.

The habit of being absorbed by the constant distraction of your response of fear is an involuntary process that recycles the past in a continuous loop. And although a catchy song stuck on repeat, yesterday's conversation regurgitated, or a stimulating movie mentally replayed don't always elicit fear, they do highlight the tendency of thought to focus on the past. More usually it is the thought of the pleasure we want to repeat or the pains we want to avoid that draws us back to the past; the twinge of an old injury, a rerun of a disappointment or a success, reminiscing about or missing someone's presence. Then there are the thoughts that lead us into darkness with feelings of regret; "if only i had done that differently" says i. guilt's punishing retro-visions remind us we can't go back; we made our karmic bed, now we must lie in it. And we are all familiar with worry. worry expects a repetition of the past. "what if something dreadful happens?", "how will i cope?"

"worry" is a stark example of how habits of thought, even about the future, are backward-looking by definition. A habit brings the past into the present, and justifies itself because it seems reliable. A memory of pleasure is invoked when i says, "i need a drink, a smoke", and "i can't function without my morning coffee". appetites for pleasure mask fear; "do it while you can. we're here for a good time, not a long time". Others look forward to avoid looking backward; "i can't wait to get away".

our relationships, too, are conducted by the ghosts of the past. Don't we approach people with some trepidation, hoping we don't repeat our foolish blunders? Don't we bring our errors into a commitment by either being intolerant of or excusing theirs? Don't we use tried and tested strategies to impress and manipulate?

The only time we stop invoking the past is when we are jolted back into the present by a ringing telephone, the call of a needy child, the sight of a messy duty we have put off, or a hunger pang. Further afield are the news of human events, tragedy and excitements. Unless we are aware of the origin of these events we roll along with the after-glow of the past and tailor-make our future with it.

*"Enter by the narrow gate; for wide is the gate and broad is the way that leads to destruction, and there are many who go in by it. Because narrow is the gate and difficult is the Way which leads to Life, and there are few who find It."*[70]

Is the "narrow gate" Your Now?

Yes.

Why do few find it?

Few find It because we are so busy responding to the problems we brought into the present from the past, we miss My Present.

Must we exit the dimension of time?

Not at all. time does not have its own dimension. Remember, "time" is a human concept, a thought. Can a particular thought construct its own dimension? Is a thought worthy of its own dimension? The concept of time is on the same horizontal time-line of past, present and future it defines, an imaginary line. The Greater dimension, which is the **only** dimension, is what precedes My Thought, and this is not imaginary, because it can't be conceived in the mind. This Greater Spiritual dimension is accessed by breaking through the time-line "in" your present. It is appropriate to use our imagination here, because it's as if we plunge "vertically" into My Present. A vertical line doesn't travel horizontally but goes deeper and higher. This is "when" We are, always Now.

The ancient symbol of the cross with its vertical line beckons us to take the plunge into the Now by breaking out of the constraints of the past to embrace the Joy that has always been and always will be Now. Unfortunately for us, the cross has come to represent the one-sided

---

[70]   *The Holy Bible*, New King James Version (Tennessee: Thomas Nelson Inc., 1982), Matthew 7:13–14

sacrificial interpretation of the Crucifixion by which we remain tied to a scarce and troubled past, but we can re-invigorate the symbol. From now on, every time you see a cross, let it represent your Resurrected Self standing Patiently in the Now, Eternally offering you Your Good.

The alternative is that we laboriously trudge along in our present, evading our responsibility for having created the reason to trudge. Gradually we spend what we believe to be our allotted time in days filled with repetitive and futile obligations. Perhaps you don't think your effort is futile. Perhaps you enjoy striving for a better future. Still, focus on a "better future" leaves Me out by definition, and you will find your hopes dashed again and again until you collapse from sheer exhaustion. For whether by human standards you succeed or fail, when death finally catches up with you, it is as if nothing happened, because if you give time power, your life and everything in it must dissolve into a memory.

i certainly don't want to dissolve into a memory.

Then don't be the fool that is fooled by time. Can a concept of time Really affect the You that Is Infinite, Eternal and Immortal? "time" is just a thought in your mind, a false assumption that incorrectly substantiates the "you" that thinks along with every thought you think and emotion you feel.

emotions are felt in the now. Wouldn't focusing attention on my emotions bring me into the now?

your now, not My Now. If you recall, emotions are **your** thoughts felt in the body and merely perpetuate the past. For instance, envy wants something, and "wanting" implies a past lack. malice holds someone to a past judgment, and guilt and regret attach importance to a past mistake or indiscretion. sadness looks back to a loss, and sympathy resonates with the loss of others.

Are happy emotions Your Now?

Not if that happiness is attached to an event you created. happiness derived from outside your Self is "not-sadness". The not-sadness can't last because the event can't last. And the not-sad event can't last because i and its fear is steering thought in the background. Discern the difference between not-sad "happiness" and the spontaneous Feeling of Joy that does not depend on any "thing" or "person". Enduring Happiness Is the Joy of Your Infinite Spiritual Consciousness that you Consciously Receive but don't conceive. The Mind, in turn, Reflects Joy back to you as a Joyful Event. If you can, Remember the Warm Timeless Contentment of early childhood. This Feeling is the Joy that never left you. you left It for the superficial quick-fix of the senses, senses that show you your past fear to which you react again with fear.

It is timely to remind ourselves of Truth-fundamental #3 again because It holds the secret of Now. Thought Is the Substance of the Perception we call Matter, but It must **always** be so, because the Truth doesn't change.

Don't the changes i see count?

No, they don't! change doesn't affect the Truth. If you make "change" important, then "time" is important. "things" will keep changing but what does it matter? They are just T(t)houghts made manifest. You are the Source of Thought, Eternal and Immortal. Know this and you can Relax with change. you need not fear change. Remember, You are not the body in space and time. change doesn't spell Your end.

But the bodily change we call death is an end.

death is nothing but the end of a stage in a sequence that heralds the beginning of a new stage, like moving from childhood to adolescence. Wasn't the end of childhood the beginning of adolescence? Were we distraught that childhood was ending?

No, i noticed more that adolescence was beginning.

It's an important observation. you were more concerned with your present than your past in that instance, which made a smooth adolescence a possibility. The end we call death should be just as easily traversed, for it is merely the beginning of another chapter in Life, part of My continuous Now. We might also look at it this way; if the senses are our yardstick, we can say the end of the visible is the beginning of the invisible. But Spirit was always invisible, so what really changed?

During our "visible" stage, our appearance changes to reflect our changing consciousness, which not only grows with the intellect's development, but has the potential to be lifted out of intellectual constraints altogether by a Conscious act of Trust. The more we function from the Soul, that is, the more we **let** Spirit through the Mind, the less Its physical appearance concerns us, until one day we will find we are walking along without the body. To those left behind in material sense, you "died". But you won't skip a beat. you merely walk seamlessly into another stage of Life.

Nothing "physical" stays the same because change is the nature of T(t)hought. But You are neither physical nor mental. Do not be concerned with change. our appearance is a wonderful Gift, a miraculous Blessing, a golden Opportunity to Transcend the necessity to appear. But if we think the body **is** us, we throw away the Gift, we bat off the Blessing, we waste the Opportunity. Let us usher in Our Ascendence by Understanding that both "birth" and "death" are Spiritually meaningless.

As if not being able to remember our birth isn't enough to convince us of the fallacy of death, have you ever Noticed we are the only creatures that worry about death? Could there be a link between this lack of preoccupation with a limited body and the way animals, birds and insects seem to avoid the majority of complaints we suffer. And could the afflictions with which they do suffer be our reflection anyway?

```
i have always wondered why we seem to suffer
more than other creatures, why we are the sickest,
unluckiest, saddest, most foolish and frightened
creatures in the world. There is a huge discrepancy
between humans and the rest of Nature.
```

That's because other creatures don't have the capacity to be Conscious of their Self As Consciousness. we are unique in this respect. our lack of Consciousness causes a lengthy stint in an illusory bubble, but what does it matter if there is only Now? The moment you recognize the illusion, you Realize it was never there. To put it another way, the potential to collapse time into the present, and then plunge into My Present, is the same potential to Be Conscious. It always existed. our potential isn't erased when our body disappears. For that matter, nor did our potential begin when our body appeared.

So we don't pass our potential to our children?

No, because potential is not of the body. genes do not carry the Immortal Soul. It's the other way around. your genetics are the exact reflection of your present level of consciousness. If time is important to you, then your genes will reflect the imperfection of the imperfect self that carries this burden of the past. It is best, then, to un-learn what time has taught us and teach our children about their own Timeless potential. Our Genes will respond.

Let us learn from other creatures. They Live in the Now. They haven't swapped the easy-flowing Beauty and Magnificence **of** the Now for Life-denying and Life-robbing worry **in** the now.

The uninterrupted Receipt of this "Flow" we call "Instinct". Instincts are actions that take place without conscious thought, actions that align **with** Life and Love and, importantly, have no concept of time. Consequently, non-human creatures neither rejoice at the birth of their young nor grieve at the death of their elders. Both are Instinctual occurrences having no bearing on Eternity. The Happy Ebb and Flow continues.

Instinct is the involuntary urge a Bird has to build a nest, a Bear has to hibernate for the winter, or a Spider has to build a web. Human Babies have the same Instinct to suckle at their mother's breast. Likewise, we had the Instinct to be "born" which accounts for our loss of memory of it. we lose our Instincts after the intellect takes over our mind including the dreaded change we call "death". This is **why** we dread it and turn it into a painful and frightening anticipatory experience!

Continual Happy Flow is thus the province of the animal kingdom.

humanity is unique in that it has let itself be governed by the drill-sergeant of its self-created problematic life, and must climb out of the hole it has dug for itself. To join in with the Happy Flow of Consciousness is our

Purpose. we do this by accepting that what we think and do N(n)ow affects what appears in the N(n)ow of the "future". we are not Really bound to the past unless we keep thinking our own thoughts. Every moment we have is a Fresh opportunity to change our future from a continuous present fraught with problems to a continuous Present of Flowing Peace and Happiness. W(w)e are always in the N(n)ow. Why not allow It to Be Good?

`Wouldn't it take time?`

Paradoxically, time seems necessary until we realize there is no such thing as time. While the thinker is in control of the mind, the time it seems to take to decide to swap your thought for My Thought will parallel the change. Let us, then, use time wisely, and use every moment to enter the *narrow gate*.

`How do i go about it?`

The goal would be to Consciously Trust our Intuitive Impulses most of the time. But that means transitioning from your now to My Now, because Conscious Trust only happens in My Now. It makes sense, then, that we utilize a couple of tools to help us make that transition. These tools are known as "Mindfulness" and "Meditation".

`i thought Mindfulness was Meditation.`

From the Spiritual point of View, the two are different. In a nutshell, Mindfulness brings us into our now, and Meditation into My Now. Mindfulness is a necessary prelude to plunging into My Now. The two tools work in tandem.

Mindfulness is a widely accepted practice. It is:

*"keeping one's consciousness alive to the present reality"*[71]

What it does is:

*"cultivates present-moment attention or focus and an attitude of acceptance of (rather than reactivity toward) moment-by-moment experience."*[72]

---

[71]   Thich Nhat Hanh, *The Miracle of Mindfulness*. (UK: Rider, 2008), 11

[72]   Dr. Craig Hassed, Dr. Richard Chambers, *Mindful Learning*. (Boston: Shambhala, 2014), 6

The function of Mindfulness is to simplify perception down to its content alone. we do this by not-reacting to what we are sensing, for it is only our reaction that proves we value the contents over the moment they occupy. Mindfulness separates our thoughts from the moment they occupy, encouraging focus on the moment rather than the thoughts or emotions.

"Mindfulness" is also known as "Karma Yoga" because it is "Action" (Karma) leading to Unity (Yoga) or Wholeness. This is True because Mindfulness prepares the Mind for Meditation.

Mindfulness is not a stranger to us. we naturally practice It when we do something we love. During the activity the mind becomes relatively still, and because a still mind feels good, we associate the feeling with the activity and want to repeat it again and again. This involuntary Mindfulness can happen for those who love needlework, craft, painting, playing a musical instrument, or some other hobby. Or it can happen by simply getting outdoors amongst natural surroundings; playing sport, travelling, bush-walking, gardening, bird watching or fishing. Whatever activity it is, though, we love it **because** our subjective world of thought and our knee-jerk reactions to it cease as we concentrate on the activity alone.

i have noticed i stop thinking when i am painting, but my best ideas come when i am in the shower!

Daily tasks are a great example of involuntary Mindfulness. And, less often, we access a great depth where Inspiration and Invention come forth. Though we would have transitioned into involuntary Meditation if an Original Idea entered our Mind.

But let's not jump too far ahead, for we want to make both processes conscious and deliberate rather than involuntary. This will have the added benefit of extending the Receipt of Creative Ideas beyond the shower! But nothing happens without a Connection. Mindfulness prepares the Mind for that Connection, so let's concentrate on Mindfulness for a while.

Mindfulness is a conscious practice where we concentrate purely on the contents of the present (our sensory experience). If we can manage to hold that concentration, the fear that drags our past into our present and extends our present into the future stops. In effect, we "collapse time" into the present where our perception is unencumbered by thought and our reactions to it.

For instance, you could **consciously** shower by simply focusing your attention on the sensation of water on your body and the process of washing your body. If that doesn't appeal to you, any mundane activity would be appropriate. A sink piled with dirty dishes might confront you. Rather than allowing thought to wander into the past or the future as the pile is tackled, focus entirely on the action of washing the dishes.

What if i start thinking while i am doing the dishes?

your thoughts will inevitably interrupt your peace. Minutes may even pass before you notice that you have been thinking. Such is the habit we inadvertently encourage. When you do finally notice that you are thinking, it is important **not** to push the thoughts away aggressively or with judgment, because that is just more thought. Similarly, don't indulge in disappointment in your failed efforts. Use Mindfulness again to gently bring your attention back to the task.

Any "thing" occupying the senses can be fruitfully used in the practice of Mindfulness. And any sense can be utilized because the senses are in the present with the thing they perceive. For instance, the sense of touch can be felt when you breathe. Try getting into a comfortable position away from any distractions, close your eyes and focus on the sensation of the rhythm of the breath touching your nostrils. Again, as soon as you become aware of thoughts entering your mind, as they inevitable will, bring your attention back to the touch of your breath on your nostrils.

Unfortunately our perception is not just made up of breathing and doing mundane tasks. we often see things to which we react negatively. So when you feel you have become proficient with benign situations, try being Mindful during a discord you see on the television news for example. Watching the horror of war or crime without flinching is challenging. But perhaps even more challenging is not reacting to the thought that jumps in to criticize your own stable mind as "heartless". This is when Remembering Truth-fundamental #3 becomes useful and necessary. Sit quietly and translate the tragic images of the situation back to thought, because that is all it is—thought from which you have not yet extricated your self, thought designed to continue your feeling of vulnerability. Next, Realize that this thought isn't real because it harks from a memory. Finally Realize who held the memory. it wasn't Me, so let it go.

If you can manage to dodge the guilt-trip, the intellect has other tricks up its sleeve to keep your past troubling you. However, if you are forewarned you are forearmed. you may hear your self justifying the horror of the nightly news as information you need to be safe, prosperous and healthy. you may convince your self that opinions about news events keep your mind active. Or you may rationalize that life is interesting if you have a grievance or two to complain about. But the intellect doesn't stop there. it says that some problems are actually good for you; an unpleasant duty will build your character; the pain of an injury must be endured as part of the healing process; and disappointment will lead you to something better. All attempt to neuter your displeasure around particular problems in order to maintain these problems or create similar problems in the future.

But i don't want problems.

Not consciously, but, Remember, problems justify your existence. They stave off your Awareness of existential fear with fear of tangible things and conditions. And we come to why Mindfulness is so necessary. It loosens the intellect's hold on your mind for enough time to create a space for My Thought to enter and replace fear. It's a bit of a trick on our part. Although the intellect should feel threatened in that moment of loosening, it doesn't, because i conducts Mindfulness. And here, too, is the major reason why Mindfulness is not Meditation and why the intellect is happy to confuse the two. The intellect feels threatened by Meditation because when we Consciously decide to Meditate, our Intention is to deactivate i. Mindfulness is thus like yoga training for the mind, gently encouraging us to loosen the rigid tendons of our thought, preparing the Mind for the main act.

Don't misunderstand. There are many benefits resulting from practicing Mindfulness as a single discipline, including increased concentration and memory, and a feeling of well-being and productivity. But these merely make **your** now better.

That's good.

your good is not-bad; temporary and imperfect. If you are happy with that, by all means, stop there.

The greatest benefit of Mindfulness, though, is the preparation it gives us for My Thought to enter the Mind. If our reactions to our imperfect now are kept in abeyance, there comes a moment when we tap into the "vertical plane". That's what you tapped into in the shower. we enter the *narrow gate*. we come in contact with the Undisturbable Joy of our Perfect Self. we touch that primordial Feeling of deep Relaxation and Peace. It's the same Feeling that earlier helped us make the distinction between our normal thoughts and the Intuition, and what Eastern practices call "Bliss". It's as if our whole body right down to the cells and nerve-endings have been tied up in knots and suddenly untied. we don't notice the level of tension until there is none. The Release is palpable. It's like we flick the reverse switch back into forward gear and it Feels so Right.

It is at this crucial moment that our practice Transcends our now. It even Transcends the welcome benefits of Mindfulness. Unfortunately, though, unless we Know to Acknowledge Joy's Source and Relax into It, the moment of Bliss that would Reflect back to us as proof that we in fact **did** Connect, is interrupted by shock. "What was that?" invades our thought, followed by a wish to get the Feeling back. The knots re-establish, the familiar tension returns, and Bliss becomes a memory that i wants to recapture for its self. Of course, it can't, because this secret selfishness of purpose further blocks the Feeling of Joy. **I** can't be personalized or directed towards any selfish purpose. **I Am** All-inclusive, Incorruptible, Immovable and Complete in My Self (every Self) in the Now. i's manipulations are acts of futility. This retrograde desire is the very reason why the practice of Mindfulness should, but doesn't usually, include some Understanding of what Mindfulness can lead to; the Revelation of My Present.

Unless you are prepared for Bliss and Understand that the Effect is everyone's Shared Soul-state, and that it is not for you to use as your personal portal to peace, you will find the practice of Meditation difficult if not impossible. i has not agreed to Its Transcendent outcome—Peace for everyone, at all times, in all places.

Meditation, then, is the natural extension of Mindfulness, because we can't Meditate without somehow bringing our self into our present moment. But once we plunge into the Now, there is no little i. This is what Meditation does and why It is so important not to stop at Mindfulness; Meditation deactivates i.

We should also be aware that there are many forms and hybrids calling themselves "meditation", and we should honour each one as they are all on the Right track. But the Meditation that deactivates i is the only form of Meditation that will deliver My Promise of Permanent Harmony in a practical way.

Let us then be warned. i's intention to get a benefit for its self from meditation destroys Meditation.

What's the point if i don't get a benefit?

The benefits from Meditation include the benefits of Mindfulness, but now they will be Permanent, because you Understand that Permanence is not **for** you. It's bigger than you. we are reminded again of the meaning of Conscious Receiving. we open our Mind to Love and **let** It do Its Thing. This One Pure Intention directs the intellect to work **with** the Intuition, not instead of It.

you are only asked to Connect. That's the only point of Meditation. Unless you Understand this, the intellect will again keep step. Notice it sets out plausible reasons why you should Meditate, but at the same time undermines these very reasons by making them **about** you. "i will do better at my job if i meditate", "i will be more peaceful", "the right people and circumstances will be drawn to me".

Watch your motive to Meditate. Any motive other than to Connect feeds pride. Do you want to seem "in the know" to your friends? Is Meditation fashionable? Less noticeably egotistical; are you fascinated with the idea of Meditation, just attempting it to satisfy a curiosity?

All deny You! Get in first and pre-empt the intellect's strategy. Set your Intention to Connect to My Thought, practice Mindfulness to get you started, and wait. When you Feel the Bliss, check in. Is there an agenda? Are you waiting for an answer to a problem? Are you expecting your life to improve? Are you wanting to be lifted out of your i-ness? Connect to the Source of the Intuition on Its terms, not your terms. Anything less is your thought sneaking its way in to manipulate the mind, activating and invigorating i and its secret hope that Meditation will help it get what You already Have!

you can't get, in a bogus future, what You already Have Now. This brings us to the subject of "prayer". Prayer Is a synonym for Meditation, but what do we do when we pray? Don't we ask the god-of-matter for things we don't think we have? Or to change a bad situation into a good one? Or for protection?

*"Prayer is a cup held up to be filled"[73]*

```
Filled with what?
```

With the Undisturbable Joy of Your Being, the Feeling you cannot Know, but can experience As the Harmony that Transcends fear and its forms altogether.

```
Can i not ask for anything?
```

Ask to Connect. Then do your part by Remembering that what you sense is actually thought, not matter. Then suspend your thought and allow My Thought to enter your Mind. As you Feel the switch, it is quite appropriate to ask for what i cannot Know.

```
Like what?
```

Ask for Guidance. Ask to find out all about Love, Grace, Infinity, Immortality, Eternity, the 3 Omni's (Omnipresence, Omniscience and Omnipotence), and the Truth-fundamentals. Ask for discernment to tell the difference between intellectual thought and Intuitive Thought,

---

73  Mary Strong, *Letters of the Scattered Brotherhood*. (New York; Harper and Row, 1948), pg

between i and **I**. Ask for the Strength not to be tempted to use Truth for self-aggrandizement, self-preservation, self-defence and self-protection, but to wait for Direction and Guidance. Ask for the Courage to follow that Guidance, to submit your self to It.

Ask for the Wisdom to Know you can't store up Spiritual Treasures, for they Renew themselves every moment. we don't rely on yesterday's feeling of Bliss or last week's Vision. Our expectation is for nothing, just to sit quietly in the Presence of Our own Consciousness, like being in the company of a loved one, just content to be together.

Ask for the Resolve to remain Silent. Just as Nature declares not Its Order, we in Silence demonstrate It. Ask for the Strength to resist the temptation to divulge this Pearl to the uninitiated, to Understand its Sacredness and Preciousness and although it is the Intelligence and Power of the Universe, it is fragile until Our Consciousness is strong enough to face the backlash of the collective intellect. Secrecy is paramount.

Ask for the Integrity, Discernment and Strength to follow Ideas that will be at odds with the prevailing thought. Ask for Clarity of word and deed, for our Intention to be Pure.

Then Listen, waiting Patiently for a Response. If you are Sincere, you will get a Response, but, again stressing, it won't be a Response that you can envisage.

Meditation has a reputation for being a difficult and lofty pursuit, an esoteric oddity reserved for austere monks or closed-eyed, cross-legged New Age zealots chanting "Om". Meditation doesn't exclude this display of dedication, it's just that this old stereotype doesn't serve us anymore. Meditation makes Conscious Trust more achievable, because It makes Conscious Trust a discipline, which brings It into our day-to-day life.

Upon awakening in the morning, pre-empt the habitual anxious buzz, and set the tone for the day by tuning in to Me. Relax into your day by Connecting to Me and **letting** Me lead you. Once you are proficient at Connecting you won't have to close your eyes, and you can practice extending your interludes to include short Connections during the day for a minute or two. Remember, be neutral instead of reactive to outer events.

Wait for a moment to Feel My Presence. you can do this as many times as you remember to do it.

It is not so much the duration or the frequency of the Meditation that's important, but correction of the order of T(t)hought. When you put My Thought first, Love controls your everyday life. That's the benefit.

Sounds wonderful. How will i know it's working?

Apart from Recognizing the Feeling of Joy and Freedom from your childhood, your fear diminishes. desire for things calms down. you worry less. you don't feel the need to push your point of view as much. What people think of you is not important to you anymore. But nor are you apathetic. you find Fulfilment in service to others. An effortless Balance and Flow takes over. As a result, the people in your play become more cooperative, kinder. Finding that you are not defending your self, judging or laying blame, you Feel Happier. This Happiness is, however, not based on logic. There is no comparison to past experience.

In addition, your body responds to the Natural Balance and Flow that your imposition of thought covered up. guilty appetites for addictive foods, drinks and habits gently and unforcedly fall away. Finally, problems of every nature disappear, again for no rational reason, but they are just no longer present anymore. Nor do your loved ones suffer as many problems, or their problems are of a less serious nature. Just the same, when a problem does arise, you don't panic, you know how to handle it.

With the help of Mindfulness and Meditation, Conscious Trust allows the Hand of Truth to burst the bubble of ignorance, because it is the unencumbered Now that will Release you from the burden of time.

> *"Those verily who, renouncing all actions in Me and intent on Me, worship meditating on Me, with whole-hearted yoga, these **I** speedily lift up from the ocean of death and existence."*[74]

---

[74]  *The Bhagavad Gita.* (Adyar: Theosophical Publishing House, 1953), 12th Discourse:6

# CHAPTER 14

———◉———

# i is for immoral

So far in this section, we have looked at ways we can support Conscious Trust. Now we get to the issue that hampers us the most—guilt.

guilt is the fundamental reason why the bubble of ignorance forms in the first place. we are all individually responsible (guilty) for believing in a separate material universe, even though this "existential guilt" is unconscious.

It's not really guilt then.

Technically, you're right. guilt, by definition, is the awareness that we have done something wrong. No one can feel guilty for something they don't know they did! But **I** will still use the term, because if we knew about this crippling mistake, we **would** feel guilty.

The reason we are unconscious of existential guilt is because guilt is quite an advanced emotion. It becomes active in our mind when conscience comes out of dormancy. And we should note here that the guilt in a "guilty conscience" is very different from existential guilt, yet are intimately linked to each other because there can be no surface guilt without existential guilt.

Let us revisit our diagram of the bubble of ignorance to remind ourselves where conscience sits.

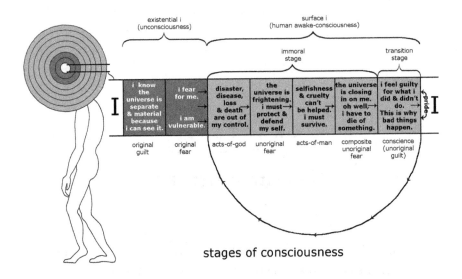

| | existential i (unconsciousness) | | | | surface i (human awake-consciousness) | | |
|---|---|---|---|---|---|---|---|

stages of consciousness

As you can see, conscience doesn't enter our awareness until the very last layer.

Why so late?

Late, because our little i's nature is to preserve its self. Admission of wrong-doing or humbling the self (a pre-requisite for conscience to enter) is thus fiercely resisted. Instead, **pride**, the intellect's muscle, and a synonym for the ego, is called in to boost i's self-preservation instinct and delay for as long as possible the activity of conscience and hopefully smother it altogether.

The first four layers of the bubble of ignorance are when i is in the ascendency and pride is an integral part of that rise. pride naturally assists the passage from childhood to adulthood, away from our parents and carers to self-survival or independence. In the pursuit of independence, pride glorifies us, celebrates and rewards our efforts, boosts our confidence and self-esteem, picks us up when we are down, and pats us on the back as we build our good reputation. The problem is that our ultimate goal is to Depend on Our Spiritual Self. This is what Spiritual growth means. Ideally, then, the time pride assists us would be brief. Stifling that Ideal, unfortunately, is our belief in a separate material universe, and instead of growing out of pride, we take it beyond young adulthood and make physical independence and advantage the goal for our whole life.

pride then takes us on a rampage. we snatch and grab what we can. we cheat and manipulate, demonstrating little or no concern for our fellow human. "It's the cost of doing business" says i. "Don't take it personally." The attitude with which we conduct ourselves becomes ruthless. "It's a dog-eat-dog world, i must get my share, get out of my way."

pride's reach beyond its useful purpose is why we call its reign the "immoral stage" of consciousness. guiltlessly, we do whatever it takes to build an impenetrable fortress around our body-oriented self. "me, me, me" is pride's catch-phrase.

And pride would continue on unhindered if it were not for the feeling of uneasiness that heralds the "transition stage" of consciousness. guilt makes its first appearance and forms a hair-line fracture in our self-assured facade. i starts to notice the struggle it is experiencing is not uncommon, and a little sympathy creeps in for the plight of its neighbour. Along with this call to conscience, i realizes its efforts to preserve its self aren't working as well as it had hoped. A little humbled, i puts one foot outside its me-fortress.

But not for long, for the intellect senses that it is losing its grip on its puppet and promptly calls on pride's service to make little i see sense. Notice on our diagram how pride sits on the outside of the bubble as if to form a crust around it. But we do not resist, for we would much rather bask in the superficial pleasure of our ambitious desires and wanton successes than pursue the uncomfortable course conscience suggests. As a result, as conscience presses in to make us responsible for our sinful acts-of-man, pride keeps pace with greater cunning and guile.

pride's Machiavellian side begins to show around adolescence, just as we are spreading our self-reliant wings. Think of an adolescent living at home, craving independence, but too proud to admit he or she doesn't have the means or the courage to move out. The parent is usually willing to support the adolescent, and the adolescent will usually accept the allowance, but, at the same time, they will hold an underlying resentment. A typical scene might unfold when a parent's wallet is left out in the open. The daughter needs money, and rather than openly ask for it, she secretly slips a couple of notes into her pocket. "dad won't mind" she rationalizes.

Why did she steal and deceive herself about it when the money was hers for the asking?

pride. Asking for money proves without doubt her dependence and humiliates the developing ego. By opting for stealing there is a chance she won't be caught, and as long as the sin remains undetected she can pretend it is acceptable. i will always take the option that saves it from humiliation, for humiliation is a little death of the ego, a little crucifixion that we resist. And if humiliation can be avoided and the sin justified, pride has done its job to circumvent conscience.

Avoiding humiliation, however, is a sign that pride is just gearing up. The vicious underbelly of pride is exposed when we openly shift the responsibility for our wrong-doing on to someone or something else. In the above illustration, pride has an opening when the daughter is finally accused of stealing. With feigned indignation, she could throw blame on the accuser, "how dare you accuse me of stealing", or deflect guilt in the form of shame, "i'm devastated that you would accuse your own daughter of stealing". On the other hand, if she happened to sense defeat, she might give the martyr a run, manipulatively turning guilt back on her accuser in order to absolve her self. "Alright then, you win. i'll just have to get used to being treated like a baby."

As we mature, pride settles into a rhythm. The thrill of the melodramatic battle carried forward from adolescence is an occasional lure of pride, but pride's normal style is to excuse daily misdeeds. Don't we justify taking what isn't ours by calling it a right? Pinching stationary from our boss as if it is a perk of the job, or taking advantage of a government handout when we don't really need it "because they made it available" are two examples of this rationalization. The overt sin could be stymied by conscience. But pride disables our moral compass and becomes the hidden fundamental sin. pride compels the sinner to sin, justifies the sinful act, and sits unchallenged behind remorselessness.

Though, we rarely pick up the hypocrisy, for at the same time as we remorselessly justify our own immoral acts, we condemn our fellow-human for their immoral acts and demand remorse and restitution from them. The high moral ground becomes pride's favourite position. I am sure you have noticed that as we become more and more aware of injustice and inequity in the world, pride takes us on what we believe is a self-less crusade to fix these wrongs. Unaware that we merely shift blame from our existential self to other people and institutions, we take pride in our new-found social conscience. "It's the government's fault that the poor and disadvantaged suffer", "business should do more" says i, outraged. i puffs out its chest at the contribution it is making towards a better world. However, making the world better denies that the World Is already a Perfect Reflection of our Self, the denial giving i the opening to take pride in its apparent self-less-ness. But taking pride in self-less-ness **is** selfish, a ruse to glorify i once again, to delude its self that it is doing the right thing and being a good person. "i am good" says i.

What's wrong with that?

i cannot claim Goodness. Goodness is My Domain. Attempting to usurp My Good merely feeds pride and keeps everything Good, including Justice and Equity, from being Revealed.

In our lack of Consciousness, we cannot See how the intellect engages pride through every layer of the bubble. In the transition stage, conscience comes along, but represents a slight inconvenience to the intellect before it works out that conscience is just another opportunity to gain advantage and exalt i. But, if we are alert, we find we have the same opportunity to let conscience operate in the service of Consciousness, for the True role of conscience is to decommission pride. If we are Aware that we inadvertently preserve the guilty i with pride, we can welcome conscience. Humbled by our deepened sense of responsibility, we can move through all the excuses and justifications for our wrong-doing and all the false causes for discord to where we discover that we are not responsible at all. we cannot be responsible for an illusion, only for believing it is real. And so we drop the belief Knowing that this was the only purpose of conscience. conscience is not required once we are Conscious that there is no guilt or an i to be guilty. The only **I** is Me, You. We are all Guiltless in Our Invulnerability.

But before we even get to first base toward this Realization, we must Recognize that conscience is here to help.

179

One of the earliest efforts to decommission pride and activate conscience in human awareness is recorded in the story of Moses.

The Hebrew name for God is Ehom, translated, **I Am**. When Moses Saw the Light of Consciousness, like every Illumined Individual down the Ages, he Recognized His Self as That. "**I** Am that Ehom" he said;

*"I Am that I Am."*[75]

Unlike his fellow Hebrews who were understandably wild, bitter and frightened after being subjected to years of harsh conditions of bondage to the Egyptian Pharaoh, Moses' Mind was Spiritually prepared to Consciously Receive the Revelation that the Self has Dominion of the Mind for Universal Good and the prideful self is our only enemy. The Revelation also gave Moses the Wisdom to Know that he couldn't tell his brethren the Whole Truth, because they were at the "immoral stage" of Spiritual evolution. They believed victimhood was out of their hands, and, consequently, that their unruly behaviour within their own ranks, and the reactions of spite, hate and revenge toward their captors, was totally justified.

Moses' first and immediate Intuitive instruction was to lead the unfortunate group out of physical danger. During this long and arduous journey, demonstrations of Spiritual Consciousness poured through the Mind of Moses.

*"The pillar of cloud by day and the pillar of fire by night"*[76]

and the

*"dividing of the waters"*[77]

---

[75] *The Holy Bible*, New King James Version (Tennessee: Thomas Nelson Inc., 1982), Exodus 3:14

[76] *The Holy Bible*, New King James Version (Tennessee: Thomas Nelson Inc., 1982), Exodus 13:22

[77] *The Holy Bible*, New King James Version (Tennessee: Thomas Nelson Inc., 1982), Exodus 14:21

...allowed safe passage and escape from the Egyptian army, but the "miracles" had the added benefit of building the Hebrews' Trust, preparing their minds to Receive the Intuitive message Imparted to Moses and which he was to later share with them. This message had the authority of their familiar "god" to command they change their attitude and behaviour for their own good, yet would deliberately fall short of revealing "where" this message was really coming from, or why it was necessary.

Why did Moses hold back?

The leap from a complete lack of Consciousness to Consciousness is too great. Skipping stages is not possible. Moses' group had a long-standing religious tradition of worship to, and faith in, the intelligence and power all of us have assigned to matter, the "vengeful" god-of-matter. Notwithstanding the futility of following a god that the self we want to deactivate actually invented, it still represented the self's only source of hope in that instance of oppression and brutality. To smash that hope would not only have caused a riot, but would have been counter-productive to their Spiritual evolution.

Why?

At the "immoral stage", information that speaks of **I** before i knows that there are effectively two "I's", and that the one they identify with is a non-entity, is too much to assimilate. Worse, the attempt to explain the Idea that God Is the Self runs the high risk of encouraging i to believe its judgmental and intolerant "vengeful" self (the only self it knows of) is "God". This lays out a welcome mat for i by fueling pride, a disastrous outcome. Moses Knew the barriers he faced, barriers still in place to this day.

Then, as now, a middle step is required, a transition. we must become aware that i is the cause of its own troubles and there is no god to pick up the pieces. The responsibility must be firmly placed in our lap before we can see there are no real troubles to be responsible for. The necessary middle step paves the way for us to Understand that our Freedom is not a false god's responsibility. No god can make a false self Free. The Universal Self (God) is already Free. our only responsibility is to Consciously surrender our false self to this Truth.

Fortunately, this middle step has already been well laid-out for us in the remarkable document known as the Ten Commandments, a moral code of conduct designed to turn justification for immoral conduct into responsibility for it. you will notice the Commandments compel **you** to take action against the instinct of pride. There is no "god" to fall back on.

Before we examine the Ten Commandments from this new angle, though, we should be aware that as we go about removing pride, we will remove what amounts to the protective layer over guilt and expose another danger; the tendency to get stuck in surface guilt. For if we agree we are the cause of our troubles, it is only reasonable that we pay the price. The "vengeful" god-of-matter suddenly gains legitimacy. Through it, we can atone for our sins. "it's my karma" says i, "i'll just have to work through it". But guilt was never meant to be bathed in, it was meant to help us make the transition to Consciousness. You are not i. Therefore an important but hidden message of the Commandments is that Good can't be Revealed while you think a god or karma is punishing you for your wrong-doing.

Let's examine this great teaching. Not only to inspire us to take responsibility for our sins, but to work through that step to the total release from responsibility. Because, ultimately, if We are not i, We never committed a sin for which to take responsibility. Herein lies Our Freedom.

### 1. *"you shall have no other Gods before Me"*[78]

Before we can Understand there is no wrong for which to take responsibility, we must uncover the i that thinks there is. If we have set up the god-of-matter, we make the job impossible. The first step, then, is to admit we have denied Our Self by assigning power and intelligence to matter. The second step is to realize we have taken pride in a self that thinks it is subject to that power and intelligence. There is nothing *before* Me, certainly not justification for a sinful non-entity.

---

[78]  *The Holy Bible*, New King James Version (Tennessee: Thomas Nelson Inc., 1982), Exodus 20:3

*2."you shall not make for yourself any carved image, or any likeness of anything that is in heaven above, or that is in the earth beneath, or that is in the water under the earth; you shall not bow down to them nor serve them. For **I**, the Lord your God, am a jealous God, visiting the iniquity of the fathers on the children to the third and fourth generations of those who hate Me, but showing mercy to thousands, to those who love Me and keep My Commandments."[79]*

At first glance, this Commandment makes Consciousness out to be harsh and conditional. But it is merely conveying the uncompromising nature of Truth and Its Law of Consistency. That is why **I** am *jealous*, not in the human sense, but because **I** don't share My Good with an erroneous belief. Look at "jealousy" in the sense that there can be no compromise. Either you Listen to Me and benefit, or you ignore Me and perish.

it is pride that wants to make this Law look unreasonable while simultaneously assigning human attributes to the god-of-matter and missing the point. The point is Consciousness cannot be found in an image of Consciousness, material or mental. There can be no exceptions. All distract you from discovering Consciousness Is You.

But then we come to the powerful pressure of religious tradition. our families, in good faith, hard-wire our minds at a young age with philosophical and religious beliefs that invariably include symbols and statues of deity. These traditions were handed down to them in equal good faith. Not unhelpfully, cultures develop a sense of community and belonging by carrying out daily rituals of worship that involve these visual props. And not surprisingly, the props become part of the participants life, giving form and meaning to what can often be a difficult existence. Yet this is the *iniquity* we visit on ourselves and our family to the *third and fourth generations.*

The way to break the chain of *iniquity* and find *mercy* is to inwardly refuse to let the props dominate. Rather, let them remind us to go within. The moment we Understand that Love doesn't compromise, and it is we

---

[79] *The Holy Bible*, New King James Version (Tennessee: Thomas Nelson Inc., 1982), Exodus 20:4-6

who visit iniquity on ourselves, we can lift up our traditions into Unity and Wholeness.

*3. "you shall not take the name of your Lord God in vain, for the Lord will not hold him guiltless who takes his name in vain"*[80]

The *Lord God* in this context is not the intellect of Genesis 2. We can discern that this *Lord God* is Consciousness by studying the meaning of the Commandment.

Before we do that, however, it must be made clear what "guiltless" means. Understandably, we might think the word "guiltless" means "free of guilt", which presupposes we **were** guilty. This is however **not** what "guiltless" means in this context. To be Guiltless is never having done anything to be guilty of. Guilt-less-ness is the Eternal Innocence of our Infinite Spiritual Consciousness. **I Am**, We are, Guiltless in our True Identity and nothing can change that. Therefore, the Commandment is trying to tell us that we have made a choice to identify with a guilty self, and he who *takes his name in vain* demonstrates this!

Ok. But what does taking the Lord's name in vain mean?

It means to deny Truth or condemn Consciousness by speaking of It in an improper or irreverent manner. But wouldn't that be an absurd thing to do? Because, of course, We are the Consciousness that we take in vain! Yet we do it because we don't Know We are **I**.

In your lack of Consciousness, you have separated i from **I**, given Me the role of god-of-matter, and subjugated your self to this false thought. So can this false god protect or hold Your Guilt-less-ness for a false you? No. A lack of Consciousness can't be protected from guilt because to lack Consciousness **is** to be guilty. you forfeit the Consciousness of your natural Guilt-less-ness by the act of taking your Consciousness in vain. In

---

80    *The Holy Bible*, New King James Version (Tennessee: Thomas Nelson Inc., 1982), Exodus 20:7

other words, **I** cannot make you Be Conscious of Your Guilt-less-ness. By denying Your own Consciousness, you create guilt.

As long as we deny, reject and deride Our True Identity, Our Guilt-less-ness is rejected with it.

> *4. "Remember the Sabbath day, to keep it holy. Six days you shall labor and do all your work, but the seventh is the Sabbath of the Lord your God. In it you shall do no work: you, nor your son, nor your daughter, nor your manservant, nor your maidservant, nor your cattle, nor your stranger who is within your gates. For in six days the Lord made the heavens and the earth, the sea, and all that is in them, and rested on the seventh day. Therefore the Lord blessed the seventh day and hallowed it."*[81]

Since we are so accustomed to stimulating the mind with outer busy-ness, it is best to set aside formal periods of time to switch channels, to Meditate. But the Commandment has a much deeper meaning.

The division of days into a week of seven is symbolic of the disciplinary training of the mind we undertake for "six days", and on the "seventh" we Rest in the clarity of the Mind we prepared earlier. you need not take the numbers literally. Just Remember, since you carry your Mind with you, you can retreat to your Sacred Sanctuary at any time, even while you are working at your daily duties. As you practice Mindfulness in this way, you realize the responsibility for what you achieve from work is not on your shoulders at all, but on Consciousness, on Me, and the practice of Meditation facilitates that life-changing Recognition of True Responsibility.

Everyone *within our gates*, within range of our Consciousness, benefits. No more "work" means no personal effort of i is necessary as We bear Witness and participate in the Presence of Consciousness. Keeping the Sabbath holy means you cannot cheat by making others work in your

---

[81] *The Holy Bible*, New King James Version (Tennessee: Thomas Nelson Inc., 1982), Exodus 20:8–11

place. Your Consciousness fans out and embraces the holiness of all. Then any work you do becomes the continuous and Effortless Joy of following your Intuitive urges rather than pushing against your guilt and fear.

*5. "Honour your father and your mother, that your days may be long upon the land which the Lord your God is giving you."[82]*

If our circumstances are less than ideal, we must not blame our parents. we cannot hold them guilty. On the other hand, we should not give them personal credit for our fortunate circumstances if only for the reason that fortunate circumstances are misfortunes in disguise. our parents, then, are exactly suited to us, because they are part of **our** reflection. If we would release our self from any perceived dissonance or false privilege, we must release our father and mother by honouring them, for by honouring them we honour our Self through the act of honouring. That is, we simultaneously Release them and our self to the One Self Eternally.

*"Call no man your father on earth, for you have one Father, who is in heaven."[83]*

*6. "you shall not murder."[84]*

murder is an act-of-man because it seeks to protect or defend i. But what is there to protect or defend if We don't die? murder, then, reinforces

---

[82]  *The Holy Bible*, New King James Version (Tennessee: Thomas Nelson Inc., 1982), Exodus 20:12

[83]  *The Holy Bible*, New King James Version (Tennessee: Thomas Nelson Inc., 1982), Matthew 23:9

[84]  *The Holy Bible*, New King James Version (Tennessee: Thomas Nelson Inc., 1982), Exodus 20:13

the reflection that i builds that compels it to be *"a murderer from the beginning"*[85].

Immortality cannot die. Yet i thinks it is ridding its self of its enemy not knowing its enemy is its own self. When i is attacked, pride will justify murder as self-defence and muzzle conscience. Not knowing there is no justification for an unconscious act, and as if to play into the hands of pride, society sends out mixed messages about murder. Nations sanction murder in war, and as a punishment for crime. i even thinks it is acceptable to murder its self as a misguided attempt to get out of difficulty. But can you get out of your false reflection by any other means than an act of Consciousness?

Actually, murder becomes an impossibility when we Understand Our True Self, because, first of all, we wouldn't have any reason to kill if We Understood We are all from the One Source. And secondly, what would be the point of killing the indestructible Self? It would only show our lack of Consciousness if we did.

But what if it is my duty to murder, as in war? Should i abstain?

To answer the dilemma of duty, let us consult the Bhagavad Gita:

*"Verily renunciation of actions that are prescribed is not proper; the relinquishment thereof from delusion is said to be of darkness."*[86]

Krishna's disciple, Arjuna, received this advice as he was facing a duty he could hardly bear, that of slaying or being slain by his extended family and fellow countrymen who were gathered on the battlefield ready for combat. The choice to harm his kinsmen or be harmed by them highlights the circular and desperate futility of duality. If Arjuna chose to harm, he would be saddled with a living hell of guilt. On the other hand, if he chose to submit to harm, he would be branded a coward. Both challenged

---

[85] *The Holy Bible*, New King James Version (Tennessee: Thomas Nelson Inc., 1982), John 8:44

[86] *The Bhagavad Gita*. (Adyar: Theosophical Publishing House, 1953), 18th Discourse:7

pride which made the choice impossible for pride. Yet it was exactly this challenge to pride that offered the destruction of pride that **was** the choice.

> *"he who regardeth the dweller in the body [i] as a slayer, and he who thinketh he is slain, both of them are ignorant. He [**I**] slayeth not, nor is He slain; He is not born, nor doth He die; nor having been, ceaseth He any more to be; Unborn, Perpetual, Eternal and Ancient, He is not slain when the body is slaughtered. Who knoweth Him Indestructible, Perpetual, Unborn, Undiminishing, how can that man slay, or cause to be slain?"*[87]

Krishna meant that if i is a non-entity, who would be doing the slaying and who would be slain? As there is neither the slain nor the slayer, where is the problem? Only in the belief that there is an i to be preserved or destroyed. Therefore, *renunciation of actions that are prescribed*, that is, avoiding actions that we find to be our duty, only keeps us bound to the bubble of ignorance.

So it's ok to contradict this Commandment if it's my duty?

Paradoxically, we don't contradict the Commandment by doing our duty, we uphold it. If we avoid our duty, in this instance by conscientiously objecting when the powers-that-be say we must go to war, we force someone else who may not have the "Protection" of Consciousness to go in our place. Effectively, we violate the Commandment, because we sentence that unconscious person to what we feared erroneously. But by Knowing the Self can't "die", our Consciousness becomes the Power of Safety, even in a war-zone.

Contradictory as this sounds, doing our duty (if it is a law) does not preclude us from Receiving Spiritual Protection. On the other hand, doing our duty doesn't mean we automatically Receive Spiritual Protection. But by avoiding our duty, we fear a consequence of an illusion, and we violate the second Commandment. For fear serves pride and keeps our false self

[87] *The Bhagavad Gita.* (Adyar: Theosophical Publishing House, 1953), 2nd Discourse:19–22

and its illusory reflection in place. Only by fulfilling our duty without concern for the result for our little selves are we released from the bondage of pride. But that's not all. The reason we wanted to avoid our duty, the discordant situation we feared, is rendered powerless, because **I** don't die and therefore the capability to murder or be murdered is removed.

7. *"you shall not commit adultery"*[88]

you cannot betray another and be self-less at the same time. infidelity is an act-of-man that boosts pride and is therefore immoral.

```
Adulterers probably just want to be loved.
```

pride will attempt to justify the sin and invoke sympathy. "poor me" says i. But adultery is nothing more than an attempt to get from our reflection what we haven't Received. There is no way to Receive Love if you haven't first Acknowledged that Love Is the Nature of your own Being and Shared It. Sharing demonstrates you Received Love and completes the cycle of Joy. And because i excludes what it seeks, it creates its own lonely cycle.

Adultery is thus a denial of the opportunity to Know the Self. The resultant loneliness creates a seeking for Love in bodies, a transient pleasure that substitutes for the Love we have shut out. pride is standing by to excuse the act, but the body is not an instrument to be used for the service of pride, because pride protects the guilty. Only conscience clears the way to discover the body can't get Love, for conscience makes a space where Love can eventually be Received, Known and Shared.

But more than taking a relationship to a whole new level, Love Forgives past wrongs, for what is past is gone in Present Wholeness. i and its needs are no more. betrayal is not possible in this atmosphere, and pride has no footing.

---

[88]    *The Holy Bible*, New King James Version (Tennessee: Thomas Nelson Inc., 1982), Exodus 20:14

### 8. *"you shall not steal"*[89]

you can't Understand that **I Am** Your Infinite Provider if you think taking from someone else is going to benefit you. The two ideas contradict one another.

stealing is another act-of-man that comes in many forms, from pilfering and cheating to embezzlement and grand larceny, and not just possessions. i steals innocence, virtue, and confidence, but it can't really do these things, for it has no real authority.

stealing is stark proof of i's position in the immoral stage far from the reach of conscience or any sense of remorse. Actually, i sees the underhanded manipulation of cheating as a fair strategy in the business of life. "i need it", "they can afford it" says i. pride will justify its act on these grounds. But when you steal, no matter how you justify it, you are again attempting to get what you have not Received. Not only do you demonstrate that you are ignorant of Your innate Good, you alienate others and cause suffering. Obeying your conscience and using self-restraint, on the other hand, has obvious benefits. People learn to trust you and your life is more harmonious as a result.

Yet this forced right behaviour is only a prelude to the Understanding that, like dying, stealing is a Spiritual impossibility.

### *"The earth is the Lords and the fullness thereof."*[90]

**I** Embody every Thing in My Consciousness. A thief can't really steal, because the thing he allegedly stole was never anyone's property in the first place. Title to property is, at best, a temporary guardianship. we can't take any "thing" with us when we disappear from this mortal coil. No "thing" is ever ours to personally own, and certainly not at the expense of someone else, because every Self "owns" everything. Every Thing is the Shared Perception of My Thought. **All** that **I** have is already yours by Divine Inheritance. The Reflection never leaves Its Source.

---

89  *The Holy Bible*, New King James Version (Tennessee: Thomas Nelson Inc., 1982), Exodus 20:15

90  *The Holy Bible*, New King James Version (Tennessee: Thomas Nelson Inc., 1982), 1Corinthians 10:26

Understanding that "things" are a Reflection of Your own Infinite Consciousness allows you to Trust that if you have a physical "need" it will appear at the exact moment that you require it. But stealing from another is a violation of Your Self, and only your self suffers under karma. There is no need to worry, compete, struggle or resort to stealing. Leave everything to Me.

*9. "you shall not bear false witness against your neighbour"[91]*

conscience would suggest this Commandment simply means to desist from slandering your neighbour. This is good advice, but why do we want to slander our neighbour in the first place?

Because it makes us feel better by comparison?

But why does it make us feel better? Why do we get so much satisfaction from judging, criticizing and condemning others? Because we don't have to look at our own faults. What we don't know is that our neighbour is merely reflecting our own shortcomings back to us.

First of all, what does "bearing false witness" really mean? it means we look at something we created. it is false **because** we created it. But the delusion is multiplied when we look at our neighbour falsely, because, as we previously noted, another person has the same capacity to experience the True Reflection of Love as we do by Listening and Trusting. But Sharing Love with them is **how** we experience It. So when we bear false witness against our neighbour, we not only deprive them of the chance to Know their True Nature through our Sharing, we reject our own capacity to access and experience that same Self. When we condemn them, we deprive our self. our condemnation, then, is never justified.

condemnation is sometimes justified. There is injustice in the world.

The injustice you point out is a veiled criticism of the supposed

---

91  *The Holy Bible*, New King James Version (Tennessee: Thomas Nelson Inc., 1982), Exodus 20:16

perpetrator. But **you** made the injustice you see. It is **your** karmic reflection. Look deeper. Remember the lesson of the Crucifixion/Resurrection. Think how easily we take offence when someone criticizes us, and then, to defend our self, we immediately turn the blame on them for being critical. Aren't we just playing the game by condemning? we condemn **them** when it is **we** who are reacting to something that isn't True. What can hurt Invulnerability? we become the victim (or the spokesperson for the victim) for whom sympathy and an apology or some other compensation or retribution is demanded! "What a wicked, vile person" we say. But by throwing the judgment back, we throw a smoke-screen over the Consciousness that could Free everyone from the tangle of responses. we give power to the little i that believes it is powerless if it **doesn't** respond defensively to criticism.

So the victim becomes the perpetrator by taking the high moral ground, for which it is really a victim of its own false witnessing. Taking offence keeps the powerless i that is guilty of judging in place.

So i have to stop judging.

Not by an act of will. you cannot stop judging if you feel justified to judge. Understand **why** you judge. you identify with the victim and feel right to judge the perpetrator. But if you Know the victim is really the creator of the perception that compels the perpetrator, you see how you merely project your guilt (your reluctance to take responsibility) onto another by blaming them. If you can manage to consciously delay this automatic reaction, suddenly there is a space to Feel Compassion for the perpetrator and an opportunity opens up to break the cycle.

At the Sermon on the Mount (a message that obviously preceded the Crucifixion/Resurrection and is just as misunderstood), we learn again it is not about settling scores or making perceived wrongs right, because this reinforces the false perception of injustice. It **is** about **not** retaliating in the Knowledge that **I** cannot be hurt. There is no thing or person to fear.

> *"you have heard that it was said, "an eye for an eye and*
> *a tooth for a tooth", but **I** tell you not to resist an evil person.*
> *But whoever slaps you on your right cheek, turn the other*
> *to him also. If anyone wants to sue you and take away your*

*tunic, let him have your cloak also. And whoever compels you to go one mile, go with him two."*[92]

But they get away with it.

So what? Are **You** diminished?

*"Do not judge according to appearance, but judge with Righteous judgment"*[93]

The appearance of lawlessness fools us. *Righteous judgment* means it is not our function to superiorly point out the sins of others, or to feel resentful about letting them "get away with it", because we committed the sin of bearing false witness in the first place. It is our incorrect perception that instigates the whole miserable picture. we can even expand what "bearing false witness" means beyond criminal violations to our perception of accident, sickness and poverty. Don't we bear false witness when we look upon someone and judge them to be injured, ill or poor? This is not an excuse to ignore the needy or refuse to help. Quite the contrary, and we will get into why in more detail in the next chapter. For now, ask your self, can **I**, Permanent Good, Be afflicted in any way? Aren't we again looking at the reflection of our beliefs and propping up the believer while we do it? Take responsibility for your reflection and you release the other person from blame and unjust suffering, because You See them for who they Really are; Whole. This is what Consciousness does! Both you and they are released together or not at all.

*"Judge not, that you be not judged."*[94]

Remember, the judge feels good in judging. i feels morally superior. it feels it is standing up for Right. But Right already Is. Therefore **I** do not

---

[92] *The Holy Bible*, New King James Version (Tennessee: Thomas Nelson Inc., 1982), Matthew 5:38–41

[93] *The Holy Bible*, New King James Version (Tennessee: Thomas Nelson Inc., 1982), John 7:24

[94] *The Holy Bible*, New King James Version (Tennessee: Thomas Nelson Inc., 1982), Matthew 7:1

need you to intercede for Me. Judging in My name only proves that you doubt Me. Do not judge, and if someone judges you as "bad", rightly or wrongly, inwardly reject it, but don't react. The humiliation you feel is not Yours. The word "humiliate" means to humble the self. Welcome it. To Understand "who" is feeling attacked, embarrassed or diminished enables you to switch identities and watch the little self refrain from employing its deadly self-defence strategy of pride.

I am not able to be enhanced or diminished. **I Am** Complete and Infinite. Therefore do not bear false witness against your neighbour by denying him his Completeness and Infinity, for you only deny your own.

When you allow Me to take My Rightful place at the Source of the Mind's Reflection, bearing false witness loses its appeal, because we stop deflecting guilt. Finally we See that bearing false witness is a universal mistake. you can't deactivate i if you bear false witness, because to be guilty of this mistake is to be i. The scaffolding of pride and judgment that propped up i's guilt is dismantled, for **I** take responsibility for My Reflection. Now **I** bear True Witness to My Permanence and Perfection.

...which brings us to the final Commandment:

> *10. "you shall not covet your neighbour's house, wife, manservant, maidservant, ox, donkey or anything that is your neighbour's."*[95]

Following neatly on from Commandment number nine, we bear false witness, but this time on our self. we judge our self unworthy of success, for why else would we covet?

i is right for the wrong reasons. i **is** unworthy of success, because **I Am** Success. **I Am** Unlimited Abundance. i doesn't know that its feeling of unworthiness stems from its lack of Consciousness of Truth, so it reflects its unworthiness back to its self appearing as its failure and the other's success.

---

[95] *The Holy Bible*, New King James Version (Tennessee: Thomas Nelson Inc., 1982), Exodus 20:17

coveting is our resignation to a lack of Consciousness, for what could we desire of our neighbour that is not available to Infinity?

we have no right to claim Spiritual demonstration without Consciousness. If we compare our self to our neighbour we are bound to find pecking orders and inequities. At the bottom end of the order, our unworthiness intensifies and turns on our neighbour as hate. i hates its neighbour for his demonstration of abundance at what seems to be its expense, and pride is too proud to let go of the hate. i, again, is guilty for not taking responsibility for its reflection, and cuts its self off from discovering the Truth of the situation; **I** have Infinite Abundance to Share with My neighbour. There is no hierarchy in Infinity.

If **you** see an inequity, it is **you** who is not Sharing the Love of Your Self. Consciousness Is Love, and Love Is the Law of multiplication, not division. Do we have less Love by Sharing? No, we increase It. The unfoldment of Infinite Consciousness doesn't end, because Love doesn't end. If We are Consciousness, We are the Receiving point where Love Flows "out" into manifestation to Provide more than we "need" and which **we** Share with our neighbour. If it appears we don't have Success or Abundance, it is not our neighbour's fault. Love Is a cup running over. Love has no favourites. Love doesn't leave anyone out. Love Is Awareness of this Truth. What then is there to covet? Love Shared Is Love Received As Fulfillment and Joy, Success and Abundance for all.

The idea of coveting, then, leads us back to Our True Identity, and full-circle back to the first Commandment. You shall have no other gods before Me. Don't place any conditions between your self and your neighbour as if matter is god. we Forgive our neighbour by releasing our hate, and Love rushes in to Illuminate the dark corners of our mind, and out again to melt the perceived inequities and lacks in our world.

> *"He uttered His Voice, the earth melted."* [96]

To Receive the full benefit of the message of the Ten Commandments

---

[96]   *The Holy Bible*, New King James Version (Tennessee: Thomas Nelson Inc., 1982), Psalm 46:6

we must deactivate i, for if we keep i, we keep guilt, and this priceless message will be seen purely as a treatise on conscience and nothing more. conscience is very much like Mindfulness in that it is a stepping stone to something Greater. Therefore we must not linger. Begin to see conscience, not as a strained and unwelcome obligation to suppress our "natural" instincts to preserve our little self, but as an often uncomfortable but necessary way-station along the Path to Illumination. Don't let pride set you back.

# CHAPTER 15

# i is for injustice

With a greater Understanding of how the Spiritual meaning of the Ten Commandments deactivates i, we should now build on that Understanding by examining one of the most significant reasons why we don't actually get to the Spiritual meaning of the Ten Commandments. That reason is that we don't think we need to. we believe that we can bring about a peaceful and "just" world through our good and right actions.

But this reasoning is flawed because a just world does not come from being a good person or doing the right thing. First of all, it's unrealistic to expect everyone to be good and right, and second, everyone's idea of "good" and "right" is different. No, a Just World comes from the Realization that there is no such thing as a "wrong" person, and no such thing as a "right" person.

◇◇◇◇◇◇◇◇◇◇

True Justice Is Love, but we have chronically obscured Love behind an acceptance of the "fact" of "right (not-wrong)" and "wrong". The Mind is therefore unable to Receive and Reflect Permanent Right. Let's check. Have we reformed humanity yet?

No, but why?

In a large part, because our justice system inadvertently encourages the reaction of sympathy for one side of the crime, usually the victim.

What's wrong with sympathy for the victim?

197

Nothing if we Recognize its value as a call to conscience, as a stepping stone to Consciousness. The trouble is we see it as a personal virtue and stop there.

Again, what's wrong with that?

A sympathetic nature indirectly reinforces injustice. The ninth Commandment (*you shall not bear false witness against your neighbour*) touches on this idea, but it is such a block to Consciousness that we should expand on it.

If you recall, where "good" is sought in the world, "bad" must be, because Permanent Good cannot be Reflected by a belief in vulnerability. Hence when pride makes "good" into a desirable personal quality, "bad" must enter with it. Unwilling to admit we carry "bad" within our self, we project the "bad" onto others. Those "bad" people, to be bad, must do the wrong thing **to** the "good" people. perpetrators are "bad" making the victim and their sympathizers "good".

However, we should remember from the lesson of the Crucifixion/ Resurrection that any reaction to mental or physical abuse assumes there is an i to be hurt that then prevents access to our Perfect Self. Therefore, sympathy, a reaction on behalf of the victim, aids and abets the i we should let die. It is not at all obvious, but sympathy takes us in the wrong direction. Twice as unhelpful as self-pity, sympathy accepts i in its ability to be hurt **and** feels "good" and "right" in its sympathy. sympathy becomes the measure of our care for one another when it should be seen as fostering the very misery for which it feels compelled to care. True Care steps in and assists without sympathy and dissolves the scene at the same time. Therefore when we wrap up sympathy in self-righteousness, the Truth is rejected in favour of the tragic scene that prompts a further reaction of sympathy.

If you can follow all this, part of "doing the right thing" in a "caring" society is the unintended consequence of ensuring the existence of wrong-doers. we work **against** perpetrators and **for** victims. we rarely sympathize with the perpetrator, and if we do, we end up condemning the victim, a scenario just as unjust. The result of our sympathy, then, is the reflection of injustice in the form of crime, abuse, inequity, violence and tyranny, the very situations that produce victims that call for sympathy. Moreover, we do it for pride. victims are not necessarily "good" but by sympathizing with them, **we** are "good", which makes sympathy something pride is eager to develop and encourage.

So i shouldn't have sympathy for the victims of the world? Seems rather hard-hearted.

you should, because sympathy is the call of conscience. But do not get stuck there, because, remember, a guilty conscience is not the destination.

How should i move through sympathy then?

Recognize that guilt recognizes guilt. You are not guilty. And if You are Guiltless, so is your target of sympathy. Therefore the intellect is right in the sense that it **would** be hard-hearted and callous if we were in a position to help the wounded and grief-stricken and didn't. But, by the same token, the emotional involvement that sympathy demands is not necessary to **be** of help. When My Care works through you, there is no conscience-call to be sympathetic. That ship has sailed.

In fact, the person who calmly and unemotionally assists the victims of injustice demonstrates that they are letting My Care through **by** being unemotional. For **I Am** Love and Love is not deceived by the false perception of injustice. **I** Know that the harmed are actually Safe. Love lifts the Spirit of the harmed in a way that empathy with the grim scene cannot.

Unhelpfully, bleeding-heart emotions fuel fear for a self-in-a-body. Therefore, by joining in the sadness, you bear false witness. you contribute to the perception of injustice. you deny the person's Invulnerability and cloud your own.

Having said that, it's understandable to be sympathetic to suffering, because you don't yet know you are contributing to the scene. you can't go from not-caring at all (and being unemotional) to letting Me Care (and being unemotional) without a bridge of emotionality. i's emotionally charged form of "care" is a transition to a Spiritual level of Care, My Care. For **i** must be pushed from being selfish to selfless and sympathy is the way.

The danger, though, is that we confuse Care with sympathy. sympathy is not the goal, Care Is. And even though the intellect will firmly disagree, it doesn't change the fact that the two are not compatible.

Watch sympathy and its close cousin empathy, for when they are extended beyond their use to prompt help or serve your fellow human, they are pride in disguise.

What's the difference between sympathy and empathy?

"sympathy" is the arms-length aching pity for the suffering, whereas "empathy" goes a step further and gets down in the trenches of emotion with the victim. empathy follows through on sympathy; sympathy **for**, empathy **with**.

Neither sympathy or empathy attack, but stand up for attack of the perpetrator. empathy, in particular, holds a secret put-down to those who don't share in its values, a silent superiority that says "i am good". But this self-assessment lacks sympathy, for it intimidates and condemns the apparently unsympathetic and marginalizes those who sympathize with the wrong-doer. The intimidation usually works. Not wanting to be tarred with the same brush of hard-heartedness as the wrong-doer, we join the band-wagon of "compassion" for the victim and leave the wrong-doer out in the cold. we bow to the pressure, for our pride can't bear to be accused of callousness or lack of empathy.

i thought empathy was a good thing. Isn't it compassionate to be empathic?

True Empathy **Is** Compassion. Empathy with an upper-case "E" Understands that i suffers for no Real reason, but i is not in any position to escape its own ignorance. But this goes for the perpetrator as well. Perhaps more so, for he does not have the sympathetic crowd with him. The Kindness and Consideration of Empathy Is Universal, but cannot Flow Freely unless we maintain a psychological distance from judgment. Empathy acts after and through the Remembering that no one can be left out. That's how it **can** be Empathic.

empathy with a lower-case "e", on the other hand, joins in the trouble and looks for a person or group of persons to blame. But is there anyone to blame for a false perception of wrong-doing? And can there be True Compassion when some people are excluded from that compassion? Empathy heals through inclusion, empathy deceives and divides.

For the Purpose of Awakening, we can treat sympathy and empathy the same, because both reinforce the perception of injustice by nourishing guilt. In the face of accusations of cruel dispassion and heartlessness, don't **you** feel guilty for not putting your self in the muddy shoes of another? From beginning to end, the whole psychological setup is to emotionally blackmail you into acting on a misperception. Therefore, don't let guilt for not succumbing to sympathy and later empathy bait you into believing the forms of injustice are real. emotions that support the belief in injustice actually crusade for death. What is crueller, blocking the Thought that could dissolve the whole sorry scene, or maintaining the sympathy that reinforces the horrors for which it is sympathetic?

human sympathy has a double-standard that exposes its stripes. human compassion is conditional. And if some souls don't deserve sympathy then sympathy must be a ruse. you can't demand Justice while you contribute to someone else's lack of justice.

Justice (the All-inclusiveness of Love) is blocked because persons can't be wrong, yet wrong is only ever linked to persons.

Ever noticed "bad" can apply to events, conditions and people that we fear, but only people are accused of being "wrong"?

```
i hadn't noticed.
```

A back-ache or a tooth-ache is "bad" but not "wrong". On a bigger scale, a destructive flood is "bad" but not "wrong". It is "bad" that people drown. It is tragic but not "wrong".

```
These things feel wrong.
```

They can Feel incorrect on a Soul level, but not morally wrong. The Soul doesn't have morals. morals are a stepping-stone **to** the Soul, part of the transition to Consciousness. persons, only, are deemed "wrong".

```
Why is that?
```

Because a person has the ability to **know** he can be "bad". conscience has introduced us to "wrong" in the moral sense. But "bad" is always an error of judgment. A person is never intrinsically "bad", just ignorant of his inherent Good. And if a person is never "bad", then a judgment of "wrong" must be doubly wrong.

we make the wrong-doer guilty for our own incorrect judgment. That is, we disown and project our guilt onto the so-called perpetrator in order to keep our hurt reactions in place. Suddenly we are innocent and able to judge the one to blame for our hurt. But when we judge, don't we bear false witness against our neighbour? Didn't we just establish that a person can't be "wrong"?

It was this stalemate (that still exists today) that Inspired a re-think of the Ten Commandments. Not that this moral code was suddenly incorrect, but now humanity was ready to Receive a deeper meaning, to go to the next level, to make it possible to break the stalemate. It was Jesus who, when the time was right, narrowed the Ten down to Two Commandments.

i didn't know he had Two Commandments.

He didn't call them "Commandments". Though it is helpful to call them Commandments for the sake of comparison. The first Commandment is similar to Moses first Commandment which is *"you shall have no other Gods before Me"*. It has been updated to this,

> *"you shall Love the Lord your God [Consciousness], with all your Heart, with all your Soul, with all your Mind, and with all your Strength."*[97]

The second is a twist on the ninth Commandment that recommended *"you shall not bear false witness against your neighbour"*, but this one is much less open to misinterpretation,

---

[97] *The Holy Bible*, New King James Version (Tennessee: Thomas Nelson Inc., 1982), Mark 12:30

*"you shall Love your neighbour as your Self."*[98]

Immediately, we might want to know why eight of Moses Commandments are missing. Was taking the Lord's name in vain and making and worshipping idols now permissible? Did we not have to honour our parents or keep the Sabbath sacred? Was it suddenly allowable to kill and steal and commit adultery? Was coveting not wrong anymore? No, because if we Understand the meaning of Love, we don't need any other instruction. Everything else falls into place.

Why not just have one Commandment then? Why do we need two Commandments to Understand Love?

Because Loving our fellow human is the way we demonstrate our Consciousness of Love. If we brand someone a wrong-doer, we must be judging him as unworthy of Love. In doing so, we demonstrate **our** lack of Consciousness of Love. It is therefore no use Loving God (Consciousness) if you don't afford Man the same Love, because if you don't Love Man you demonstrate you don't Love God (Consciousness). They are the same!

i'm not sure an abusive person, a bully, a murderous dictator or a terrorist is worthy of Love.

Loving your neighbour doesn't mean we should love the dreadful things a person does. It doesn't mean we ignore acts that hurt others. Of course, we segregate the person from the rest of society, but we do it with Compassion, and, at the same time, we look through this façade of immoral behaviour in the knowledge that it **is** a facade. What is it covering up? This is the question we should ask ourselves. If we judge our neighbour as unworthy of Love, our mind is closed and **we** can't Receive Love. That's why we fall back into judgment and one-sided sympathy. But that's why we need the second Commandment—to remind us that our neighbour; family or foreigner, friend or foe, is **the** avenue to the Love that we Recognize and Acknowledge in and as our own Consciousness. The Two Commandments are like One Commandment with two essential

---

98   *The Holy Bible*, New King James Version (Tennessee: Thomas Nelson Inc., 1982), Mark 12:31

components. For if we try to Know our Self (Love our Consciousness) without Loving our neighbour or vice versa, we will fail.

our resistance to look through what a so-called wrong-doer does is precisely why the wrong-doer offers us the greatest opportunity to Understand Love and bring It into our experience, for our negative reactions are the most intense against a wrong-doer. And the more heinous the crime, the more we cringe. "i can't understand how someone could do such a thing" says i. Yet the Truth remains; his True Self Is **our** True Self. And if we bring him in, we discover our Self. If we leave him out, we leave our Self out.

How does that stop his wicked behaviour?

Stopping the behaviour is not our primary goal. The behaviour will be rendered powerless as a natural result of our Consciousness. For it was only judgment of him that gave him a platform of power. our fear is the culprit, for we cannot look through wicked behaviour while reacting to it. we forget, Invulnerability can't be threatened.

Let's navigate through the blockage of fear. In addition to the lack of need for eight of the Ten Commandments, we should Notice that the tone of the Two replacement Commandments are markedly different from the old versions, because they specify what **to** do rather than what **not** to do. This is significant because, before, we could "do the right thing" and "be a good person" by **not** stealing, **not** murdering, **not** committing adultery, etc, and still remain offended by these actions of others. The Commandments didn't say **not** to be offended, they only said not to bear false witness, not to judge. However, not-judging only goes half-way. To go the full way we must not react to perceived violations of "right" and "good". we must find a way **not** to be offended.

In the past, our hurt reactions, our outrage and offence, didn't mean we were not a good person. In fact, our outrage and offence demonstrated our goodness! In addition, we could remain offended or hold a grudge or a resentment on a long-term basis without violating the Ten Commandments. It wasn't "wrong" to be a victim. Although many of the Ten Commandments hint at owning your existential guilt and fear, there is no Commandment dedicated to not reacting. "you shall not be a victim" is unachievable to a victim. They are a victim **because** they think they are not responsible. And from this blameless position, the victim thinks he has a right and a responsibility to blame the offender/perpetrator. Not to be left unmentioned, there is power in the reactions of resentment, vindication and blame. Certainly we feel the victim is entitled to react by judging. we have sympathy for their gripe which means we take the gripe on.

But if we are to evolve Spiritually we must climb out of the rut that says it's possible to "not bear false witness against your neighbour", not judge, but remain offended. Again, we didn't see the two positions as incompatible. we could regard the person unfavourably, and, because we didn't think our thoughts had any bearing on our experience, we could forcibly suppress our hate but not give up the reason we hated. we could not-judge and, to all appearances, be upstanding, righteous individuals. Technically, we adhered to the Commandment. The literal understanding of the ninth Commandment never asked more of us.

But now more is asked. For you cannot "Love your neighbour as your Self" **and** remain offended in any way because to be offended is to deny Your Self's Invulnerability and blame your neighbour for your sense of loss. To be offended is to blame, to make guilty, to bait the conscience of someone else in order to avoid facing your own guilt. For you made the picture of inequity in which you made your self a victim.

The next guilt-hiding tactic is to challenge the one we blame to back down first. "i won't do the right thing by you until you do the right thing by me" says i, ensuring they won't, because you can't possibly see the right they do in the mirror of "withholding" you hold up to them. you can't reap the Love you don't sow. By attempting this you demote "love" into a bargain, which isn't Love. Insisting that the one you blame backs down first misunderstands the whole Idea of Love.

It's hard **not** to be offended by people who do evil things.

"evil" is **our** lack of Receipt of Love perceived **as** a person, or **as** what a person does or doesn't do. Love can only come **through** a person **after** we open **our** Mind. A person, therefore, is never intrinsically evil.

Think of those we are quick to judge as evil like the infamous "Hitler" or "Idi Amin". our fascination with these characters is fueled by our anger at the atrocities they orchestrated. They are held up as an examples and "warnings" not to repeat the same mistake. But it is **our** failure to Receive Love that crystalizes into a "Hitler" or an "Idi Amin". we like to think of them as different, but they weren't born evil. They and others we describe as evil-incarnate have become the unfortunate embodiment of the collective Loveless human mind. **our** subsequent fear of acts-of-man reflects back to us as the serious and tragic reality of genocidal maniacs.

    Sounds like You are suggesting they were
innocent and the victims guilty.

humanly, it's the other way around. But if we are to Release ourselves from perpetual victimhood, we must realize both our reactions and the reactor contribute to the reflection of hurt. True Love is not the thought that reflects Hitlers and Idi Amins back to Its Self. This is inconsistent. evil intent cannot flourish in the Presence of Love. To allow Love through, we must let go of our hateful grudges and have Compassion for the perpetrator too.

we are **not** innocent if we believe we are hurt. we are **not** innocent **because** we believe we are hurt.

    If my sympathy for acts-of-man is misplaced,
is my sympathy for victims of natural disaster
misplaced too?

**I** must reiterate that sympathy is only misplaced if we **don't** recognize it as conscience compelling us to serve our fellow human. Otherwise, sympathy is pride. sympathy is misplaced if we sit back and think sympathy is enough, or if we use sympathy as the excuse and justification to criticize and condemn a perceived perpetrator.

If we can See this, we also See that hurt can come from any source, natural or man-made, but if we have sympathy for victimhood, we blame man, and we turn the one avenue of Release (man) into a source of hurt. This cuts off our Release altogether.

we can't blame man for natural disaster, but Man can be our Savior from these events too. For if we Know what Love Is, we must be Loving our neighbour as our Self, and we would also Know that Love could not put any "person" in the path of "natural disaster". Suddenly we release the god-of-matter too. It was always our failure to Recognize Our Guilt-less-ness that gave matter its apparent power. By Loving our neighbour, the whole structure of discord, including injustice, collapses.

# PART 4

## Conscious Trust

# CHAPTER 16

———◎———

# i is for insecure

In this final section of the book, we will consolidate our study by looking at how Conscious Trust can help us reach our potential of Consciousness. All the things for which we strive; Safety, Health, Prosperity and Love, are out of our hands. our purpose is therefore not to hold all these balls in the air in some deluded belief that we can. They are already established in Consciousness.

In our unrealized potential, though, ignorance fans out into these four main areas of human struggle; lack of Safety (insecurity), lack of Health (illness), lack of Prosperity (impoverishment), and lack of Love in Relationship (isolation). All of us struggle with at least one of these big four areas, and most two or more.

The secret is that these four challenges are not really separate challenges but the same challenge seen through the prism of the fearful little i's split mind. It is helpful, then, to study these four areas individually and at some length. For as we develop one area of Consciousness, we develop Consciousness of the Whole and eliminate all the others. Along the way, too, we introduce and learn to apply the two important tools of Gratitude and Forgiveness. Just as importantly, we round out and strengthen our Understanding of perhaps the main tool in our Consciousness toolbox— Conscious Trust Itself.

insecurity is an obvious starting point, because i is a state of fear and, as such, insecurity (feeling unsafe) underpins every other area of struggle. That is, our anxiety is heightened and our sense of danger exposed when we feel ill, suffer financial pressure or when a relationship ends or turns sour.

On the plus side, because vulnerability and insecurity are synonymous, the study of insecurity offers us clear and relatively straightforward reasons to begin Conscious Trust or to continue It with added vigour.

Despite the many reasons why we feel insecure, We **are** Safe. But the Mind cannot Reflect Safety while we let the mind reflect our fear back to us as dangerous situations that we seem powerless to control. From vast global threats such as hurricanes and earthquakes right down to tiny molecular germs and poisons that threaten to wreak havoc on our bodies, danger seems to be part of life.

On top of that, we listen to fearful voices. Those charged with our protection unwittingly began to coax us to turn away from Truth as soon as we could comprehend what danger meant. "don't run too fast or climb too high, you might fall down and hurt yourself", "don't talk to strangers, they can't be trusted", "don't get dirty, you might catch germs", "rug up, you might catch a cold", "don't pitch your tent under a tree, a branch might fall on you", "don't eat berries off that bush, they might be poisonous", "don't swim out too deep, you might drown".

But not only were we taught that we were unsafe by simply breathing, our early instructions to "be safe" were woven with the guilt that our parents unconsciously inherited and passed onto us.

How so?

Remember our parents waving us off at the doorstep? "take care", "safe trip" they'd say. we still hear it from friends and family. we say it too because it seems like a caring thing to say. But the "farewell" not only tempts a fate we didn't mean to tempt by way of our pre-emptive worry, it also reminds us of a burden we took on at an early age; "don't make me regret not wrapping you up in cottonwool", "i couldn't live with my self if anything happened to you". The child was made to feel responsible for the parent's peace of mind. And so we learnt that safety in the world is not just about our own welfare, it's about our loved ones as well. "you are responsible for my fear" is the powerful underlying message that sets us up for failure, for we **are** responsible, but not through fear. fear makes us accept discord and demands we protect the guilty i that created it.

It's up-side-down. we protect the wrong thing. we should be Protecting ourselves **from** i, not protecting i. Besides, it's futile to protect that which has the goal of fear. Of course, we fail and feel guilty for it.

Safety Rests in the Awareness that there is no power that can hurt anyone, because the so-called power of "danger" is a false perception. True Perception is the Revelation of Conscious Trust. That is, when we let our Mind be used correctly, we Realize (make Real) that we are all Invulnerable in our True Identity.

"danger" is a picture we all agreed to create of others being hurt to prove to us that **we** can be hurt. If someone else is vulnerable, we must be too. And so an ongoing goal of our life is to protect our self and our loved-ones from danger. The problem is our understanding of "security" makes us think we are choosing safety, but we are really only choosing not-danger temporarily before the picture reverts to danger once more. we never stop to ask "who created the picture?". For if there is any protective action to take, it is to Protect our self from i and its belief of danger.

Protection, then, is not a defence against anything outside us. It's a double-layered inner Spiritual Protection against the believer **and** its belief. In this case, against i **and** its belief of danger. Watch that you don't stop at one layer. The thought that practicing Spiritual Protection can protect **i** from danger will sabotage My Promise of Safety and Security.

Why won't Spiritual Protection protect i?

Because, by definition and by nature, i is not safe. i wants to be safe, but that very desire presumes Permanent Safety is impossible. The only way to Be Permanently Safe, then, is to relinquish the desire to be safe.

**That** feels unsafe.

It feels unsafe because you think you are being asked to put little i at risk. But the risk is in believing i can be protected!

Let Me explain further. If you desire safety, you naturally seek protection from danger, and if you seek protection from danger, Spiritually or otherwise, you imply that danger exists. you then reflect forms of danger back to your self from which you want protection. Suddenly you are caught in the inescapable cycle of fear that desires safety. But You were never caught in the cycle. It was i. i's desire to be safe caught you in its net of vulnerability.

`How can i give up the desire to be safe if i don't yet believe` **I** `Am Safe?`

If it was possible for you to forget the Truth of Your Safety, it must also be possible for you to Remember It. Spiritual Protection is always available and Conscious Trust is the way to Remember. This is the hidden message of Psalm 91. Let us examine it.

> *"He who dwells in the Secret place of the most High*
> *Shall abide under the shadow of the Almighty.*
> *i will say of the Lord, "He is my refuge and my fortress;*
> *My God, in Him i will Trust."*
> *Surely He shall deliver you from the snare of the fowler*
> *And from the perilous pestilence.*
> *He shall cover you with His feathers,*
> *And under His wings you shall take refuge;*
> *His Truth shall be your shield and buckler.*
> *You shall not be afraid of the terror by night,*
> *Nor of the arrow that flies by day,*
> *Nor of the pestilence that walks in darkness,*
> *Nor the destruction that lays waste at noonday."*[99]

`The Psalm speaks of danger.`

you don't ignore danger's apparent presence. The Psalm implies that *He who **dwells** in the Secret place of the most High* has some sort of special gift at his disposal. So what does "dwelling" mean and where is this *Secret place of the most High*? The *Secret place of the most High* is your Mind, your Secret Sanctuary, and *dwelling* means to practice Conscious Trust. "dwelling", then, means to switch mind-channels from the fearful thoughts that **you** are thinking, or beliefs that you have taken for granted, to Listening to

---

[99]  *The Holy Bible*, New King James Version (Tennessee: Thomas Nelson Inc., 1982), Psalm 91:1-6

the Voice of Truth, My Thought, your Intuition. It means to let Me Guide your actions.

So what is this special gift at your disposal if you dwell? Dwelling or Consciously Trusting also means to **abide**, and where do you "abide"? you **abide** *under the shadow of the Almighty*. In other words, when you dwell or abide in Conscious Trust, you are Protected from all manner of discord. It's as if you travel in a protective force-field. But you haven't erected anything in defence of danger, you have removed danger by Consciously Trusting that You are always Safe. Not in any blind faith type of way, but by Consciously disengaging from the thought-system that has reflected danger. you disengage because you Understand it isn't telling you the Truth. Then you **wait** for the Truth to replace it. dwelling is waiting. For what? In time, danger seems to part ways for you. That is, you don't avoid danger (because there is no actual danger to avoid), but, in Effect, danger dissolves to Reveal Safety. we dwell in Defence-less-ness.

The Psalm goes on to tell us what to expect in our Defence-less-ness:

> *"A thousand may fall at your side, and ten thousand at your right hand;*
> *But it [danger] shall not come near you."*[100]

The bullet-proof attitude of youth is correct then? It won't happen to me?

The bullet-proof attitude is false hope unless and until you become proficient at dwelling in Conscious Trust. If you think forms of danger have power over you, your belief will come true. The forms become powerless only when you Realize they never were powerful.

Sounds a little harsh to everyone else. i feel sorry for them.

Defence-less-ness implies a warning not to revert back to reacting to

---

[100] *The Holy Bible*, New King James Version (Tennessee: Thomas Nelson Inc., 1982), Psalm 91:7-8

the pictures of danger with sympathy for the fallen, because sympathy reinforces the picture of danger and therefore actually contributes to it. Defence-less-ness through dwelling in Conscious Trust is the only way to Prevent danger and actually help people.

But the Psalm says thousands fall, so how does my Conscious Trust help?

Think of the airline safety procedures we all sit through before takeoff. In the case of an emergency, you are reminded to fit your oxygen mask before you assist others. This is because you won't be much help to anyone else if you are incapacitated. It's the same with Consciousness. The help you are able to facilitate depends on your Consciousness.

Real help Rests on Knowing that the thousands don't really fall at all. Do I fall? Can I fall? Everyone's True Self is unaffected. Of course, as we have said before, this doesn't mean we stand by and watch people suffer. That would indicate a morally deficient consciousness that has not yet moved into the transition stage let alone able to dwell in Conscious Trust. conscience, the sign that we have entered the transition stage, demands that we assist those in need of physical assistance. But even as we go about assisting in earthly ways, we Know that the greatest assistance we can afford is Consciousness, because Consciousness offers a Permanent solution and does not depend on our physical presence. Consciousness is Omnipresent, in all places at all times. So from wherever you happen to be, close at hand or across the world, those with an open Mind will be silently and automatically lifted out of the slavery to their own emotional reactivity by your Consciousness, because the Consciousness you Receive is theirs too.

Then wipe away those crocodile tears of sympathy. The Mind is only Free to Reflect My All-inclusive Safety when you have the Understanding, Strength and Courage to reach beyond the cries for sympathy. True Strength and Courage does not react to the perception of danger but Calmly faces it with Conscious Trust.

Those who can dwell in Conscious Trust offer salvation to humanity from its collective bubble of ignorance. Let us follow some dwellers of the past and See how Spiritual Protection works.

There was a Hebrew King and Prophet named Hezekiah. Hezekiah's people were faced with an enemy army threatening to destroy the city with powerful material weapons. He gathered his people together and said;

> *"Be Strong and Courageous; do not be afraid nor dismayed before the King of Assyria, nor before and all the multitude that is with him; for there are more with us than with him. With him is an arm of flesh; but with us is the Lord our God to help us and to fight our battles. And the people were Strengthened by the words of Hezekiah king of Judah."*[101]

As it worked out, the enemy army fought amongst themselves and was destroyed, a most unusual turn of events considering the army was so materially powerful.

What happened? And why did Hezekiah call the army's power "arm of flesh"?

The *arm of flesh* is the belief in a vulnerable body. This is what the army really carried. The material weaponry merely demonstrated the belief. weaponry is a show of force that seeks to intimidate just as much as physically destroy the target of its aggression. This *arm of flesh*, however, doesn't count on or even know it is possible to dwell in a Greater Power. For in the Presence of Consciousness, the tactic of intimidation and aggression always backfires. Not only because Defence-less-ness and Invulnerability can't be intimidated or destroyed, but because the belief that vulnerability can protect itself is exposed as a contradiction. Hezekiah had this Consciousness (the *Lord our God*) to Protect him. In addition, Hezekiah's Consciousness Inspired Confidence, and his people were Protected as a result. But it's important to Understand that Spiritual Protection isn't a protection against bloodshed. Again, It is a Protection against believing i can be protected.

Why didn't Hezekiah's Consciousness protect the warring army?

Because, by inciting war, the enemy army demonstrated that they were

---

[101] *The Holy Bible*, New King James Version (Tennessee: Thomas Nelson Inc., 1982), 2 Chronicles 32:7–8

not open to this Protection. They believed invulnerability was something that could be won, and won through physical might and power. But this misguided thought only proved that they were impotent, not Omnipotent; vulnerable, not Invulnerable.

Had Hezekiah believed he and his people could defend against vulnerability, the warring army may well have succeeded, because the battle would have been fought in the bubble of ignorance where i is unprotectable.

More recent events serve as added illustrations that the *arm of flesh* is impotent in the Presence of Consciousness.

During World War II it was protocol for chaplains to serve in the American army and navy. Roman Catholic, Jewish and Protestant denominations were represented, but there was a small group of chaplains who had studied, accepted and practiced the mystical teachings of Mary Baker Eddy.[102] Under their watch, there were significantly fewer casualties. Ralph Bailey served as a chaplain for a year of active combat during several European campaigns. All around his area of authority there was heavy loss of life, but hourly "Preventive work" and instruction by Bailey, Hezekiah-like, Protected Bailey's particular group of soldiers from harm. In his own words;

> *"Our officers and men were urged by me to claim the Protection of the first statement in the ninety-first Psalm: "He who dwells in the Secret place of the most High shall abide under the shadow of the Almighty," with emphasis on the word "abide." The result was a magnificent record of not one man killed by enemy action from the time i joined the outfit in the Mediterranean in May, 1944, to VE-Day in southern Bavaria in May, 1945. Those who were wounded shared in this protection to the extent that all will, in so far as i could ascertain, fully recover."[103]*

---

[102]  Mary Baker Eddy. *Science and Health with Key to the Scriptures.* 1875. (Massachusetts: The Christian Science Board of Directors, 2009)

[103]  *The Story of Christian Science Wartime Activities 1939 – 1946.* (Massachusetts: The Christian Science Publishing Society, 1947), 169

Another chaplain, Milo Guild, was assigned to the naval vessel "S. S. Exchequer". He was known to make hourly use of the statement from the Old Testament;

*"I am with thee, saith the Lord, to save thee."[104]*

In June 1944 the Exchequer received orders to proceed from Swansea, Wales, to the Isle of Wight. In an already busy stretch of water the enemy sensed easy pickings and on both that voyage and its return the battle raged around the ship. Those on board the Exchequer witnessed several sinkings of transports, destroyers and other craft in their vicinity, but not once did enemy fire touch them. As the troops commenced operations at shore, they were barraged from overhead, but the Exchequer unloaded and reloaded her troops without a mishap. In fact, throughout the entire operation;

*"there was not a man lost aboard the "Exchequer," nor did the ship so much as experience "the smell of fire," even with explosions and destruction in evidence on every side."[105]*

Back on land, another chaplain, Joseph Ware, was assigned to conduct funeral services for men who were victims of aircraft accidents. Prior to his assignment, there had been five or six funerals a week. Fatal accidents abruptly ceased after Chaplain Ware began his work, although *there was no apparent diminution of activity.*[106]

Perhaps the chaplain's greatest contribution was to demonstrate that we can do our duty, put our body in harm's way, and, by opening our Mind to Our Invulnerability and the Love of Our Self and our neighbour, not only do we remain Safe ourselves, but we offer Safety to those open to Protection.

Seems miraculous.

---

[104] *The Holy Bible*, New King James Version (Tennessee: Thomas Nelson Inc., 1982), Jeremiah 30:11

[105] *The Story of Christian Science Wartime Activities 1939 – 1946.* (Massachusetts: The Christian Science Publishing Society, 1947), 173

[106] *The Story of Christian Science Wartime Activities 1939 – 1946.* (Massachusetts: The Christian Science Publishing Society, 1947), 176

From the Spiritual Perspective, so-called miracles are the norm. discord is the aberration. Hezekiah, and the chaplains Bailey, Guild and Ware simply Knew that there was no i to protect and nothing from which to be protected. The whole fearful scene was a construction of the mind believing in vulnerability. By not reacting, they effectively removed i from creating the picture. Then by Consciously Trusting that **I Am** Safe, they could each sit Receptively in the Secret Sanctuary of their Mind (dwell in Conscious Trust) and **let** Safety and Security Be. They Knew i didn't do It, **I** did.

Surely it takes more to stop large-scale wars and genocide.

human tragedies like genocide are a result of the lack of Presence of a transparent Mind of a Conscious Individual, the sad result of no one Knowing they can withdraw from the belief that i can and should be protected. Through the misunderstanding of Empathy we cling to the idea that the "enemy" should be obliterated, which justifies "defensive" aggression, often in the name of "god". But what god would choose sides? "god will protect my side" hopes i, not knowing its god is the universal belief in the power of a separate material universe to which **every** human subjects themselves. ignorance is the real danger and **guarantees** the conflict and heavy itinerant losses.

In addition, the false dependence we put on something outside us to protect us encourages apathy (the opposite of sympathy). A mind glazed with apathy and indifference doesn't have to face guilt on any level. Moreover, in the absence of a Conscious Individual who is "dwelling" somewhere on the planet, an individual with evil intent can easily play on apathy, de-humanize it into cruelty and mercilessness, and whip up enthusiasm in the wrong direction. tragedies like genocide result.

But why wait for someone else to do what you were born to do? The waiting will be in vain, because you can't Understand let alone See what you don't Receive. It's up to **you** to Consciously Receive the Realization that none of us are vulnerable in Reality, for where can the evil intent land? It was only ever in your mind. In the Presence of Consciousness, war-mongering egos cannot gain the momentum they need for large scale tyranny and conflict. The evil intent is undermined and even extinguished before it gets out of the starting block.

Isn't it arrogant to think i can do that?

i didn't do It. One Conscious Individual is a majority.

Am i equally Protected from natural dangers like wild animal attack?

There is no hierarchy of dangers, no effects that are more or less dangerous than another. All are powerless in the Presence of Consciousness.

*"All phenomena are empty"*[107]

Adi Shankara was an Illumined Individual who lived in India in the 8th century. Shankara was attracted towards the Spiritual life in his childhood. It is said that one day, while bathing in the Purna River, he was attacked by a crocodile. Sensing he was in mortal danger he decided to "renounce the world". That is, he recited the Vedantic mantras of renunciation and immediately the crocodile left him.[108]

Shankara used the Vedantic mantras in the same way the chaplains used passages from the Bible, not as magic formulas, but as tools to lift them into the Peaceful atmosphere of the Mind where danger did not tempt them to react. Shankara didn't do anything **to** the crocodile. He did not resist it or fight it. Nor did the crocodile respond to something outside it. The picture of danger was always illusory. It simply took Consciousness to dissolve the mentally reflected picture of danger. In other words, in the Presence of his Illumined Consciousness, the "danger" couldn't operate. it lost its power. There was no believer of danger, therefore no belief of danger to reflect.

---

107   Brainyquote.com Bodhidharma http://www.brainyquote.com/quotes/quotes/b/bodhidharm267267.html

108   Advaita-vedanta.org Sankara's Life http://www.advaita-vedanta.org/avhp/sankara-life.html

But i am not a chaplain or a child mystic.

It doesn't matter. Just as there is no hierarchy of dangers there is no hierarchy of persons able to avail themselves of Spiritual Protection. Jesus, one of the greatest transparencies of Consciousness that we know of said;

> *"Very truly **I** tell you, whoever believes in Me will do the works **I** have been doing, and they will do even greater things as these."[109]*

He wasn't appealing for us to believe in him personally. "Me" is the Consciousness of every one of us. He tried to tell us that we all have this Impersonal potential embedded within Our Consciousness. All it takes is Conscious Trust in Me, Your Me, not his "me".

Are terrorist attacks empty phenomena too?

***All*** *phenomena are empty.* The Consciousness that Rests in My Safety cannot be harmed. It is only our doubt that this is True that leaves us open to danger and allows discords like terrorism to flourish. It follows then that the madness of terrorism is its weakness, but cannot be fought with the weakness that says the terrorist is powerful.

The terrorist's power is in our fear, and his lack of fear in which he chillingly takes pride. The terrorist's lack of fear is not a result of Consciousness, but a result of a **lack** of Consciousness that has deluded itself into thinking its martyrdom is godly. And our fear obviously still throbs under the pretense of defiance. our mistake is that we share the belief in this bogus god-of-matter with the terrorist. Therefore it is our belief in separateness (the god-of-matter) that simultaneously allows terrorism and lets those of us that want an end to terrorism down. A person or group of persons who lethally combine a lack of conscience and a swollen sense of pride is no threat to Consciousness and cannot upset Its Equilibrium.

The only defence against this madness, then, as always, is to Be

---

[109]   *The Holy Bible*, New King James Version (Tennessee: Thomas Nelson Inc., 1982), John 14:12

Defence-less. Dwell in Conscious Trust. Take responsibility for your reflection and then let it go. Sink into My Safety. Not under the false impression that defiant solidarity will somehow deter the terrorist, but that a thought against Love cannot penetrate the Thought of Love in Consciousness.

What about the global threat of climate change? we can't even agree that it is real let alone agree on how to stop it.

The answer is the same as with any other threat. Dwell in Conscious Trust and the course of action to take will be Revealed to you.

But it seems completely different from any other threat.

It's the old doomsday fear rebadged and globalized. But it does hold some valuable lessons for us, so let us examine what is going on. First of all, if all phenomena are empty, climate catastrophes are too. Dwell in Conscious Trust and wait. Eventually you will Hear that humans **are** responsible for destructive climate change, but not for the reasons you think. Any over-use of Fossil Fuels and deforestation is done in the name of self-preservation and therefore is a response to existential fear. Consequently, any erratic weather patterns resulting from such actions must be part of the false reflection of fear. Of course, this doesn't give us the excuse to sit back and do nothing. greedy, self-indulgent and wasteful behaviour should be changed, but not at the aggravated demand of shrill accusatory voices that seem to be attracted to this issue. Nor should our inability to back-peddle our use of Fossil Fuels at warp speed be a subject of guilt or a reason to lay blame. The surface reasons for "climate change" and the arguments about what we do about it are almost irrelevant. They miss the point!

What's the point?

"climate change" brings a commonality of every discord into sharp focus. humanity's problem is not with the latest thing or person or situation it fears. it's problem is with Me.

With You?

223

Yes, because **I** say You are Invulnerable. you want to be right about who you are. you want to keep your identity. And that identity must remain unsafe. In counter-attack to My Assertion that You are not i, you must prove Me wrong. you must perceive something that makes you vulnerable! And what could offer greater proof that i is vulnerable than a crisis that threatens the planet and all its inhabitants? If you win this argument, you win against Me. But is a win that kills you and your environment really a "win"?

Not at all.

Still, this is what this crisis is all about. If you are right about "climate change", the "you" you think you are will die. If you are wrong, that "you" will lose its pride—another death.

Seems very silly.

If you can See how absurd it is, then "climate change" has become a blessing rather than a disaster. It offers us the greatest opportunity to Awaken yet, because it has never been this blatantly obvious how we create lose/lose situations. And, if you remember, lose/lose in human terms is win/win in Spiritual terms.

Remind me how lose/lose is win/win again.

The death of i, its humiliation, is the "rebirth" into your Spiritual Identity together with the dissolution of every problem. The question is, are you willing to be wrong? Not just about "climate change" because this is just the latest reflection of discord. The question is, are you willing to be wrong about i and its belief of danger having power over My Thought? The stakes are very high now, so your answer warrants careful consideration. The situation is showing you that to lose the Tug-of-war with Me sets you Free.

Can't you See? "climate change" is the decoy. It symbolizes your inability to Awaken. It's the intellect and its puppet that pose the real threat. They will kill you before they let you see Truth.

So Relax. The Truth doesn't change, and the Truth Is that the Climate is part of My Reflection of Invulnerability. The Climate can't be destructive without our ignorance that It is not destructive. The intellect orchestrates every disaster and, if necessary, sends in pride to deflect our guilt. In this case we **have** taken on guilt. we agree that we are responsible, but then we have immediately funneled guilt into a massive political blame-game on a global scale. To reverse this unsolvable dilemma, all we have to do is take back our Dominion by "dwelling" in Conscious Trust. The Climate must "obey".

> *"Now it happened on a certain day that He got into a boat with his disciples. And He said to them, "Let us go over to the other side of the lake." And they launched out.*
>
> *But as they sailed He [Jesus] fell asleep. And a windstorm came down on the lake, and they were filling with water, and were in jeopardy.*
>
> *And they came to Him and awoke Him, saying, "Master, Master, we are perishing!" Then He arose and rebuked the wind and the raging of the water. And they ceased, and there was a calm.*
>
> *But he said to them, "Where is your faith?" and they were afraid, and marveled, saying to one another, "Who can this be? For He commands even the winds and the water, and they obey Him!"*[110]

Jesus was reminding the disciples of their Dominion when he said *"Where is your faith?"*. Faith is Conscious Trust. It looks gently on the dangerous scene without panic, in non-reactivity, and along with your corrected behaviour (if you think you contributed), the *raging of the water ceases and there is a calm*. The thoughts of man are always responsible for perceived disaster, yet Peace emerges out of the fog of human thought to quell it when we Understand what Faith really means.

In the end, we are only doomed to our own false reflection, which means We, the Source of the True Reflection, are not doomed at all.

> *"If i am in error, the loss is surely mine; but if i am in the right, it is thanks to that which my Lord has revealed to me."*[111]

---

[110] *The Holy Bible*, New King James Version (Tennessee: Thomas Nelson Inc., 1982), Luke 8:22-25

[111] *The Koran*, translated with notes by N. J. Dawood (England: Penguin Books, 1956), 34:48

i gather you are saying that even though i feel unsafe, **I** am actually Safe at all times in all places.

Yes, it's your Consciousness of Safety that translates as the Law of Safety. Consciousness doesn't have a locality. Although, in your potential, as your bubble of ignorance becomes more and more porous to Truth, an area of Influence seems to extend around your body. This helps to explain the *thousands that fall* to your left and right in Psalm 91. If your consciousness still includes the possibility of danger, then you will still see it. It's a paradox, but Consciousness unfolds incrementally and spatially. Put it this way, you take your C(c)onsciousness wherever you go, and the deeper and stronger your Connection to Me is, the wider My Influence extends.

While i am still a novice, then, does it mean that whatever i leave behind in my travels is **not** protected? i'm thinking of my home and car. When i leave them behind, do i leave them vulnerable?

your H(h)ome and C(c)ar are within your C(c)onsciousness. They are an extension of you, so it's like you take them with you.

The reason i ask is that it concerns me that sometimes i deliberately go against Trust. i lock my home and car. By doing that, i don't want to exclude my home from the Protection of Consciousness. Then again, when i don't lock up, it feels arrogant somehow, or like i am testing my Trust.

If you still have some reservations, it would be foolish not to take precautions, because fear reflects back to you as the things you fear. In the transition stage, Safety Reveals Itself gradually. Continue to dwell in Conscious Trust and you find you become less obsessive. But it will not be forced. Consciousness doesn't ask you to lose your common sense. One day you will "forget" to lock your house, and when it finally occurs to you, you won't panic because you will Know it wasn't absent-mindedness. Protection will have become automatic. Your Consciousness goes before you to make the crooked road straight, but it also leaves a Safe trail behind you.

Does that mean when i travel in cars, trains, planes and ships, i am safe?

**You** are never unsafe. Just as the Climate is not intrinsically dangerous, nor is the Car, the Train, the Aeroplane, the Ship, or any other Form of Transport. We can travel in Perfect Safety because We have Dominion of the Mind through which Vehicles of Transport appear. They didn't appear on their own.

i still worry about my loved-ones being involved in a disaster.

you cannot Realize Your Invulnerability if one other person is **actually** vulnerable. If you think it is possible for one person to be unsafe, then Invulnerability must be a fallacy. But Invulnerability Is True. Relax into this Freeing Awareness. Because It Protects your loved-ones too. The Beauty of Consciousness is that It must be Universal.

This Realization is also how we extinguish the childhood guilt we took on and involuntarily pass on as adults. Just Remember, your loved-ones are not responsible for your Peace of Mind. And you bear false witness if you think they are unsafe. Therefore, the next time you are tempted to say, "drive carefully" and "take care", as if your well-wishing could override the fearful forms to which you unconsciously contributed, stop and pause. Then say "have a wonderful trip", because the Knowing that they too are Safe Acknowledges My Universal Safety, and It Is so.

# CHAPTER 17

# i is for illness

When we think of the subject of "health" we normally think of the balanced functioning of the body. But Health is a Universal Concept. Therefore, if we Understand and Acknowledge the Infinite Source of a Healthy Body, we will also enjoy Healthy Relationships, a Healthy Business, a Healthy Environment and even a Healthy World.

Though, since we already associate "health" with the body, let us start here.

A Healthy Body Is the Reflection of Consciousness. The body is not healthy on its own, because there is no such thing as a Body separate from the Consciousness that operates It. A R(r)eflection of C(c)onsciousness, no matter what I(i)ts S(s)ource, is just a mental image in and of the M(m)ind. It never externalizes even though it looks as though it does. We must remember that we are not "in" a body, We are C(c)onsciousness appearing A(a)s B(b)ody.

So why does the body get sick?

The body doesn't get sick without you. The consciousness that feeds the mind with the belief that the body can make you sick is sick. And when the mind is fed with a belief, the body must follow, because according to Truth-fundamental #3, thought is the substance of the perception we call matter. I'm sure it wouldn't have escaped your notice that the vast majority of us escape the ravages of danger, but from the common cold in winter to the infirmity of old-age, and every twinge and pain in between, we all suffer from illness.

Why is illness so prevalent?

We are each an Individual expression of Infinite Spiritual Consciousness, so in our **lack** of Consciousness, the body becomes our personal point of convergence for the consequences of the misconception that we are "in" a body. Inferred is the idea that the body has its own intelligence and power to make us sick. This incredibly disempowering thought exemplifies our sense of vulnerability and forms into unhealthy patterns of emotions and thoughts that themselves show up as bodily malfunctions. But that's not all. The thought that the body has power over us feeds thoughts that reflect back to us as additional "causes" of illness such as poisonous plants and substances, and deadly insects and germs. These "outer causes" further reinforce our belief that we are vulnerable and the cycle continues, even though none of these "causes" are really causes at all. They are effects or symptoms of a false belief—the belief of separateness.

you might think that correcting this idea would solve our health issues, and it would, but i doesn't want to correct this idea, not because it doesn't want to be well, but because i would no longer exist. i exists **because** of the belief of separateness. In the same way as i reflects unsafe scenarios back to itself to prove its vulnerability and serve its continued existence, i unconsciously encourages illness.

But illness is much more ubiquitous than danger. And that is because illness has two huge payoffs or rewards that undermine our conscious desire to be well beyond simply proving vulnerability.

Payoffs?

Yes, and until we become aware of them, it is virtually impossible to complete this appearance without pain and/or debilitating dysfunction.

The first payoff is that we are not judged for being ill. This is in stark contrast to the response of banishment, criticism and ostracization we attract for doing something we know is wrong such as lying, cheating and stealing. When we are ill we get sympathy! we get attention! For some, it is perhaps the only time their loved-ones feel compelled to gather around.

The second payoff is that we don't have to feel guilty for being ill. Again this is in stark contrast to the times when we do wrong and feel the undeniable pang of guilt. When we are ill it's not our fault. Although we might feel a little guilty for coughing or sneezing on someone, we are not blamed for being ill. Nor do the infected blame us for making them ill. And when it comes to the decrepitude of old-age, we are totally forgiven. illness is "just one of those things" says i. "the body breaks down in one way or another". And if we are dealt the illness-card early we simply endure it like we endure bad weather.

Furthermore, because our sick self is the subject of sympathy, we have a guilt-free opportunity to use illness to get out of our obligations. "i can't look after you if i'm debilitated" says i in silent relief. But we cut off our nose to spite our face, for the inevitable outcome of illness is death.

But then illness lets us die too. you may or may not have noticed that illness makes victims of us, but there is no perpetrator. illness therefore is easily attributed to god. "it must be meant to be" says i fatalistically. Thus we put illness in the acts-of-god category of discords along with natural disasters like earthquakes. But what does this mean? For a start, by making the god-of-matter responsible for illness, it means that we must really be "in" a body that dies. But more than that, it proves that god is truly vengeful, that god doesn't let us off the hook for our past acts of omission and commission, and, therefore, if we die from illness, we can rest assured that we paid our debt, we can die with a clear conscience.

Some consolation you might say! But the guilt-free pay-off of illness goes further still. During our life, illness provides a rite of passage to the intellect **because** our voice of conscience is not invoked. When we are ill, the intellect's only opponent is sidelined. Without the pesky interruption of guilt, we use the looming inevitability of illness as an excuse to indulge the senses, for where else can pleasure be sought? If god made illness, i reasons, then the pleasure of the senses must be the offset to the pain of illness. Besides, who would deny a little pleasure to an entity doomed to die?

## What's wrong with pleasure?

Nothing at all. In fact, Joy is Pleasure in the True sense of the Word, and That is your Spiritual Inheritance. But you don't need any earthly reason to Feel Joy. Therefore, it's not so much the forms of pleasure or indulgence of it that sets us back, but **desire** for pleasure, for desire for pleasure demonstrates without doubt our belief of separateness.

## How do You make that link?

Before **I** explain the link, let me explain what **I** mean by "desire", for the definition of "desire" has become very narrow. It has come to mean to seek pleasures of the flesh such as eating for the taste and texture beyond the biological need for food, or sexual gratification beyond a monogamous relationship. "desire" includes these but is not limited to them.

## Is desire "wanting fulfillment"?

More than wanting fulfillment, "desire" shows its fullest meaning in **where** we search for that fulfillment. we search for fulfillment in matter, via the stimulation of the senses. "desire", then, is dependence on matter that we substitute for Dependence on Me. And this brings us to an important point. Not all desire is matter-dependent, because the Desire for Consciousness reaches behind matter and therefore does not stimulate the senses. So, in order to easily distinguish Desire from desire, let's call matter-dependent desire "sense-desire".

Now we can Understand why the desire for pleasure demonstrates without doubt our belief in separateness, because when we have a desire for something material and then gratify that desire, we think our effort and/or the world of effect provided it. desire for pleasure therefore shuts the door to any Acknowledgment of the Real Source of Joy, and with It, the experience of Forms of Joy.

But that's only the half of it. Brewing under our ill-considered sense of pleasure is a tragedy, for in duality, to seek pleasure on such spurious grounds is to invite pleasure's opposite—pain. Indirectly then, sense-desire leads to death because sense-desire makes us choose pain over Love and pain makes us choose death over Life. The question "what is really pleasurable that ends in pain and death?" is never asked.

Unaware that it is racing towards an unwanted outcome, i ravenously submits to the temptation that its sense-desire reflects back to it. And with the pain of illness looming on the horizon, especially as we age, we have the perfect excuse to indulge in instant gratification of our desires. Under the protection of the guilt-free payoff of illness, self-gratification is elevated by our sympathy into an indefensible positive. we exempt ourselves from any negative that self-gratification might have had, for illness gives us a reason to keep doing it! That is, we wave off any notion that sense-desire and its natural self-gratification might be unhelpful and, instead, give both a seemingly self-less and broadly worthwhile purpose. fear of sickness justifies and makes "get what you want because you die anyway" a worthy goal.

The result is a weird twist, for although we consciously dread illness and do everything to prevent it or overcome it, sense-desire works unconsciously in the background to guarantee illness.

Fortunately, there is a Spiritual teaching known as "The Four Sublime Truths" of Buddha that brings consciousness to the connection between the part of us that secretly welcomes illness through its payoffs and the part of us that thinks worldly pleasure for its own sake is a good thing. Both parts attract pain and death by going for a temporary and unsustainable pick-me-up, a choice that also inadvertently rejects the Permanent Joy for which we Truly yearn. In turn, this appears as the "outer" causes of illness and every other type of "ill-health" we experience.

The First Sublime Truth; *The Truth of suffering.*[112] points out that our material existence including birth, sickness, decrepitude and death is the definition of suffering and sorrow. Apart from birth, which is usually celebrated, who would disagree?

Why would Buddha include birth in that list?

Because our own birth into mortal existence demonstrates that our consciousness accepts a purely material existence. If we accept that we can

---

[112]  Kunzang Thekchog Yeshe Dorje. *The Treatise of the Ship Captain's Sword.* (Sikkim, India: Deorali Chorten Gonpa), 26

be sick, deteriorate into decrepit old-age, and die, we must accept that our birth contributed to the suffering and sorrow of these three.

The Second Sublime Truth; *The Truth of the cause of all suffering.*[113] explains the reason for this sick sequence of events, and its concurrent pain and anguish—material dependence, the seeking of satisfaction (or the prevention of dissatisfaction) in and from the material world—sense-desire.

Buddha called sense-desire "ignorance" because any seeking for or by a non-entity is a recipe for dissatisfaction or suffering. sense-desire sets the karmic wheel of our discordant existence in motion, renews it and continues it. Not least the idea that we can escape our pain through death. Because consciousness was never "in" a body and doesn't die, sense-desire actually extends our misery beyond one mortal appearance. Here too is another reason for placing birth in the same category as death.

Reincarnation is implied then?

re-incarnation assumes we "incarnate" in the first instance. Spiritually speaking, we don't. our consciousness appears **as** a body. re-incarnation also implies a past, but there is only Now. Though, while we appear to live in time, the idea is useful. our mortal existences are like repeated opportunities to Awaken. we reappear again and again until we switch our point of View and become Aware of what appearing represents. What keeps the apparent cycle going and the body visible is sense-desire, because sense-desire proves that we depend on matter.

But surely babies don't indulge sense-desire?

Babies have not developed their intellect so they have no reason or compulsion to indulge sense-desire. However, Buddha said birth is not exempt from the cycle of ignorance. So even though it shocks us to see babies suffering horrific defects, disease and premature death, we must Understand that children, unless they Individually bring a high degree of Consciousness into this appearance, will fall subject to the prevailing collective belief in illness, decrepitude and death from which we, as part of the human race, have not disengaged. Therefore, it is up to us to develop

---

[113] Kunzang Thekchog Yeshe Dorje. *The Treatise of the Ship Captain's Sword.* (Sikkim, India: Deorali Chorten Gonpa), 28

**our** Consciousness, which puts the intellect back in the correct Order behind Love and Reveals Harmony on every child's behalf.

The Third Sublime Truth; *The Truth of the cessation.*[114], not surprisingly, instructs us to cease depending on matter by ceasing sense-desire. Not by practicing austere self-denial rights and rituals, but by treading the middle-path between the two extremes of self-mortification and self-indulgence. Nirvana or Permanent Harmony is Revealed when we do. However, this is very difficult when we don't know that sense-desire and self-gratification cause the discord we always attributed to the god-of-matter. we need some suggestions to lead us in the Right direction.

The Fourth and final Sublime Truth; *The Truth of the path.*[115] offers these suggestions. The Way is known as the *Sublime Eight-fold Path*[116]; Right Views, Right Thoughts, Right Speech, Right Conduct, Right Livelihood, Right Effort, Right Mindfulness and Right Meditation.

We don't need to go through each instruction because we have covered them in our study to a large extent. What stands out is that Buddha uses the word "Right".

What does he mean by Right?

Right Thoughts and Actions are Buddha's version of the Ten Commandments. Unlike the Ten Commandments that tell us what **not** to do, Buddha's Sublime Eight-fold Path tells us what **to** do.

Why?

"you shall not..." doesn't work on sense-desire because we don't want to give up what makes us feel good. In any case, you can't say "you shall not be sick" or "you shall not do anything to relieve pain" or "you shall not do anything to avoid sickness". Just like "you shall not be a victim", the demands are nonsensical and unreasonable. we have no way of discerning we are responsible, not only because we don't think we are responsible for disease, but because our responses to disease seem perfectly reasonable.

---

[114] Kunzang Thekchog Yeshe Dorje. *The Treatise of the Ship Captain's Sword.* (Sikkim, India: Deorali Chorten Gonpa), 29

[115] Kunzang Thekchog Yeshe Dorje. *The Treatise of the Ship Captain's Sword.* (Sikkim, India: Deorali Chorten Gonpa), 31

[116] Kunzang Thekchog Yeshe Dorje. *The Treatise of the Ship Captain's Sword.* (Sikkim, India: Deorali Chorten Gonpa), 33

Buddha's *Sublime Eight-fold Path* of Right Thoughts and Actions doesn't mention illness at all, but gently encourages us to align our self with Spirit. By setting out what **to** do, rather than what **not** to do, we eventually make the link between illness and sense-desire ourselves. For it is no coincidence that our illnesses **and** our sense-desires vanish when we let our Spiritual Self run the Mind.

Importantly, too, Right Thoughts and Actions cancel out the first payoff of illness. sympathy for the victim of illness is returned to its proper function as the call of conscience to serve our fellow human in his ignorance that He **Is** Health. For beyond that, sympathy stands in the way of True Care by breathing life into the victim and its ills.

True Care heals, because It Sees the Perfect Self that was never sick. Care Is Love and Love never was, is, or will be ill.

Doesn't illness present us with an opportunity to express Love?

Caring for the sick **is** an expression of Love. It is a saintly expression, but Love is not limited to caring for the sick, nor does it require sickness to be expressed. In fact, Our Consciousness of Love **Prevents** sickness. Be careful, then, not to let illness dictate your actions. sickness, especially in later life, demands that our loved-ones drop whatever they are doing and care for us. The idea is even built into our marriage vows; "in sickness and in health" we pledge. sickness draws sympathy and calls it love, but is it love to have your loved-ones suffer the sadness and pain of watching you lose your faculties, functions and dignity in old age? Love is offering Hope to your loved-ones by setting a Healthy example.

The Four Sublime Truths dig down through the layer of sympathy to release disease from its label as an unavoidable cause of suffering, because disease is **not** really a **cause** at all. we have been incorrect to say it is. In Truth, disease **and** suffering are both **effects** of the illusion of separateness that compels sense-desire and its outcome of self-gratification. i is the cause of disease **and** suffering. i is guilty of both, but ultimately of nothing, because Nirvana or Consciousness Is the only Cause, and It Is Healthy and pain-free. self-gratification is therefore a demonstration of ignorance and must be brought to Light as such.

Right Thoughts and Actions, then, gently steer us towards the One

Right Desire; to Consciously Trust our Intuition, because Right in Its Eight Forms is what we Hear when we Listen. Rightly Understood, we act **after** we Listen to our Intuition. My Thought leads the way. Everything falls into place because self-less attitudes and behaviour Reveal the Joy of Our Self, canceling out self-gratifying motives.

Would the desire to be healthy be classed as sense-desire?

A desire to be healthy will make you sick which justifies self-gratification. So, indirectly, yes. For why would you desire health when you can tune in to Me and embody Health Now, without thinking?

So i can eat anything i want and not exercise and still be well?

No, because implicit in this suggestion is the idea that you don't need to follow through on My Intuitive advice. It implies that **I** will keep you healthy despite your self-indulgent and unhealthy behaviour. Apart from the fact that Consciousness of Health can't impose on a **lack** of Consciousness of Health, if you are Listening to Me, your appetites for unhealthy foods and behaviour will naturally diminish.

Still, your question exposes a common misperception. we Intuitively Know that fresh food and regular exercise is good for us, but then we make the mistake of saying the fresh food and regular exercise **themselves** make us healthy. See how we transfer the P(p)ower from Consciousness to matter? It isn't the fresh food and regular exercise that keeps us healthy, it is the **Source you Hear** that tells you that fresh Food and regular Exercise Is Health Itself. you follow this Intuitive advice. The **Source** of Health, Me, and the **following of Intuitive advice** appears As your Healthy Body.

Now you can see why the Source will not protect you from processed food and sloth. These ideas are yours. By thinking them, you remove your self from My Protection. Your Health is not at risk. This and only this is why you are drawn to "healthy" foods and activities. you Hear Me dimly, but then you misinterpret My Call. The food and activities are nothing of themselves just as the body is nothing of itself.

Would You give me Intuitive advice to take medicine if i was sick?

If you have opened your Mind to Me, but are not quite ready to Hear that You already Embody Permanent Health, Love will appear in the form that you **are** ready to accept. If medicine is the help you need, it will appear. But **I** don't respond to your sickness. **I** Respond only to your openness of Mind to Receive.

It must be Understood that opening your Mind to Receive doesn't mean **I** come down from My Orbit into the bubble of ignorance. Spirit is **not** working **through** the medicine and the food and exercise unless you already Know Spirit and Matter are not separate. Don't separate them. In line with Truth-fundamental #2— Love (Consciousness) appears **As** Medicine, Food and the call to Exercise. Otherwise we make E(e)ffects causes and transfer the power to matter. **I Am** the only Cause.

It is a common mistake to make E(e)ffects causes. Don't we hope the medicine will "cause" the disease to disappear, and the food or exercise will "cause" the disease to stay away? In the case of medicines, sometimes the particular symptoms will indeed disappear, encouraging us to spend billions of dollars funding drug "cures". But fear is intrinsic in the idea of "finding a cure for disease" in just the same way as "keeping the body healthy". Therefore, in both cases, the belief in disease remains intact to form, either for the first time, or again and again.

> *"i'm saying that the source [of the trouble] is basically in thought. Many people would think that such a statement is crazy, because thought is the one thing we have with which to solve our problems. That's part of our tradition. Yet it looks as if the thing we use to solve our problems with is the source of our problems. It's like going to the doctor and having him make you ill."*[117]

So the idea that prevention is better than cure is wrong?

[117]  David Bohm. *Thought as a System*. (New York: Routledge, 1992), 2

prevention can work temporarily in duality, but the disease we said we were going to prevent was never real anyway. The idea of "disease" is inherent in the preventative motive and must contribute to its appearance, not its disappearance! The idea of prevention makes us feel like we are choosing health, but we are only really choosing not-illness for a while. True Prevention of illness is similar to Protection against danger. The Prevention must be double-layered; against the believer **and** its belief; against falling under the spell of i and its belief that it can be sick or cured.

Then early-detection tests must be counter-productive.

There is no harm in them except the tests assume that you can be sick. Actually, they expose your expectation of sickness, otherwise why would you be testing for sickness? The test reinforces the idea that your body can get sick by itself. By all means, undergo the test, but be Aware of the real danger. The "cause" of sickness is the consciousness that believes that you are in a body, and that the body can make you sick. Then you give the test power to confirm your powerlessness. Don't give Dominion of the Mind away to a test. There is no danger in sickness **or** the test except the danger **you** assign to them by forgetting that You are Invulnerable.

On the other hand, if the early-detection test is a compulsory government initiative, your objection to take part is like dodging the imperative to go to war. it implies fear. Are you afraid the test will reveal a hidden disease? Do not be afraid. If the test reveals a problem, you have the opportunity to switch S(s)ources and Reveal its insubstantiality. If not, your healthy report will contribute to the nation's healthy statistics because you silently Acknowledge the Source of your Health.

Remove the barrier that **you** can be sick or well, and paradoxically, you are "cured" of the possibility to experience illness, because Health is never in danger of getting sick so it can't be made well. The only You there Is **Is** Permanent Health.

The wounded hoards and the conventional wisdom that supports and funds disease have good intentions, but *the road to hell is paved with good intentions.*[118] They join hands and march to their deaths in solidarity for

---

[118]   Goodreads.com Bernard of Clairvaux http://www.goodreads.com/author/ quotes/2734978.Bernard_of_Clairvaux

the fight against disease. Don't follow them. Turn around and Live! our Intention should be to "Reveal Permanent Health", not prevent disease, because disease is a false perception, and to take measures against it simply reinforces the perception. Consciously Trust that All Is Well.

You mentioned that my sense of vulnerability reflects back to me as poisonous plants and insects. Are you saying they are not really poisonous?

A "poison" is so named for its adverse effect on the body. Yet no substance that enters the body, of itself, has any intrinsic power to benefit or harm. It is the i behind the mind that decides these outcomes and projects the power onto the effect thus erroneously making it a cause. The substance is then made deserving of our desire if it is "wholesome" or of our fear if it is "poisonous".

Let us then neutralize desire and fear once and for all by comparing two objects that we believe have opposite effects on the body.

What about apples and arsenic? Apples are wholesome and arsenic is poisonous.

Very well, let's examine these objects and our assumptions about them. The thought of "apples" and "arsenic" immediately conjures up pictures of good and evil. To be the "apple of one's eye" is to be the object of affection, apple-pie wholesomeness is desirable, and "she'll be apples" implies optimism. More practically, we accept an Apple as part of a healthy diet.

Arsenic, on the other hand, has a dark and foreboding image. Even though it is a naturally-occurring Element, It is feared as a threat to our body, and hence our life. But fear does not affect My Reflection. Can Effects be causes of Health or dangerous to Health? Can Effects benefit or harm the Cause? This is the wrong Order.

Let us follow it through. First of all, there is the assumption of a "me" to be acted upon, implying that the Apple has a power for health and the Arsenic has a power for illness, even death, over "me".

Ok, but it's common knowledge that apples are full of vitamins and minerals to support my health which is probably why i feel good when i eat one.

In this instance, the mind translates the collective belief of the healthiness of apples, backed up by the "good" bodily sense-experience of eating an apple, into the conviction that apples are good for "me". In this way, the One and only Infinite Power of Consciousness and Its Health is erroneously transferred to the object. The Divine Law that ensures Good appears **As** Apples is commandeered. "apples are good," says i.

Now let's look at Arsenic. How do you know it is poisonous? Have you tried it?

Of course not, are You crazy? i have read about victims of arsenic. It was a popular poison used to commit murder in the nineteenth century because the symptoms mimicked cholera and went undetected. Since then i have heard of whole populations being unintentionally poisoned by arsenic-contaminated water supplies.

This time the conviction builds a fear around the object giving it a "power" to kill. The Divine Law that ensures Good appears **As** Arsenic is, in this instance, reversed. "arsenic is bad" says i. Arsenic is vicariously assigned our fear.

But arsenic was poisonous before the belief that it was!

Was it? thought comes before perception of thing, remember, not the other way around. **we** made Arsenic appear poisonous because we isolated and concentrated it in turn giving tacit approval to unscrupulous minds to use it inappropriately. This confirmed once again our vulnerability when we were poisoned. But did you Know Arsenic is in Apples, more potent in the juice of Apples?[119]

---

[119] www.fda.gov Questions and Answers: Apple Juice and Arsenic http://www.fda.gov/Food/ResourcesForYou/Consumers/ucm271595.htm

No, i didn't know that.

Yes, and as well as being a constituent of Apples, Arsenic is a naturally occurring Element in Soil, Water and Air, and appears in many of the other Fruits, Vegetables and Grains we consume. However, the intellect wants you to give away Dominion of your Mind to "things" and leaves out the evidence that doesn't suit its case.

These are just traces of arsenic and therefore not harmful.

The deduction that traces are harmless overlooks the fact that high concentrations of Arsenic don't appear in Nature, so we say small concentrations are harm-less because "harm" was our premise. Why not make harmlessness our premise? Arsenic is never harmful to Me in My Omnipotence. humans manipulate what **I** appear As, as if **I** could be improved, and then blame the "thing" for being a poison.

So arsenic isn't poisonous?

It is poisonous to the doubt that It isn't. The point is, the I(i)dea of isolating Arsenic can be both harmful and helpful depending on whether the True Source of the Idea to isolate it was Acknowledged or not. If you admit that the Idea comes from Me, Love Protects the manipulation of Arsenic just like we can manipulate naturally occurring Metals and Minerals into Tools and Buildings and Vehicles without harm. Compounds of Arsenic are used in Industry as Paint pigments and even in Medicines. But if i thinks **it** is doing the manipulating of matter, the reflection of fear that prompted the manipulation will bring both "good" and "bad" results to the body i thinks it is. When you leave Me out, Good is missing. you are on your own.

In asking whether a substance is poisonous or not, you only go half way. you forget to ask "to whom is it poisonous?" arsenic is poisonous to i, but You are not i, so Arsenic is not Really poisonous! The power you assign a poison is in **your** mind. It is **you** who has to agree to make the power effective, because the mind is the only way things can be given power, and by no one else but you. Don't give any object the power to make you sick and die, and you won't be able to use Elements like Arsenic inappropriately.

But don't stop there. What is the next step? It's critical. Don't give an object the power to make you well either. An Apple has no intrinsic power to give You Health. Transcend dualistic thought and its thinker altogether. I can't be healthy or sick, alive or dead, because **I Am Immortal Life and I Govern the Body because It is My Reflection. Nothing more, nothing less.

So i can take poison arsenic and live?

No. i can't take anything and live. The test would only appease the intellect and reinforce the i that felt vindicated when it appears to be finally poisoned, if it is not carried off in a straight-jacket first. If you take Arsenic to test its powerlessness, the need to test only proves you don't believe it, and the underlying **conviction** in harm attached to the substance would probably "kill" what you **think** is you. you don't go looking for trouble to prove there isn't any.

But i thought you said arsenic wasn't poisonous. Either it is or it isn't, surely?

While you are in the process of Realizing your potential to be Conscious, the body has a role in helping you learn that you are not body. It's a paradox we have discussed before. Infinity appears As My Effects and each one has a part to play within that Infinite arena. All My Elements, including Arsenic, have uses. The branch of a tree is useful in the growth of Apples but you don't eat the branch of an apple tree. you eat the fruit because it is more palatable, it tastes better. you discriminate. The fact that you don't bother consuming the branch of the tree is a good example that you **do** Listen to your Intuition. Love leads us along. you drink Water when you are thirsty, you go to sleep when you are tired.

i take an antidote when i drink poison.

Yes, you would take sensible measures if you believed Arsenic was a poison, because it **is** poisonous if you believe it. This is why you don't consume concentrated forms of Arsenic on its own or by choice. It has other uses. Importantly though, if you **did** happen to ingest Arsenic in larger doses than naturally occurs, just as if a so-called deadly insect bit you, as long as you are *dwelling* in Your Sacred Sanctuary and Consciously Trusting that **I Am**, You are Protected.

*"they will take up serpents; and if they drink anything deadly, it will by no means hurt them; they will lay hands on the sick and they will recover."[120]*

## Am i Protected against germs too?

If Germs Exist, they must Be Good. If you say germs are "bad", then they don't Exist. you can't have it both ways in Consciousness. In Reality, Germs are an Effect of Consciousness and no threat. As always, the mind has power over the body, and if i is in charge of the mind, it takes on the belief about germs to its own detriment. Because i believes it is in a body that dies, anything that leads to death is feared. germs are then associated with our demise and their power thus authorized. But it is fear that steps into the scene feeding the idea that the body's immune system cannot match the germ, while its partner death stands by unchallenged at the gate of the mind to prove it true.

If **we** disengage from the collective belief in disease and death, can its sickly reflection survive? Can there be an illness without an i to die? Can sickness sustain itself without you to believe it and give it substance? No. It loses its power, for the only power it had was our ignorance about its lack of power. disease and death are not laws, so the germs that supposedly cause disease and death are not lawful.

## Where does that leave the germ?

The Germ is a decoy and a scapegoat, like Arsenic.

Just as Arsenic has no intrinsic power to harm, a Germ, no matter what its type or apparent viciousness, has no intrinsic power to harm. Nor does the body have any power to host viciousness without your consent. It can't be otherwise. Remember, matter has no intelligence or life of its own. W(w)e have D(d)ominion.

Similarly, Consciously denounce the power of every so-called cause of illness. Can pollen, dust or any other irritant cause My Infinite Intelligence

---

120  *The Holy Bible*, New King James Version (Tennessee: Thomas Nelson Inc., 1982), Mark 16:18

to falter? Can a virus override My Governing Influence? Can a Gene, if it is My Creation, be enabled to disrupt other Parts of that Creation? The affirmative answer consigns Me to oblivion, or makes Me the author of debilitating germs, chronic allergies, destructive viruses and faulty genes. But isn't My Body My Reflection? And wouldn't Germs, Allergens, Viruses and Genes also be My Reflection. Would **I** pit one against the other? The two T(t)houghts are incompatible. **I** Am Omnipotence. There is no power in a germ, an allergen, a virus, or a gene, for not-bad or for bad. More deadly is the belief that matter has power over Me.

Surely i can't get out of the genes i inherited.

Most of us are convinced that genes (DNA) control the body. If we have parents who died early through illness, the unconscious belief that our inherited fate is sealed is difficult to overcome and tends to manufacture our destiny, hence the belief is perpetuated. But recent discoveries should help us relax our anxiety somewhat. It has been shown that we can retrain our mind to "create" healthy beliefs, and by doing so, potentially alter our genes. After all, genes are our belief appearing.[121] It turns out that we don't inherit our diseases or our attributes from our parents, we inherit their beliefs about disease and, under that, the belief that our body controls us. It's the mind that we turn over to belief.

i should accept that my mind causes my disease?

Yes, but, again, the mind is not a cause. The Mind is My Effect. The believer, i, no matter what it believes, is the "cause", but no "cause" because i doesn't really exist. If there was no believer, there would be no beliefs of any kind and the Mind would be clear to Receive and Reflect My Thought of Permanent and Perfect Health back to Its Self, You!

To believe you control the mind is to be out of control of the false reflection. But to allow the Mind to be controlled by Consciousness of your True Self is to overcome the false reflection and the i that thought it could control it. your only Real inheritance is your Spiritual potential of Permanence and Perfection that includes your Perfect Health.

---

121   Bruce Lipton, Ph.D., *The Biology of Belief* (California: Elite Books, 2005)

But if i let my True Self control my Mind what
would become of psychology and psychotherapy?

They wouldn't be required, but for as long as we think we are in charge (which makes matter in charge), mind-sciences are essential. They are an important step towards Consciousness. Remember, we cannot skip steps. The leap from dependence on matter to Dependence on Me is not possible without loosening and breaking our back-to-front thought-system to allow the Light of Spirit to penetrate. mind-therapies lay the ground-work by helping us learn to take responsibility for our reflection. Initially, though, we don't have any idea we are in a reflection, let alone know that we are responsible.

Offering a safe space, and an unbiased listening ear, the therapist can gently uncover the false causes of illness and unravel the blame. At first, we are convinced our problems are the fault of something or someone else; our parents, our ex-spouse, our child, the government, the weather, an inherited disease from our mother's side of the family, etc.

Once we purge ourselves of this angry and frustrated pent-up energy, the load lifts and we arrive at the next crucial layer. we find the problem was always in our hands, for **we** held the resentment, **we** decided to marry the wrong person, **we** didn't get treatment early enough, or the illness served **us** by allowing us to get out of an obligation. In the end, though, we must all come to the same grim conclusion; **we** made a childhood decision, even though it was involuntary, to listen to our intellect, to identify with i. we thought we had to survive on our own and support our self. That's the original mistake we made. **we** are responsible for using the Mind incorrectly. And so we come face to face with our existential guilt.

But what then?

If we are not ready to learn that i is a false cause, we deflect the responsibility back to the obscurity of karma or the supposed lessons of "god". we might turn to religious interpretations such as that of the Crucifixion and, like a get-out-of-jail-free card, incorrectly deduce that Jesus sacrificed himself that we could somehow feel forgiven while maintaining the guilty i. The contortion of thought leads us astray, but religious interpretations are not to blame. They are just another example of our inability to look under guilt.

mind-therapies and religious interpretations can't reach past self-blame, because they don't Recognize the Guiltless, Defence-less, Invulnerable **I**. And they can't reach **I** because they can't reach beyond the mind. Neither the mind-therapist nor the theologian, unless they themselves are Illumined, are qualified to take us beyond the mind. Even the Illumined among us can't face our existential guilt for us. They point us in the Right direction, but alone we must face the Truth that we can't avoid problems as long as we identify with i.

`Isn't it useful to uncover the cause of my`
`aches and pains?`

Useful only to discover You are not i. Rolling around in mental and physical causes of our suffering is another lure to stay vacillating between disease and not-disease. If our goal is to Transcend i, revealing causes that aren't really causes merely caters to and encourages the self-indulgent self. Why not cut to the chase? The root cause of your suffering is identification with i. It's that simple!

> *"Therapies can work on your body.*
> *They can work on your mind.*
> *They can work on your emotions.*
> *You are not the body.*
> *You are not the mind.*
> *You are not the emotions,*
> *so what is therapy doing?"*[122]

You are Consciousness, not mind, not body. Yet the Mind is our avenue of Consciousness, and we should be Mindful that any thought other than My Thought is detrimental, and leads to despair and hopelessness.

`Depression?`

Yes, amongst other mental illnesses.

---

[122]  Captizen.com Swami Rajneesh quotes on therapies and therapists http://www.captizen.com/swami-rajneesh-quotes-on-therapies-and-therapist/

## But not everyone is depressed?

we are all depressed to some degree. we must be, because we can't access Joy. humanity is, by virtue of its state of fear, in various states of depression or not-depression. Sometimes the depression reflects back as an actual brain imbalance, and if it runs in the family, we have the belief in inheritance to contend with too. But the severity of depression and its physical symptoms does not alter the approach we should take. It pays to remember that, in duality, even with our best efforts, it is difficult to maintain a positive attitude, because "positive" is really "not-negative" and must succumb to the stronger pull of negativity from time to time. Likewise, "optimism" is "not-pessimism". The condition known as "depression" is therefore the failure of the promise of optimism; a promise it couldn't keep because its premise is pessimism. What Hope can be extended to an entity that has a natural affinity with negativity?

True Hope is Confidence that the Spiritual Power of Good Exists, and, because It's Our Self, It is closer than our own breath. A glimmer of this Truth is all that is needed to spark Hope. There is no Hope otherwise. For the depressed, this Hope is chronically absent. That is why they are depressed.

depression is the narcissist of pride. i is mesmerized by its own reflection so deeply that it creates a black hole of thought whose voices inside and outside the head offer death as a permanent escape.

## So suicide is not an escape?

suicide is a tragedy for all concerned, a tragedy for the one who took their own life and for the ones left behind. The rest of us shuffle our feet and avoid looking at the grief-stricken in the eye. But if we really want to be Released from the understandable but ongoing torture of the special intensity of grief that suicide instils, we must honestly and squarely face what is really going on. The Spiritual Perspective offers us this Release.

If we can momentarily distance our self from our reactions, we might be able to See that suicide and our reaction to it is entrapment within the bubble of ignorance epitomized. Notice that at every turn, i is indulging its self. Wasn't the suicide victim selfish to commit such an act, and now aren't we selfish in our reaction? "**i** am haunted by what **i** could have done to prevent it", "**i** wasn't planning to be a widow", "**i** won't see my child grow up", "**i** have been robbed of grandchildren". And who would not resonate with such an outpouring, hoping it won't happen "to **me**".

The fact is, suicide creates the mother of all victims in its fallout, because the sympathy grief demands is untouchable. Those of us watching on think sympathy helps, and it does to a certain extent, but then it becomes smothering and inappropriate somehow. we don't know what else to do, but it's as if we are forbidden to move on. And the Intuitive Solution trying to reach through the fog of grief is cut off at the knees by a fierce back-lash for daring to drop sympathy, for who would want to cause a callous amplification of grief? So we all remain silent in our horror and our wish to offer or receive comfort is almost spurned.

The Solution for us all is to Realize that no one has ever "died", and so the "departed" haven't either. When **you** "die", **You** will Be Alright! You Are Always Alright because You were never "in" a body and never will be! And if You are not in a body, neither is your Loved-one! Their body simply disappeared as it appeared so many years before and will reappear again. With this Realization, perhaps self-pity can soften its grip on grief, and sympathy graduate into the True Comfort and Support for which it was meant. Then together, in the Strength of Love's Embrace, we can feel privileged that the dear one Graced our presence at all. And although it is still supremely tragic that they chose to orchestrate their own disappearance, they do Live on. Not just in our memory, but Really and Truly.

To evolve in Consciousness should be our only concern. If we can manage to take our reactions to suicide off the table, we stop contributing to the ever-worsening picture of suicide in the community. If this seems cold-hearted, we should ask ourselves, are our current approaches working? Realize that they can't work because they play up to the i that is by nature depressed.

It sounds strange, but to Really Live, Be Healthy and Happy As the Body, you must die to i. Why not do it now? This is the only death there is. Once you die to the concept of the self, physical death will die with it, and the voices of doom and grief will be silenced.

What will happen to my body when i die to the concept of my self?

Ironically, the quality of Its appearance must improve, because It Is part of My Reflection of Good. And when Your Purpose for this episode is finished you will be cheerfully ready, because, as always, **I** will Be "with" you. Conscious Trust will ensure a gentle disappearance without pain or illness. you will lay the body willingly and gently aside like an empty wrapper and move on, either to appear as another, or remain invisible, because the B(b)ody was never anything other than a R(r)eflection of invisible C(c)onsciousness. The M(m)ind will continue to R(r)eflect your level of C(c)onsciousness as it has always done. And if you Know this, you have already risen out of depression.

The senses will of course contradict Me. sickness is constant and compelling evidence that death is real, in no small measure due to the apparent deterioration of old-age. decrepitude steps forward to prove to you that you were right to doubt that death doesn't exist. Some victory! Is death the measure of success? To the intellect it is!

But we do get old.

You are as old and as young as Eternity. Does Eternity have an age? During this appearance, we mature, but that doesn't spell deterioration or loss of faculties unless your idea of maturation includes the painful break-down implied in the concept of "old age". Unfortunately, most of us have an age in mind when we should switch to being "old" and the descending slide begins. "youth gone, what chance do i have to be fit and healthy" says i.

An astonishing experiment on a group of elderly men conducted by Harvard psychologist Ellen Langer[123] in 1979 should give us reason to question our assumptions about aging. The experiment demonstrated that the inevitable deterioration of function and vitality aging seems to herald is optional.

Dr Langer and her team retrofitted an old monastery in New Hampshire, USA, replicating the decor of 1959. There were Life magazine

---

[123]  Ellen J. Langer, Ph.D. *Counterclockwise; mindful health and the power of possibility.* (New York: Random House Inc., 2009)

pictures on the wall, Alfred Hitchcock movies on the TV, news of the cold war and music of Nat "King" Cole on the radio. Even the clothing and gadgets were authentic to 1959. No detail was left out. No post-1950's magazines and newspapers, or even pictures of themselves were allowed. The men were to live there for a week as though 1959 were the present. They were to speak and think about their 1959 selves in the present tense.

At the conclusion of the week-long retreat, the men had more joint flexibility, increased finger length due to the ability to stretch out their fingers despite having "arthritis", measurably increased mental acuity, and improved height, weight, gait and posture. Outsiders who were shown the men's photographs at the end of the study compared to the one's taken at the beginning remarked that they looked significantly younger. In other words, the so-called aging process had in some measure been reversed. It was a stunning result.

Was the aging process permanently reversed?

No, because as soon as the old stereotypes were reintroduced into the mind, the body responded. But it wasn't the study's purpose to permanently reverse aging, it was to demonstrate that the mind is the determining factor in aging, not time or biology. The study proved just that, and very powerfully.

To permanently reverse aging we must go further. Let us not be satisfied with the body we create with all our fears and expectations of illness and deterioration. Let us plunge into My Now where our ever-Present, Ageless, Indestructible Self resides. It shows you that illness, old age and death are false perceptions of i. Conscious Trust corrects your false perception.

So the sickness will go away?

It was never there. It was in your mind, but remember, you have Dominion of your Mind, and **I am** not sick. **I Am** Health. you can't make this True because It already Is. But you control the appearance of the R(r)eflection by whether you allow Me through the Mind or not. Sit in Silence with a Receptive ear and Consciously Trust. Then one day you Notice the pain is not worrying you anymore, that ailment has gone away, the lump or rash has disappeared, and the black dog has stopped following you.

*"A thousand may fall at your side, and ten thousand at your right hand;*
*But it [illness] shall not come near you."[124]*

Those who do not dwell in the Secret Sanctuary of their Mind cannot See that they were never ill. Resist, then, falling into the trap of false hope or sympathy. Your Wellness is no coincidence. Nor is it a betrayal to those that are not yet ready to Receive this information. The immediate beneficiary of your Conscious Trust was always going to be your own body. Welcome the confirmation. But more than that, see your Wellness as a watershed moment, for you can't be Well on your own for long. If you are Well, you must have come to the Realization that the *fallen* are not Really sick, even though they appear to be. Consciousness, being Universal, means your Realization of Wellness is theirs too. The false reflection vanishes when you decide to relinquish the i of everyone. This is the secret to "Spiritual Healing".

i always thought Spiritual Healers were just better at praying. Either that or they have the power of mind-over-matter.

Spiritual Healers are better at Praying because they Know what Prayer Really Is. Prayer doesn't ask an apparently aloof, indifferent and cruel god to heal the person that this same all-powerful god apparently made sick in the first place. Prayer does **not** establish Health. Prayer **Acknowledges** that Health Is already established in Consciousness. Now. Not tomorrow or at some time after the right words are uttered with conviction, emphasis or even with a noble intention, because this demonstrates our **lack** of Consciousness. Could Omnipresence, Omnipotence and Omniscience respond to a lack of Understanding of what Omnipresence, Omnipotence

---

[124] *The Holy Bible*, New King James Version (Tennessee: Thomas Nelson Inc., 1982), Psalm 91:7-8

and Omniscience Are? To be absolutely clear, Spiritual Healing is not about bringing the Presence, Power and Intelligence of our True Self to our false self. There is no god that you can pray to that will make you well, because this god-of-matter made you sick. Spiritual Healing is the discovery that only i can be sick, but as You are not i, You can't be sick.

In fact, prayer used in this incorrect way is not different from "mind-over-matter", it **is** a type of mind-over-matter. mind-over-matter is the belief that we can use the power of the mind to change our material circumstances, in this case, to change sickness into wellness. The fact that matter **is** mind can afford a strong intention its effectiveness, but for this reason, can't be mistaken for Spiritual Healing. If i is conducting the manipulation, its premise is sickness and any "good" effect won't last. More importantly, misguided intention to "make the body well" fails to see that emotional, mental or physical pattern-adjustments might be necessary before healing naturally occurs. To impose our will is not only incomplete but can make matters worse in the long run. Moreover, matter is **already** mind, so the idea that we can use the mind to alter matter demonstrates our ignorance that our thought of sickness produced the sick matter in the first place.

Then does Spiritual Healing really work?

Spiritual Healing only works if both the Healer and the patient have an open Mind to Receive Truth. Obviously, the Healer is the more Conscious of the two. The patient's openness is his Confidence in the Healer. Still, the Healer Knows that there is nothing to heal and hands his Mind over to His Consciousness to Reveal Its Self on the patient's behalf. In fact, the Spiritual Healer doesn't actually do any "healing" at all, because "healing" presupposes there is something to heal. What the "Healer" does is dwell in Conscious Trust and let Me Reveal the Health that was always Present. we just couldn't See it through the opacity of the bubble of ignorance. Therefore, we shouldn't call what happens "healing" but "Revealing". The Spiritual Healer is actually a Spiritual Revealer!

Spiritual Revealing is the Natural outcome of Conscious Trust, the Product of an open Mind. Therefore you can become your own Spiritual Revealer. Sometimes the Revealing will be instantaneous. At other times some other adjustments have to be made before the Revealing eventuates.

In the Eternal scheme of Things, it doesn't matter. A particular outcome or its timing become irrelevant.

What causes delays is i. Just watch that you are not carrying the payoffs of illness in your back pocket. The sympathy and guilt-free payoffs reveal that you are hanging on to the belief in separateness. This belief will rationalize that your life "in" a body is pleasurable while leading you to a painful death. But by returning to Conscious Trust and dwelling in My Omnipresence, Omnipotence and Omniscience you will gradually perceive a noticeable loss of appetite for worldly pleasure. Not that you swap it for austerity. you experience the Joy of merging with Your Self in the dimension of Truth where Sharing is the only Pleasure. The body, rather than being put into the service of getting what you don't Receive, is put into the Service of Sharing what you do Receive, and what you Receive Is Love. The body naturally readjusts to this All-inclusive Purpose of Mind, because, after all, the Body is Mind-Substance. That is, as you melt into undisturbable Joy the payoffs naturally lose their hold on you and drop away, and so must illness.

*"This is My Beloved Son in whom **I** am well pleased."*[125]

My Beloved Son, You, and **I** are One in Health.

---

[125] *The Holy Bible*, New King James Version (Tennessee: Thomas Nelson Inc., 1982), Matthew 3:17

# CHAPTER 18

---•⊙•---

# i is for impoverished

The subject of impoverishment throws us right back to the central difficulty of the appearance of separateness. Food, Clothing, Shelter and Money seem to be separate from us, so if we don't have a strategy and the able-bodied-ness to go out and acquire these things, we believe we will soon be sleeping under a bridge, as the destitute are often forced to do. Though if we have discovered we are not in danger or sick, we must also have discovered we can't be impoverished, because Prosperity comes from the same Infinite Source As Safety and Health. It all comes as a package.

It's hard to believe Spirit can Provide tangible things.

It doesn't. The senses report "tangibility" and you believe them. But, as we have learned, we shouldn't trust the senses. we were never impoverished in the sense that the only Things we Really Have are already part of Us; Consciousness, Love, Intelligence, Power, Integrity, Grace. Once we Know we Embody these Attributes of Consciousness, what we possess materially pales into insignificance, yet we are never at a loss.

It's very hard to Trust that Idea when i see my debts piling up.

Trust is very difficult when you find your self in a situation caused by lack of Trust. The dire implications of an empty bank balance, the sparse pantry and the increasing pile of bills compel us all to fear for the future. Not to mention the daily evidence of scarce times that we see on the television and read about in the newspaper that call for a circling of the wagons to protect us from loss. our baseline anxiety is kept idling by the spectre of impoverishment.

Yet a scarce present is the **result** of a continuing belief that we are vulnerable, the proof of existential fear. If we remind ourselves that We are, in fact, Invulnerable because We are Infinite, then we have a chance to change the outcome, because we change the fearful storyline. For when you think about it, Abundance is the fundamental meaning of Infinity. Can Infinity lack anything? Can Infinity be limited in any way? Can Infinity be divided up and handed out a bit here and a bit there? Does Infinity have favourites or exclusions?

No, but Infinity doesn't pay the bills.

**I** know it's extremely difficult to convince you that your bills would be taken care of, because impoverishment represents the front line of battle with the intellect, and you are accustomed to letting the intellect win this battle. it uses lack and insufficiency as overwhelming proof that you are vulnerable.

So let us try and dispel the impression.

impoverishment and fear of impoverishment are the direct result of not accepting the Truth-fundamentals. you have not yet accepted that Y(y)ou are 100% C(c)onsciousness, and that Y(y)ou appear **A(a)s** M(m)atter. Nor have you accepted that nothing externalizes or that both Harmonious and discordant circumstances remain in your M(m)ind as R(r)eflections. you **have** instead accepted the impression that your "good" can and should come **to** you from outside you. But there is no way that any F(f)orm of G(g)ood can come **to** you from outside, because "outside" is inside your C(c)onsciousness. Provision in any Form, even when your material and mental effort seems to be instrumental, is always a Reflection of Consciousness. impoverishment is a reflection of your lack of Consciousness.

i think the problem is i don't believe that Infinity can translate itself into abundant matter.

your thought about it can't, you're right. All you are asked to do, though, is submit your Mind to Infinity. **you** can't Know how Infinity translates Itself, all you can Know is that It does. So let Me do It. What have you got to lose?

Take a lesson from Nature. Do wild Animals, Birds, Fish and Insects worry where their next meal is coming from or where they will sleep? Does a Bear worry if its fur will be warm enough for winter? Does an Eagle worry if its wings will be wide enough to glide through the air? Does a Dolphin worry that it will have nowhere to swim? No, they just do what comes naturally **because** they are Provided with everything they need to survive and thrive. They don't do what they do **in order to be** Provided with the necessities of life, because that intent introduces the idea that their Good could be withheld from them until they do something to instigate that Flow. They **would** worry if they thought they had to get what they needed themselves. But what an absurd idea!

But You say i should Trust in order to instigate the Flow.

Humans are different. we disconnected from the Flow, but only in perception. Nevertheless perception seems real. we therefore need a way to break that false perception. Conscious Trust Is the Way.

*"I have come that they may have Life, and that they may have It more Abundantly"*[126]

Other creatures don't need money though. Isn't this the main reason we are different?

Money comes and goes like any "Thing". Do we worry that a Fruit-tree is bare of Leaves and Fruit in winter?

No. In due season the leaves, buds and fruit appear again.

---

126   *The Holy Bible*, New King James Version (Tennessee: Thomas Nelson Inc., 1982), John 10:10

Money is no different from a Fruit-tree. It appears when necessary. Besides, is it Money that you really need? Most people are surprised to learn that Prosperity has nothing to do with Money. What use is money on its own?—to go out and buy some Bread, a Coat, or a House! The Bread, the Coat and the House are the things you "need", not the money in and of itself. money is just paper, a decorative piece of metal, or a number on a bank statement. you cannot eat it, drink it, wear it or live in it. The actual money doesn't offer any protection or interact with you in any way. it is really quite useless.

It's a valuable bit of paper or decorative piece of metal, and a welcome number on a bank statement.

That's because we have specialized, and so we have introduced Money as an instrument of exchange. city-dwellers can't normally grow their own food or build their own house, and even if they could, they don't usually have the time. money enables us all to Share our individual Expertise and Talents by swapping them for the things to which we don't normally have access.

But if we see Money as something we have to go out and get for its own sake, we cut ourselves off from our Share.

Why?

Because the drive to acquire money puts the focus purely on matter. it spurns My Flow. The Talents with which we are Spiritually endowed and that represent an open Mind are smothered by that materialistic intent.

we should Notice more often that many of the Things we "need" appear without the intermediary of Money. our Family might provide a Meal, and our Friend might provide a helping hand with the Plumbing, the Cooking, or a Needle and Thread. This demonstrates that the "Things" we need are just as much within Consciousness as the Money. Money Is just another Thing. The trouble is, i puts so much thought and emotional emphasis on having or not having money, it cuts its self off from the very Consciousness that guarantees Prosperity in every Form, whether it has money or not.

Over two thousand years ago, Consciousness said;

> *"Therefore **I** say to you, do not worry about your life,*
> *what you will eat or what you will drink; nor about your*
> *body, what you will put on."*[127]

you needn't worry about any of these Things because Consciousness Is the Provider.

How do You know that's what he meant? i can't eat, drink or wear Consciousness either.

Ah, but you can, because Consciousness appears **As** Things.

> *"Seek first the Kingdom of God and His Righteousness*
> *[Consciousness], and all these things shall be added to you."*[128]

Aren't "added things" Effects of Consciousness? Consciousness Is Love. Wouldn't your guaranteed Provision of the things you "need" be the Embodiment of Love? Love Knows your "need" before you even know it's a need. In Spirit, therefore, there are no "needs".

When you Relax into My Everlasting embrace, you are Reassured that everything Is **already** taken care of by virtue of that Reassurance. That doesn't mean i's problems will be solved. It means problems and i are synonymous, for even if you had a million dollars in your hand, fear would be replaced by jubilation, but the **appearance** of abundance is just as empty and unreal as the absence of abundance. money isn't what you need, it is just the after-glow of consciousness, nothing of itself. When you try to hold it, it slips through your fingers. Seeking *the Kingdom of God and His Righteousness* is another way of saying Consciously Trust Me, and My Abundance will Flow unabated, As Money, or As whatever you "need".

Paradoxically, Money comes to us when we Know we don't "need" Money.

---

[127] *The Holy Bible*, New King James Version (Tennessee: Thomas Nelson Inc., 1982), Matthew 6:25

[128] *The Holy Bible*, New King James Version (Tennessee: Thomas Nelson Inc., 1982), Matthew 6:33

How can i ever know i don't need money?

Ponder this...

> *"For everyone who has, more will be given, and he will have Abundance; but from him who does not have, even what he has will be taken away."*[129]

That sounds back-to-front.

It sounds inequitable to the human sense of fairness. But before your indignation gives you an excuse to reject it, Notice this statement from the Parable of the talents is rather vague about what we must "have" in order to be given more, and also about what we "don't have" that ensures we lose even what we "have". A clue is given earlier in the Parable. "talents" are handed out by a man to his servants according to their respective "abilities" (which, not coincidentally, is a synonym for talents); five talents to one servant, two talents to a second servant, and one talent to a third servant. Each servant's ability not only attracts these talents in the first place, but also seems to have a bearing on what is done with these talents later. The servants with five and two talents multiply their talents by investing in more talents, and are rewarded accordingly, but the servant with one talent hides his talent in fear of losing it, and is punished accordingly. So what do you think these "talents" represent?

Could it be money?

It is significant that the word "talent" is used in the Parable, but because these talents are "invested" successfully, our material thinking naturally assumes the missing word is "money". Let us insert the word "money" and see if it works.

> For everyone who has money, *more will be given, and he will have Abundance: but from him who does not have* money, *even what he has will be taken away.*

---

[129] *The Holy Bible*, New King James Version (Tennessee: Thomas Nelson Inc., 1982), Matthew 25:29

Can this be Right? If Love wrote this Parable through Jesus, would Love endorse the inequity this interpretation suggests?

`The rich certainly seem to get richer and the poor, poorer.`

This states the obvious, but human inequity was not the lesson of the Parable.

`What about "good intentions"?`

Try it.

> *For everyone who has good intentions, more will be given,*
> *and he will have Abundance: but from him who does not have*
> *good intentions, even what he has will be taken away.*

This is more insidiously incorrect because it sounds better, more righteous, but look closely. i gives weight to its personal "goodness" believing it will be rewarded and "badness" punished. But is good always rewarded? Is bad behaviour always punished? No. More often than not, so-called good-intentioned people suffer loss and injustice, and the evil-intentioned get away with their ill-gotten gains. In addition, the unpunished moral breach of the evil-intentioned breeds cynicism and despondency and erodes the enthusiasm of the genuinely good intentioned. "what's the use?" says i.

The insertion of "good intentions" doesn't work, because underneath our good intentions is i with its emphasis on not-losing. The unintended belief of loss and motive to avoid loss lurks in the background appearing as unfairness and inequity. This is why money is not the panacea for all problems. it relies on the good intentions of the person with money. It's true that Money in the hands of good intention can be used to finance a Good Idea, the Profit generated can provide Employment, and equip Governments with Funds to build necessary Infrastructure. Money can help people in need. But money can just as easily be handled by evil intention. money can fund wars and false appetites, tyranny and terrorism.

`They say money is the root of all evil.`

we malign money when we say "money is the root of all evil" because money can't be greedy, aggressive, manipulative or corrupt on its own.

money can't even corrupt the mind. corruption is the result of our lack of Consciousness that doesn't Know it Is Provided for.

"money" and "good intentions" were the wrong words to insert. Let us add a different word to the passage of the Parable, a word that changes the whole meaning and lifts it into the realm of the All-inclusiveness of Truth;

> *For everyone who has* Consciousness, *more will be given,*
> *and he will have Abundance: but from him who does not have*
> Consciousness, *even what he has will be taken away.*

"having" is not dependent on money or good intentions. "not having" is not dependent on bad intentions. Even "doing good" doesn't work if we think we did it. What we do or don't do off our own bat ensures *even what we have will be taken away* because every thought we think and act we carry out represents our lack of Consciousness. It is Consciousness that guarantees Abundance and Prosperity. If you don't have Consciousness, loss is inevitable.

we learn that Consciousness is about Trusting that we are already Provided for because i didn't do It, **I** did! In addition, we can now Understand why the word "talent" was used in the Parable. The man gave his servants "talents" according to their individual "ability" (talent). The word "talent" represents your C(c)onsciousness, and multiplies when it is "invested" correctly (by Sharing).

The ability to Share demonstrates that you Consciously Trust that you are already Provided for. Abundance cannot be Reflected back to a consciousness of fear that indulges sense-desire and self-gratification, because you can't **get** what you already Have. In fact, if you were Conscious of Prosperity you would be busy Giving, not getting.

When i can afford it i'll give.

Giving enables you to afford Giving.

Giving means losing.

In duality, you can lose what you think you "acquired" by giving, yes. But you can't "get" what you Really "need" because you already Have

Infinite Abundance by virtue of your Consciousness, so what you thought you gave away you never had anyway.

As Consciousness unfolds, we **Receive** the Insight that we already "Have". The Things we Have are Spiritual, therefore, that's all we Receive because the Reflection is just a demonstration that we Received. we don't Receive Things, we Receive Thought. To misinterpret the Effect of Receiving as an "acquisition" for your self is to block the Insight that you "Have" because you block Its demonstration.

Now if we already "Have" what would be the point of keeping the demonstration for our self? we would only prove that we didn't Receive by wanting to keep it. What we Receive Is Infinite, and does not diminish by Giving. In fact, It increases by Giving because Giving Acknowledges the Gift's Infinite Source. The pool from which **I** Give does not diminish **because** It Is Infinite. Therefore, the more you Give, the more you Have. This is what Having means.

Giving and Receiving are two Aspects of the One Action for the Benefit of All. Giving, then, might be better Understood as Sharing. **I** Share with you, so you must Share what you Receive with others.

But sharing implies i keep it too.

Yes, but don't use the word "keep" because you deny **how** you came into possession of the Thing you must Share. The idea of keeping closes My Avenue down. Think of any successful business venture. A thriving business Shares Its Ideas with its customers. If others benefit, the business thrives and expands. Though, if the business decided to **keep** its Ideas close to its chest, the business would soon diminish and flounder. It's the same with you. **I** Share with My Self. You are My Self. But you must Share with others to continue the Flow. For if you don't Share, you won't notice people Sharing with you. you then resent sharing with them and hate them for it. feeling left out, and oblivious to your contribution to the lack, you are forced to depend on your hateful and fearful thoughts to get you by.

A closed mind becomes fertile ground for false empathy, conspiracy theories and paranoia. "i might not just lose my money, i might be swindled" says i, bewildered as to why unscrupulous people and the shadows of hardship close in on it. fear, then, becomes i's honest justification for not giving and we end up as bitter and twisted hoarders clinging to baubles of dust.

*"Do not lay up for yourselves treasures on earth, where moth and rust destroy and where thieves break in and steal; but lay up for yourselves treasures in heaven [Be Grateful for your Consciousness], where neither moth nor rust destroys and where thieves do not break in and steal. For where your treasure is, there your heart will be also."*[130]

Can i save for a rainy day?

The question is rather flawed because natural gaps are no problem. your "needs' are always catered for. It's doubt that **I** will come through on time and the fear of loss that interrupts the Abundant Flow. you will always have more than you "need" if you Share what you Have.

Sharing doesn't mean we don't Have Things. It guarantees we do! we simply Know i wasn't responsible for them showing up. i didn't do It, **I** did.

Returning to the Parable once again, the one who *has* is *given more* because he Knows the Things he *has* are the Result of Consciousness.

The Parable wasn't vague at all. It was confusing because it didn't differentiate the two has's and have's. Let's do that by inserting an an upper-case "H" where appropriate. Suddenly we Realize Having Is Consciousness because Consciousness appears As the Matter we **Have**, and lack of Consciousness appears as the matter we **have** but will surely lose.

*For everyone who Has, more will be given, and he will have Abundance: but from him who does not Have, even what he has will be taken away.*

To Consciously Trust Is to bring Having into your experience.

*"man shall not live by bread alone; but man lives by every word that proceeds from the mouth of the Lord [Consciousness]."*[131]

---

[130] *The Holy Bible*, New King James Version (Tennessee: Thomas Nelson Inc., 1982), Matthew 6:19–20

[131] *The Holy Bible*, New King James Version (Tennessee: Thomas Nelson Inc., 1982), Deuteronomy 8:3

Sounds like i can have a bit of matter then.

you don't have to give up matter, just **reliance** on matter.

*"Grace is sufficient for you."*[132]

*"No one can serve two masters. you cannot serve God and mammon."*[133]

"mammon" is the world of effect; money and things; matter. If you rely on matter, by implication, you deny the Source of Matter. And you also misconstrue what Abundance Really means.

we tend to judge wealth by the amount of money and possessions we accumulate, but True Wealth is Consciousness of your Completeness, which may look bountiful one minute and barren the next. But as a Fruit-tree demonstrates, barrenness does not necessarily indicate poverty. The Fruit-tree, just like our Consciousness, is just as Infinite when it is outwardly dormant as when It is outwardly active.

Then those that look like they are suffering financial hardship might have simply stopped relying on matter and opened up to Consciousness.

Don't confuse hardship with Spiritual Consciousness. hardship is experienced because we don't Know we are already Provided for. Consciousness doesn't demand that we experience hardship in order to prove we are Conscious. Who would we prove it to? Our Self? No, such an idea merely glorifies little i.

Don't misunderstand, hardship can provide the back-handed motivation to begin Conscious Trust and set us on the Path to Consciousness, but Consciousness Itself can't Reflect impoverishment. Anyone who suggests otherwise is operating from a lack of Consciousness.

---

[132] *The Holy Bible*, New King James Version (Tennessee: Thomas Nelson Inc., 1982), 2 Corinthians 12:9

[133] *The Holy Bible*, New King James Version (Tennessee: Thomas Nelson Inc., 1982), Matthew 6:24

Beware, then, of hardship dressed up in Strength's clothing. it says, "to succeed you must struggle", "never give up", "every no leads to a yes", and "failure only makes you stronger". hardship gives rise to the idea "survival of the fittest" and makes competition king. "it's a dog-eat-dog world", "every man for himself" says i.

material success can certainly be the result of hard struggle, but more often than not, the prize stays out of reach and the struggle continues. In duality, it's easier to fail than to succeed. Remember "success" in material terms is "not-failure". The negative pull is stronger, because True Spiritual Success is out of reach. In duality, we must fight to hold our success. But what are we really fighting to hold? material success is failure in Spiritual terms, because we sacrifice our only Hope of Freedom from worry for something that can't deliver Freedom from worry. Can money buy Health, Safety or Love? our worries remain.

It seems we will do everything we can to avoid material failure except do the one thing that will guarantee Success; rely on our Intuitive Impulses. Perhaps this is why the hardship of material failure kick-starts our journey to Spiritual Consciousness, because, although failure was never necessary, it presents an opportunity to See the Real Alternative. When we are forced to let go of the prop of matter, we are given the incentive, albeit involuntarily, to Hear our Consciousness knocking on the door of our Mind with a totally New Way to approach Success. It is a blessing in disguise.

Whereas illness brought sympathy and freedom from guilt, but couldn't be called a blessing, failure forces us to meet the dragon of our fear and guilt head on. The dragon smiles ready to bestow its blessing upon us, but, unfortunately, we usually miss the sign and listen to the intellect who misinterprets the smile for a snarl. In fear, we retreat back into the arms of the intellect who warns us not to Listen to our Intuition; "you'll have to take a vow of poverty to be Spiritual". The ill-informed slander is designed to discredit Intuitive Insight and wave the flag for personal ambition, "you can do it", "you can be successful in the world". And it is certainly possible to push through, but what the intellect fails to tell you is that your success can't be sustainable where safety is insecure, where loyalty can be betrayed, and where your gain is another's loss. Can you feel secure in your success while others are living out their vulnerability, while others have lost the security you value so highly?

`i should feel guilty for my success?`

Only if you think others can lose by someone else's success, and the way you know if you think loss is a possibility is if you think **you** can achieve success without My help.

`But there will always be people who lose won't`
`there? i can't help that.`

you believe it because you see it. But i is not innocent. you can prove it the next time someone revels in their personal success. Watch your reaction. There will be an ugly pang of envy or jealousy, because, to you, their gain means your loss. Little i feels its pride cut down. it feels vulnerable, unworthy. Apart from close family whose success you ride, if you are honest with your self you will admit there is a secret belief lurking in the dungeon of your mind that depends on the failure of others for your success, because their success will somehow diminish **your** chance.

Don't we say, "there's only so much to go around" and in an expanding population we feel an increasing stress and fear that our needs will not be met? logic dictates that every time someone gets part of this limited resource, the overall share diminishes and there is less to go around. But Prosperity is Infinite, therefore Prosperity Is the Law of expansion. you can't alter or eradicate My Law, you can only exclude your self from It by not Sharing. When you Share, everyone wins. True Success can't fail. There are no losers in Consciousness.

Yet i's material wealth can buy the pleasures of sense-desire and mask its fear and guilt. As a result, when i becomes wealthy in the world, through the world, there is little chance to grow Spiritually.

*"...it is easier for a camel to go through the eye of a needle*
*than for a rich man to enter the Kingdom of God"*[134]

---

134 *The Holy Bible*, New King James Version (Tennessee: Thomas Nelson Inc., 1982), Matthew 19:24

Truth is Eternally Patient. Even the person who comes by his wealth materially must eventually realize that True Wealth is not material. To reject the Treasures of Spirit actually invites hardship **and**, as we learned from Buddha, makes us sick. Let us then debunk the notion that Abundance is not Spiritual. There is no vow of poverty to be taken in order to be Conscious. Psalm 91 actually suggests that **impoverishment** is not Spiritual. If you can manage to *dwell* in the Secret Sanctuary of your Mind and abide with Me;

> "A thousand may fall at your side, and ten thousand at your right hand;
> But it [impoverishment] shall not come near you."[135]

Credit Me with your Success and everyone benefits.

How should i credit You?

Acknowledge Me.

What will that do? It doesn't seem enough.

Acknowledgement opens your Mind to the Receipt of Thought from your True Abundant Self. This is a pre-requisite to Consciousness. Another name for Acknowledgement is Gratitude.

i am grateful for the things i have, for my fortunate circumstances.

It's a start, but gratitude for things and circumstances falls short. It's not about what we are grateful for, but what are you grateful **to**? "thank god" says i when the drought breaks. But did **I** organize the drought? If we prayed to god to end the drought, what created the drought and prolonged it that wasn't responding to your prayer? we thank the wrong god. It's the **Source** of the Permanently Harmonious Perception we should be Grateful for and to. If we don't see Harmony, we might wonder where god went, but that god was never going to respond to a call for help. Though now it

---

[135] *The Holy Bible*, New King James Version (Tennessee: Thomas Nelson Inc., 1982), Psalm 91:7-8

doesn't matter. we can still be Grateful that there is a Source to which we can switch that will Reveal Harmony. Be Grateful that **I Am** Omnipresent. I don't disappear in a drought. you simply let your fear intercede and thought the god-of-matter had abandoned you. Then you thought by praying you could bring Me back. I never left! you left Me! So will a prayer bring Me back? No. Be Grateful that **I** never left.

Just as we have become used to two variations of C(c)onsciousness and P(p)erception, T(t)hought and T(t)hing, there are two types of G(g)ratitude. Gratitude with an upper-case "G" Acknowledges My Presence and deactivates i and its fear. Gratitude therefore offers Real Hope in the face of scarcity and guarantees My Reflection remains in place. gratitude with a lower-case "g", on the other hand, scoffs at scarcity and, in doing so, unconsciously invites it back. Then are you grateful for impoverishment?

Not at all, but maybe impoverishment is a sign that i am not being Grateful enough.

Gratitude is not quantifiable. Either you are Grateful or you are not. Also, you can't be ungrateful by not being grateful for things. you can only be ungrateful if you don't Acknowledge Me, and i does that all the time whether it is grateful for things or not. That's what causes the fluctuations i experiences. Nothing more.

What about thanking people? Does that come under Gratitude with an upper-case "G"?

It does, because **I Am** every person's True Identity. It is Right to thank people for their Generosity because that Generosity came from Me (Your Self), to you, through them. They could not have been Generous otherwise. It's your Reflection. So when you thank a person, by Association, you thank Me. Likewise, when someone thanks you, immediately credit Me. It wasn't you who was Generous. you were merely a conduit.

Gratitude, then, engenders Humility. i didn't Succeed, I did. i didn't Create your Talent, I did. i didn't do Good, I did. i didn't motivate your Work-ethic, I did. i didn't paint the Artwork, I did. i didn't compose the Song, I did. Every Thing that appears and every Thought that compelled you to act was Me.

Gratitude builds Trust, because i is decommissioned from every intent other than the Desire to give the Mind back to Me and from every act that it wants to do by its self for its self. Gratitude is a tool we can use to deactivate i. Gratitude opens our Mind to Love and dissolves fear.

To Release ourselves from insufficiency and impoverishment, then, we must Consciously Trust that even if it doesn't seem that our fundamental needs are being met, they are. And when they are being met, be Grateful that i didn't do It, **I** did.

> "*The act of expressing Gratitude is in Truth, the act of Recognizing and Acknowledging (within Your Self) the Source of all Your Good*"[136]

---

[136] Joel S. Goldsmith. *Collected Essays.* (CA: DeVorss & Company, 1986), 120

# CHAPTER 19

### i is for isolated

Our final area of human struggle is isolation. **I** left it until last because our relationship with our fellow human is the most difficult of the four challenges.

i don't disagree, but why is that?

Every Person is an Individual expression of Consciousness, but in our potential to Be Conscious, every person is also an individual expression of a **lack** of Consciousness. When two people meet, then, to varying degrees, their lack of Consciousness' bounce off one another's reflection thus multiplying the emotional reactions aroused. This tangle of unconscious expectations and responses doesn't end well. Rather than being guaranteed mutual Recognition of the One Self in Guiltless and fearless Love, two people meet guarding their guilt and fear, hoping deep down to Feel that longed-for sense of Belonging, but unable to shed their defences for fear of possible intimidation and rejection.

No one ever sees each other's True Self because we all look in our own mirror and see our self in the other. This is not the fault of the other person. No one **can** Know their own Self until they become Conscious of the Truth in others. This stalemate is the essence of our isolation.

i gather You are not talking about physical isolation.

**I** am not. Consciousness of your True Self automatically Connects you to Every Self in Timeless Spaceless Eternity even if you are by yourself in a desert or on an ocean. But in your lack of Consciousness, you can be in a crowd and still be isolated. In fact, you may actively seek physical isolation for one reason or another, so it's not the physical proximity to people that's relevant. It's your disconnection with your True Self, and by implication the True Self of others (because there is only One Self), that makes you isolated.

What's the difference between isolation and loneliness?

loneliness is the feeling of isolation. we are all isolated due to our disconnection from our True Self, but not everyone is lonely, because the disconnection is often reflected back to us as problematic people from whom we feel compelled to withdraw or avoid. In this case, our isolation is welcome.

But we can't be isolated **and** Conscious, because implicit in our isolation, welcome or not, is the judgment of some people as problematic. Even if we find one person problematic, we deflect our existential guilt, which is a denial of our True Self.

This is why the final and most potent tool in our Consciousness toolkit is **Forgiveness**.

*"Forgiveness recognizes what you thought your brother did to you has not occurred."*[137]

But he did do something to me. That's why i am forgiving him.

it's not really Forgiveness if you think he did something to you, because he can only do something to you if you think you are vulnerable. This is what you are existentially guilty of. you deflect your existential guilt onto him, then pretend to forgive him. But you can't Forgive what you think is worthy of blame. This is pseudo-forgiveness. It is a false pardon, insincere and full of resentment. Without addressing this smouldering superiority, forgiveness isn't really Forgiveness but an empty and shallow act of overlooking.

To Truly Forgive, we must Forgive our self for our existential mistake. But in order to Forgive i for existing, it is necessary to step into our

---

[137] A Course in Miracles, (New York: Viking Penguin, 1996), Workbook for students, page 401

Invulnerable Self. If you Remember, conscience helps us. When conscience directs us away from blame of other people towards self-blame, we must realize this is not the destination, because i still exists to suffer guilt.

Let us expose the game. When conscience exposes our wrong-doing, we are shocked to realize that not only have we been unforgiving, but unforgivable! Swiftly come feelings of regret. "If only i had been kinder, stronger, braver", "if only i had been a better son or daughter, a better parent, a better friend", "if only i could have done things differently." And because the past can't be altered, any apology seems inadequate, any action to make good seems pathetic. we then might try to dull the regret with self-sacrifice. "If i take on their load, i will feel better" rationalizes i. So we over-compensate for our loved-ones bad habits to allay **our** guilt. Yet it only makes matters worse to turn a blind eye to behaviour we should be gently but firmly correcting. By becoming a compliant doormat, we defend and elevate the guilty i in us **and** our loved one. And now there is another reason to feel guilty. "If only i could have been tougher." It's like saying, "if only i could have been what i couldn't be." It's an impossible situation that never Feels Right and in fact deepens our isolation.

In desperation, we might ask forgiveness of "god" not Realizing "God" is our Self, ever-available in Its Guilt-less-ness when we deactivate the guilty one. Additionally, we don't Recognize Forgiveness extended to us by others, for It is barred by a terrible and irreconcilable regret. we can't accept Forgiveness while another has suffered at our hands. It is this torture to which we condemn our self to eternal fires of damnation, because we strengthen the idea of the self by torturing it. Blindly, we willingly accept hardship as penance for our ongoing imperfection. Ultimately, sickness, injury and death become symbols of justice.

The vicious cycle continues, because we can't Forgive our self through the fog of self-blame.

So let us address our own guilt first. Let Me ask you a question. How would you Feel if someone Forgave you for your past transgressions of commission and omission?

Unsolicited? Without me asking for Forgiveness? Why would they?

Don't worry about that. How would you Feel?

i would be suspicious. i don't think it's possible to avoid the karmic consequence of my transgressions.

Giving control over to the karmic god-of-matter maintains your surface guilt. Forgiveness Recognizes that your unforgiveable past never happened! karma is a consequence of believing it did. Avoiding the consequence of this belief is therefore impossible. Forgiveness wipes the slate clean, because there is nothing to Forgive. There's really nothing to "avoid" then.

Let me get this straight. If someone Forgives me, my karma is erased?

It was never there. All Forgiveness does is Recognize this.

But wouldn't i have to Recognize it too?

Yes you would, so just imagine it. Wouldn't it warm your Heart and feed your Soul to be offered this precious and forgotten Insight about Your Self. It's Joyous and Fulfilling when someone Sees through your costume in their play, when they See who you Really are. The Feeling of being allowed to drop your pretense, often for the first time since the intellect took over your Mind, is exhilarating and Liberating.

Why don't i Recognize it?

For a start, there are very few people who have Forgiven themselves, which they need to have done in order to Forgive you. But even if someone did Forgive you, you can't get past your guilt. you don't think you deserve to Feel your own Joy of Being. So **I** will rephrase the question. What if you were never guilty?

i can't imagine it.

you can't imagine it because to release your self from guilt you must

273

also Know that **You** never did anything wrong or left the right thing undone. i might have done that, but You are not i. There is no right and wrong pair of opposites in Reality, only Permanent Right or Perfection to which you become Aware or Conscious. Use your Higher Logic to bring you to this Awareness. Can Perfection do something wrong? Above all, by feeling guilty, are you not demonstrating that you believe your action of omission or commission can diminish someone else's Perfection, as if their Perfection **could** be diminished? Isn't this idea the height of arrogance?

**I Am** Their Self just as much as **I Am** Your Self because that is what the Self Is. you can never override this Truth. your belief that the **I** of someone else could be imperfect is fantasy. Truth cannot be affected by fantasy or a belief that fantasy is real. Take all this into consideration and try again. Imagine how you would feel if you were never guilty, which means there was never, and never will be, any risk whatsoever to anyone's Joy of Being—especially **Your** Joy of Being?

i can get an inkling now. It feels liberating.

Guess what? you just Forgave your self.

Now hold this self-Forgiveness while we go to the next inevitable step. What if you could Realize the one you are blaming for the hurt perpetrated on you doesn't hold the keys to **your** Perfection? Your Perfection is not influenced by them at all. What were you thinking? By holding them accountable, by not Forgiving them, you deny **Your** Perfection! And if You **are** this Perfection, where is the loss? More importantly, where else is Freedom? Silently to your self, Forgive them.

What if they turn around and hurt me again?

Forgive them again. You don't suffer by Forgiving them. In fact, you Give them and you a priceless Gift, because, when you Release them from their wrong-doing, you release them from the guilt that preserves your guilt.

Ah—here is a test. Here is how you will know if you have really Forgiven your self and, by association, them. Can you **let** them be Free? Because if they are not Free, you are not Free.

i don't know. There is pleasure in holding on to blame. It gives me energy. It makes me feel bigger and more powerful.

Seizing the opportunity to aggrandize its self, i relishes slandering people. i lets others raise its ire and then justifies its fiery hate-tirade as a deserving response. "They brought it on themselves" says i.

If none of it is true, i look foolish. i feel ashamed.

It is humiliating to think we are wrong about judging. It's the worst reason to feel guilty because it hurts our pride. we want to retaliate; "if i can't get away with avoiding a karmic consequence, why should anyone else?" our eagerness to judge, engage in gossip, or vicariously enjoy the misfortunes of others tells of our unforgiving nature.

But, remember, humiliation serves our goal. It humbles little i in readiness for deactivation. But you can't be humble **and** judge. Besides, if one person really does deserve condemnation, then we really must be vulnerable, and if we are vulnerable, separateness must be true.

you will have to make a choice, to temporarily energize little i and remain guilty, or Be Free of guilt.

But i have to let them be Free too.

Yes. Don't hesitate. Release your fellow wrong-doer from their guilt. Forgive the mean-spirited neighbour, the vindictive ex-spouse, the bully, the greedy and self-indulgent fossil fuel user, the terrorist and the genocidal maniac, for they are not to blame. They are all actors in **your** reflection. Be Genuinely Happy that they too can Feel as Liberated as you when you Forgive them, because in that Genuineness Is **your** Freedom.

Forgiveness works on everyone or no one, but It does more. Forgiveness means we, at last, know what it means to take responsibility for the evil in the world. Not to take on the blame for evil, but to See that evil is a consequence of our existential mistake. Forgiveness of your self abolishes a threat in the world, because you withdraw the dual ideas of perpetrator and victim from your consciousness. The fog of ignorance lifts a little. Before long, the one you once judged won't feel the need to reoffend, because if you are no longer defensive, you demolish the false reflection of attack—for everyone.

Finally, when you have Truly Forgiven your self, you also find that if someone blames you for something, no longer do you take on guilt. This doesn't mean you don't apologize or try to make amends when you inadvertently hurt someone. It means guilt loses its power as a weapon of attack on you. For instance, when someone casts out the bait of the martyr, "i'll be alright, don't worry about me" or "you know how ill i am, how could you leave me?", you don't react. you don't need to defend your self with resentment. For who can resent the one he Forgives?

But they are still guilty of attacking.

If you hold them responsible in any way you have not Forgiven them. Do not hold them responsible. Forgive them in this instance too, for *what you thought your brother did to you has not occurred*. It is only your belief that they can do something to you that holds them guilty. But this makes you guilty too. Their fear of isolation is no threat to you unless **you allow** them to take advantage of your sense of obligation. you think they keep you bound to them against your will, but the binding is mutual. The weird result is, once you Forgive them, you simply and happily do what they ask, because without guilt, a space is made for Love to enter. Empathy and Compassion work through Forgiveness. When one person Forgives, all the sad and petty games that poison relationships melt away as if they never existed.

Consequently, our life naturally moves into service-mode. we find Joy in the Healing Power of Forgiveness. As we let Love through the Mind, you might say we stop living our own life. Now we live My Life, Life As My Instrument to help humanity fulfil Its Purpose, for each person's Purpose is the same as everyone else's; to Be Conscious. Put it this way, to Be Conscious of our True Self is our Purpose, but to Serve our Self in the other by Forgiving them is our Function. Why? Because by Forgiving we are Forgiven and this Serves our Purpose.

It seems Forgiveness ties everything up in a neat bow.

It does. The greatest blessing of Forgiveness is that It leads us gently out of the "transition stage" where conscience has helped us discern "right" from "wrong", but where "wrong" was only ever a concept of man in his guilt, and so its opposite "right" (not-wrong) was never going to stick. And as man is the carrier of "wrong", the poison arrow of conscience necessarily doubles back on our self. "i did wrong", "i don't deserve forgiveness" says i. It is for this reason that we can't burst the bubble of ignorance until we Understand Forgiveness is first and foremost for our self.

When you Forgive your self, you send a Light laden with Love streaming through the layers of your bubble of ignorance. This Light of Consciousness shatters the crust of pride cutting through the layers of fear and discord, exploding through the unconscious barrier, through the dark grey layers, down and down, until It reaches the core belief where this whole charade was conceived.

And there you See it—i and its fear for its self, still clinging on to its belief of separateness, mocking Forgiveness. But then you can Forgive this too. In that same moment, You merge with Me in an eruption of Joy. And when you stand in this Brilliant Light, It's infectious. Others are drawn to It because you have proven that they Have what you Have. And Now You can Share It with them. you and your fellow human end each other's isolation in the Embrace of Love that was always waiting in the Eternal Now. The impasse is crossed. The bubble of ignorance bursts.

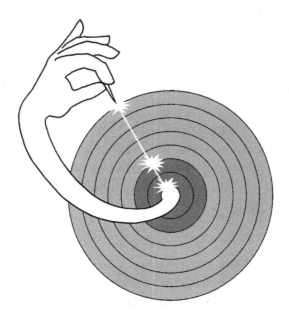

# CHAPTER 20

## I is for Illumination

Illumination, as is inferred by the name, is to throw Light onto some-thing or to en-Lighten some-thing. But we must Understand Illumination in a slightly different sense if we want to Realize our Spiritual potential, because there is actually no darkness to en-Lighten. There is no i to do the en-Lightening.

i thinks that **it** can be Illumined and its bubble of ignorance can be improved as a result. This is another mistake of thought that seeks to cling to the belief of separateness. i can't be Illumined. i is a state of darkness that we must Awaken **from** or out of into Our Eternally Light Consciousness, much like awakening out of a dream into awake-consciousness. But now we Understand that our awake-consciousness is also a dream, and sometimes a living nightmare. In fact, the bubble of ignorance is what is known as "hell". There is no hell other than this. There is no Heaven other than Illumination.

The Light never went out. we pulled down the shutters and imagined our dark room was our world. we still do. The light **we** turn on in the dark room is artificial and temporary, because this light has no Truth to it. Illumination is to discover that there is only One Light, and we can't turn it on. It is already on!

Have you ever wondered why certain stories become legends or classics? These stories don't make it into folklore by accident. we have

Felt that Light, that Undisturbable Joy, since the dawn of time in the form of ancient mythology such as the aboriginal Dreamtime, the miracles in the Scriptures, and the search for the Holy Grail. Fairy tales, old and new, transport the child in us back to the time of Hope. Dotted with mad scientists, time-travelling contraptions and magical animals, these cherished stories all toy with the Idea that we have access to an extraordinary Power. we Feel Good. Our Heart sings and Our Soul stirs. we Resonate with the Idea that we can't lose. we want to believe that when something Transcendent enters the scene everyone except the symbol of evil will live happily ever after. The Holy Grail, the buried Treasure, the Pearl of Great Price, whatever Form the Transcendent "something" takes, all symbolize the Promise that we can escape tyranny and slavery and that evil is no match for this hidden Power. The Truth behind the stories is why we never fail to be uplifted and thrilled by their irresistible storyline.

The legends invariably present us with a hero or heroine of slight stature, quirkiness or innocence facing impossible odds. This little figure is humble and flawed and full of self-doubt, yet something in him, some Strength, some Courage, some deep determination comes to the surface at the darkest most dangerous moment often surprising him as much as others. There is an insurmountable struggle and then, all of a sudden, like the phoenix rising from the ashes, the evil is defeated. Good prevails.

The hero is, of course, our forgotten Soul, our potential, the little spark, our "imaginary friend" returning from the Light in our childhood bedroom to touch the Truth in us.

As a child we Felt this innate Strength, Courage and Good within us, but we couldn't extend It because we lacked Consciousness. As It slipped behind the bubble of ignorance, we spent lifetimes in the wilderness listening to a voice that maintained that the wonderful stories that gave us Hope were just fantasy. With devastating consequences, we obeyed it when it told us to get back to our life of insurmountable struggle, stop dreaming, and be realistic.

But now Hope can be rekindled. we can turn the tables on the unauthorized voice, for we gave it the authority! we discover, with relief and deep excitement, that the legends are not fantasy, **the struggle is the fantasy**, a hellish fantasy that has tricked us to fall into a bottomless pit of fear and guilt. In the fall, fear has been made tangible and Truth an unachievable and silly riddle, but Truth only remains a riddle as long as i tries to solve the riddle. As soon as we discover We are not i, Truth is unveiled of its unconscious coat and stands Resplendent before us. The solution to the riddle is that **we** can't solve it. Any thinking keeps the solution at arms-length like a dog chasing its tail.

*"Your Strength will be in quietness and confidence"*[138]

The intellect took the i that you thought you were on a journey to nowhere that never happened. Conscious Trust allows you to sink into this startling Truth and dissolve the forms inconsistent with Reality. **I** join with My Self in a Relationship that was never Really severed.

Why does it seem to take so long?

The delay is in looking for material solutions to problems that are really mental. Yet, if there are no mental problems to solve either, the time it seems to take to solve them is just another rabbit-hole we enter into and get lost.

we must shift our attention away from matter to thought, then away from your thoughts to My Thought. Then as our individual Understanding of Me grows, as our Intent to deactivate little i Strengthens, and as the tools of Forgiveness and Gratitude, non-reactivity and identity-switching, and Mindfulness and Meditation prove their efficacy in our daily life, our impatience Relaxes. we find our self treading this world with lighter and lighter footsteps until we feel as if we are floating along without a care in the world, yet we Care deeply. The ocean of Love that was always Supporting us is Recognized, and, undisturbed, we find we can watch the

---

138 *The Holy Bible*, New King James Version (Tennessee: Thomas Nelson Inc., 1982), Isaiah 30:15

choppy surface of thought and its consequent physical activity without responding to its bait. Suddenly we Understand what it means to be in the world but not of it, and we are Free. Not free **from** anything, but Free **in** Love.

Above all, Remember that wherever we are and whatever situation we are confronted with, **I Am** Here and Now. All we have to do is Listen to our Intuition, refrain from expecting a particular outcome, and the roadmaps to Here and Now suddenly appear to Light the Way.

Each tradition has their own set of roadmaps. The Ten Commandments and the Two Commandments are two such roadmaps. The Sublime Eightfold Path of Buddha is another. The Truth-fundamentals in this book offer yet another. Even the Lord's Prayer is like a pocket roadmap, of a memorizable size, and useful because we can refer to it at a moment's notice.

It might be fitting to conclude our study with the Lord's Prayer.

That Feels Right.

Let us then translate this little gem into modern language in order to make the meaning really clear.

> *"In this manner, therefore, pray:* [Set your Intention to Listen:]
> *Our Father in heaven,* [My Presence within Me,]
> *Hallowed be Your name.* [i is not **I**]
> *Your Kingdom come.* [**I** Am Consciousness, Here and Now.]
> *Your Will be done.* [**I** determine All Activity.]
> *On earth as it Is in Heaven.* [Every Thing Is My Thought.]
> *Give us this day our daily bread.* [Let us Receive Your Thought every day.]
> *And forgive us our debts,* [And we are Forgiven,]
> *As We forgive our debtors.* [in the degree we Forgive others, for there is no one to blame if there is nothing to gain or lose.]

*And do not lead us into temptation,* [And if i can take responsibility for my reflection,]

*But deliver us from evil,* [i will discern evil as without presence, power or substance,]

*For Yours is the Kingdom and the Power and the Glory forever and ever.* [**I** always have been, am Now, and always will Be, Omnipresent, Omnipotent and Omniscient.]

*Amen.* [**I Am.**]"[139]

In modern language alone, we See that the Lord's Prayer is divided into three parts:

The first part sets us on the Right track:

Set your Intention to Listen:
My Presence within Me,
i is not **I**.
**I** Am Consciousness, Here and Now.
**I** determine All Activity.
Every Thing Is My Thought.

The second part suggests the way to remain on the track:

Let us Receive Your Thought every day.
And we are Forgiven,
in the degree we Forgive others, for there is no one to blame if there is nothing to gain or lose.
And if i can take responsibility for my reflection,
i will discern evil as without presence, power or substance.

The third part Acknowledges our Oneness:

---

[139] *The Holy Bible*, New King James Version (Tennessee: Thomas Nelson Inc., 1982), Matthew 6:7–13

I always have been, am Now, and always will Be, Omnipresent, Omnipotent and Omniscient.

**I Am.**

"**I Am**" says it all. i never was, is or will be. Now we Know how to Truly Rest in My Everlasting and Invulnerable embrace—Good Is All there Is, and i didn't do It, **I** did.

# Glossary of Terms

**Absolute:** pertaining to Truth, Love and Life; Spiritual; Divine; no opposite.

**Adam:** i, the intellect's puppet; the thinker.

**acts-of-god:** discord for which i doesn't know it must take responsibility.

**acts-of-man:** hurtful behaviour for which i does take responsibility, but without consciousness that i creates the discord that prompts its hurtful behaviour; the response of man to acts-of-god; ultimate demonstration of human lack of Consciousness; evil.

**awake-consciousness:** not-asleep; intellectual consciousness, i.

**Awareness:** Consciousness.

**awareness:** consciousness.

**birth:** consciousness' appearance as body.

**bubble of ignorance:** the reflection of discord; karma; the result of fear and guilt; human awareness.

**Compassion:** the demonstration of Love.

**conscience:** surface guilt; the discernment of right from wrong; the purpose of sympathy.

**consciousness:** awake but not Conscious; unconscious of Consciousness; lack of Consciousness; acceptance of duality.

**Consciousness:** Infinite potential; Awareness; Knowing; Truth; Life; Love; our True Self; our True Identity; **I**.

**Conscious Receiving:** the first function of the Mind; allowing the inflow of Thought, of Love, Life and Truth, not human belief; prerequisite for Reflection of Truth; necessary for Conscious Trust to be Effective.

**conscious Receiving:** partial Receiving; allowing the inflow of Thought, but then restricting It to a human purpose or use.

**Conscious Trust:** Practical Meditation; the correct use of the Mind; letting our True Self Guide us; Listening to our Intuition without a preconceived idea of what Listening will bring, or how; abiding or dwelling in the Secret Sanctuary of our Mind.

**Creative Principle: I Am;** Spirit; Truth; the Self; God; Consciousness.

**death:** the false belief of extinction; the disappearance of the body.

**discord:** the result of ignorance of Truth, the result of lack of Consciousness.

**dominion:** our unconscious holding of control of how things appear; not knowing we have control of the Mind.

**Dominion:** our Conscious relinquishment of control of how Things appear; Knowing we have control of the Mind and what this means.

**doubt:** the justifier of fear; fear's agent.

**duality:** the reflection of i's thought; the reflection of the negative pairs of opposites.

**ego:** i's survival strategy; pride.

**empathy:** identification with i; transferred guilt; shared suffering; mock-humility.

**Empathy:** Compassion; non-judgmental attitude; Acknowledgment of True Self in others; pre-requisite to healing.

**fear: existential:** i's reaction to the idea it doesn't exist.

    **surface:** i's reaction to the discord it doesn't know it creates.

**god:** the incorrect assignment of intelligence and power to matter; any idea to which i pledges allegiance; god-of-matter.

**God:** see Creative Principle and Consciousness.

**god-of-matter:** karma; god.

**Grace:** the Result of Listening and Trusting the Intuition; the Result of the relinquishment of i and its effort.

**guilt: existential:** the disowned feeling of responsibility for being i.

    **surface:** the owned feeling of responsibility for doing wrong or not doing right; conscience.

**harmony:** the reflection of temporary good.

**Harmony:** the Reflection of Permanent Good.

**heart:** the physical organ of circulation; sentimentality; sympathy.

**Heart:** Soul.

**Hope:** the Feeling of the potential of Consciousness; Relief; Comfort.

**hope:** the false expectation of a bright future.

**i:** me, you, we, us in our assumed identity; your false self; the intellect's puppet; consciousness "in" the body; awake-consciousness; Adam.

**I:** Me, You, We, Us in our True Identity; our True Self; our Real Self; our Perfect Self; Consciousness; Truth, Life, Love, Omnipresence, Omniscience, Omnipotence.

**ignorance:** the state of fear for something that doesn't exist.

**Illumination:** Consciousness; the Mind given over to Conscious Receiving.

**Infinity:** the Nature of Consciousness.

**intellect:** thought without Love; reason.

**Intellect:** Love's Intelligence; Reason.

**Intelligence:** Omniscience; Aspect of **I**; partner of Love.

**intuition:** the Intuition demoted to serve the intellect and duality; stunted Intuition; conscience; gut-feeling; psychic power.

**Intuition:** our Voice of Truth; our Feeling of Truth; our Vision of Truth.

**Joy:** the Feeling of Love.

**justice:** not-injustice; the temporary opposite of injustice.

**Justice:** a Result of Consciousness; no possibility of injustice.

**karma:** the god-of-matter; the effect of guilt.

**Karma:** Consciousness.

**love:** not-hate; the temporary opposite of hate.

**Love:** the Substance of Consciousness.

**manifestation:** the reflection, the out-picturing of thought.

**Manifestation:** the Reflection, the out-picturing of Thought.

**matter:** the reflection of thought; world; universe.

**Matter:** the Reflection of Thought; World; Universe.

**mind:** Mind incorrectly used for i's thoughts and beliefs; our inner ear pointed introspectively.

**Mind:** the instrument of Consciousness; our inner Ear pointed unconditionally towards our True Self; transparency for our Intuition; our Secret Sanctuary.

**Omnipotence:** the All and Only Power.

**Omnipresence:** the All and Only Presence.

**Omniscience:** the All and Only Intelligence, Knowledge, Wisdom.

**Peace:** the Nature of Consciousness.

**perception:** what we sense when we think for ourselves.

**Perception:** what we sense when we Listen to Thought.

**pride:** the intellect's muscle; the cover for guilt; i's primary defence strategy; the ego.

**Reality:** the Source of the Reflection of Good.

**reflection:** intermittently discordant matter.

**Reflection:** Permanently Harmonious Matter.

**sense-desire:** dependence on matter for its own sake; leads to self-gratification that demonstrates our belief in separateness.

**Soul:** Individualization of Consciousness; Heart.

**Spirit:** the Nature of Consciousness.

**sympathy:** transferred guilt; one of pride's disguises; the arms-length pity for the suffering, Call to service.

**Truth:** the Nature of Consciousness.

**Truth-fundamental:** Ideas that demolish the myths that support i;

1. **Y(y)ou are 100% C(c)onsciousness,** or, in other words, **Y(y)ou are 100% Spirit.**

2. **C(c)onsciousness appears A(a)s M(m)atter,** or, in other words, **Y(y)ou are the S(s)ource of what Y(y)ou perceive.**

3. **T(t)hought is the S(s)ubstance of the P(p)erception we call M(m)atter,** or, in other words, **M(m)atter is T(t)hought sensed A(a)s T(t)hing.**

4. **There is no P(p)erception prior to or in isolation from T(t)hought,** or, in other words, **T(t)hought comes before P(p)erception of T(t)hing.**

**truth:** i's inconsistent reality.

**Universe:** see Matter.

**universe:** see matter.

**World:** see Matter.

**world:** see matter.

# Bibliography

*A Course in Miracles.* New York: Viking Penguin, 1996

*The Bhagavad Gita.* Adyar: Theosophical Publishing House, 1953

*The Holy Bible*, New King James Version. Tennessee: Thomas Nelson Inc., 1982

*The Koran*, translated with notes by N. J. Dawood. England: Penguin Books, 1956

*The Story of Christian Science Wartime Activities 1939 – 1946.* Massachusetts: The Christian Science Publishing Society, 1947

Bohm, David. *Thought as a System.* New York: Routledge, 1992

Bohm, David. *Wholeness and the Implicate Order.* New York: Routledge. 1980

Dalton, Jerry O. *The Tao te Ching; Backward Down the Path.* Georgia: Humanics New Age, 1994

Descartes, Rene. *Discourse on Method and Meditations,* 1641. New York: Dover Publications, 2003

Eddy, Mary Baker. *Science and Health with Key to the Scriptures.* 1875. Massachusetts: The Christian Science Board of Directors, 2009

Eddy, Mary Baker. *The Christian Science Journal.* MA: The Christian Science Publishing Society, 1947

Goldsmith, Joel S. *The Infinite Way,* 1947. USA: BN Publishing, 2007

Goldsmith, Joel S. *Collected Essays.* California: DeVorss & Company, 1986

Hamilton, Bernard. *The Christian World of the Middle Ages.* UK: Sutton Publishing, 2003

Hanh, Thich Nhat *The Miracle of Mindfulness.* UK: Rider, 2008

Hassed, Dr. Craig and Chambers, Dr. Richard, *Mindful Learning*. Boston: Shambhala, 2014

Kunzang Thekchog Yeshe Dorje. *The Treatise of the Ship Captain's Sword*. Sikkim, India: Deorali Chorten Gonpa

Langer, Ellen J., Ph.D., *Counterclockwise; mindful health and the power of possibility*. New York: Random House Inc., 2009

Lipton, Bruce Ph.D., *The Biology of Belief.* California: Elite Books, 2005

Rees, Martin. *"The Anthropic Universe."* New Scientist, No. 1572, August 6, 1987

Strong, Mary. *Letters of a Scattered Brotherhood*. New York: Harper & Row, 1948


Advaita-vedanta.org Sankara's Life http://www.advaita-vedanta.org/avhp/sankara-life.html (date accessed September 3, 2015)

Brainyquote.com Bodhidharma http://www.brainyquote.com/quotes/quotes/b/bodhidharm267267.html (date accessed August 25, 2015)

Captizen.com Swami Rajneesh quotes on therapies and therapists http://www.captizen.com/swami-rajneesh-quotes-on-therapies-and-therapist/ (date accessed September 9, 2015)

Chalmers, David. "Facing up to the problems of Consciousness." *Journal of Consciousness Studies.* 2(3):200-19, 1995 http://consc.net/papers.html (date accessed July 30, 2015)

Dictionary.com http://dictionary.reference.com/browse/conscious?s=t (date accessed July 27, 2015)

Fda.gov Questions and Answers: Apple Juice and Arsenic http://www.fda.gov/Food/ResourcesForYou/Consumers/ucm271595.htm (date accessed January 25, 2016)

Goleman, Daniel. New Focus on Multiple Personality. *The New York Times, Science.* May 21, 1985 http://www.nytimes.com/1985/05/21/science/new-focus-on-multiple-personality.html (date accessed July 29, 2015)

Goodreads.com Anais Nin http://www.goodreads.com/quotes/5030-we-don-t-see-things-as-they-are-we-see-them (date accessed April 12, 2016)

Goodreads.com Bernard of Clairvaux http://www.goodreads.com/author/quotes/2734978.Bernard_of_Clairvaux (date accessed August 6, 2015)

Goodreads.com Henry Wadsworth Longfellow http://www.goodreads.com/quotes/255749-though-the-mills-of-god-grind-slowly-yet-they-grind-particle-explained.html/342438.html (date accessed August 6, 2015)

Livescience.com. What is the Higgs Boson? ("God particle" explained) http://www.livescience.com/21400-what-is-the-higgs-boson-god-grind-slowly-yet-they-grind-particle-explained.html/342438.html (date accessed July 28, 2015)

Merriam-webster.com http://www.merriam-webster.com (date accessed July 30, 2015)

Our Advaita Philosophy Ashram http://www.advaita-philosophy.info/Quotes%20and%20Links.html (date accessed July 28, 2015)

The Information Philosopher. http://www.informationphilosopher.com (date accessed July 28, 2015)

Thinkexist.com Guru Nanak quotes http://thinkexist.com/quotation/as_fragrance_abides_in_the_flower-as_reflection-grind-slowly-yet-they-grind-particle-explained.html/342438.html (date accessed January 30, 2016)

# Index

# Reader's guide

Two or more gathered together to ponder this book can multiply the possible beneficial Effects enormously. Under the clear understanding that the intellect is to be barred from taking over and indulging in argument about the content of the book, your True Self can be coaxed into an exploration of Infinite possibility. Why should the intellect be excluded? Because the intellect seeks to divide with fear and pride, whereas your True Self Shares Its Infinite bounty in unconditional Love. The outcome of the intellect's involvement is apparent in our discordant and uncertain world. Love has not yet been allowed to extend Its Influence. Therefore, any group should keep a watchful eye for any emotionally veiled or "logical" interruptions.

**Impetus for discussion or silent pondering might include the following questions:**

Do you remember back to a time in your childhood when you Knew you were Safe, despite the fears others tried, with good intentions, to impose on you?

Can you make a Connection Now with that part of you that doesn't age? Can you Feel It? If not, what thought stops you?

Can you Resonate with the Truth-fundamentals, even slightly?

Can you "locate" the Source of your Gifts and Talents and be Grateful, not for them, but to the Source?

Would you agree that you are convinced that there is a separate material universe that you were born into and will die out of? Could you bring your self to agree that this is just a belief? If not, what thought stops you?

What part of you dominates, the emotional or logical intellect (they are the same) or your Intuitive Knowing?

Have you practiced Mindfulness or Meditation, and how does your experience differ from the instructions in this book?

Can you refrain from giving your opinion when you disagree? Can you link the arising feelings of diminishment with fear?

Can you allow your self to be humiliated, intimidated, disappointed, embarrassed or offended without escalating those feelings into blame? Can you, instead, locate your existentially guilty i and Forgive it?

Can you Forgive your "enemies"?